THE IMPURITANS

THE IMPURITANS

A GLIMPSE OF THAT NEW WORLD WHOSE PILGRIM FATHERS ARE OTTO WEININGER, HAVELOCK ELLIS, JAMES BRANCH CABELL, MARCEL PROUST, JAMES JOYCE, H. L. MENCKEN, D. H. LAWRENCE, SHERWOOD ANDERSON, *ET ID GENUS OMNE*

BY

HARVEY WICKHAM

Author of "The Misbehaviorists"

NEW YORK

LINCOLN MAC VEAGH · THE DIAL PRESS

LONGMANS, GREEN & COMPANY

TORONTO

1929

MANUFACTURED IN THE UNITED STATES OF AMERICA
BY THE VAIL-BALLOU PRESS, INC., BINGHAMTON, N. Y.

CONTENTS

LIST OF ILLUSTRATIONS

THE IMPURITANS

CHAPTER I

THE PURITAN

I. THE CALLA LILY

"THE many sects and persons who fell under this definition [of Puritan]," says Trevelyan,[1] "were characterized both by an aversion from gaiety and by a passionate love of civic freedom."

There seems to be a mystery here; a strange mixture. Why should a lover of freedom hate to be gay? Is freedom, then, so melancholy? One could understand how a lover of freedom might be sad—in chains. But actually to hate gaiety!

We shall find, I think, that this love of freedom was the root of the whole matter, though certainly aversion from gaiety is the trait which most distinguishes the Puritan in the popular mind. When one uses the name to-day, one means a marplot, a spoilsport, a skeleton at the feast. Nobody would dream of calling a man a Puritan because he was a patriot, though it was undoubtedly as a patriot that he began. But the Puritan's reputation, like that of the calla, has always been chiefly associated with funerals. White was his ideal, and once he actually succeeded in achieving grey.

The Catholic Church, on the other hand, from which the Puritan rebelled, was not only authoritative but colourful. Far from denying this, when the early dis-

[1] "England under the Stuarts."

senter wanted particularly to insult his spiritual ex-mother, he called her the Scarlet Woman.

Christopher Morley, that rare modern spirit who practises letters in the fashion of a mediæval guildsman practising a "mystery," feels this affinity between colour and the Vatican even yet, and on such a secular occasion as the death of Ed Dooner, the last of the ancient inn-keepers of Philadelphia. Writing to Tom Daly anent the cold funeral meats demanded by such a solemnly joyful death-feast as was toward, he says:[2]

"There was something essentially Catholic, I mean Papist, about that place [Dooner's Hotel] as I remember it. One surrendered to it as the troubled soul does (eventually, I dare say) to the Church Universal. It was a Steve O'Grady kind of place; a parish priest kind of place."

And he goes on to speak of the "endless decencies of those hambone and whisky days, the lit'ry associations of the dear old hotel," where there was "neither pimping nor skimping"; where the atmosphere was "as masculine as firemen's suspenders—the sort of a place where bishops and men with bubukle noses were equally at home," and where "any of the genuine kidney would know themselves."

Here is a funeral, but with hint of flagons instead of flowers; a certain relish for life even in the presence of death. And it is "masculine," that is to say, sexless from the writer's standpoint.

How deeply this sort of thing frightened (and frightens) the Puritan! That it is passion, which—whether too freely indulged in or too negatively suppressed—tends to gloom, is a truth he never could grasp. He might call

[2] *Vide The Commonweal,* May 9, 1928.

a prostitute a drab, but she remained a bright temptation. He never thought of fighting her with hambones and whisky, or of hell-fire as being other than red.

Maitland, in "The Anglican Settlement and the Scotch Reformation," describes these early reformers as "those who strove for a worship purified from all taint of Popery." He is not, of course, referring to the very early reformers, especially not to Luther, whose passions were essentially political, but to those later ones who were striving to bleach not the Church but the Reformation. Again a yearning for white is indicated, and a conception of white as something freed from something else rather than as a proportionate blending of all kinds of light.

It was thus that the Puritan got his name. The *character* may be traced back to the earliest times and to lands far outside of Christendom, but the name did not come into use until about the year 1564, and is of English origin.

It is not my purpose to lay bare all the complicated and warring causes of the Protestant Reform, but one of them was certainly the existence of an austere individualist, at first unnamed, who found himself upon a ship whose pilot was a wine-bibber and a friend of sinners, whose crew reeled to the tune of endless chanteys and seemed to the sober eye to be palpably drunk and bent on going to the devil.

In a way the individualist was right. The good ship *St. Peter* unquestionably had the devil aboard—a cold, unwetted stowaway hidden in the hold and busily mixing perdition with the stock of grog. If the Puritan—for we might as well give him this appellation from the start—had cherished a taste for heady liquor, he might have set after the devil. Being constitutionally inclined to be horrified by danger in solid or liquid rather than spiritual form, he preferred to leave the ship, never dreaming that said devil had managed to slip quite a bit of poison into the vinegar.

Here was a chance to set out for those desert islands dear to all Robinson Crusoes—islands that should blossom with white flowers. And the adventurers were Defoes enough to stock a few provisions before hoisting their lifeboat's mains'l and casting off the fasts. But, what with the haste and all, and the fact that the source of supplies was necessarily the ship, the cargo was not so pure as it might have been. They took but little wine, but even their fresh water had received a papal blessing; while some went so far as to carry with them an actual love of episcopacy—things which were to lead to reproaches later on and to a reformation within the Reformation. Moreover, they had clung to a Bible composed of Scriptures selected and made canonical by Catholics, and, so far as the New Testament was concerned, actually written by Catholics. It was to take more than what is ordinarily known as Puritanism to get rid of this—a Samson head of hair is not to be cropped save by the scissors of some veritable Delilah.

"The strength of Puritanism," says Burton,[3] "lay in the results effected by the general study of the Bible." And, he adds, "The lack of a consistent theology was less felt because of the great stress" which was laid upon "serving God in spirit and in truth—by feeling and conduct rather than doctrine." The calla lily, you see, was no whited sepulchre. But, as the same writer also remarks, "This study of the Scriptures was carried on by

[3] *Vide art. "Puritanism,"* "Catholic Encyclopedia," by Edwin Burton, S.T.D., F.R.Hist.Soc, and V.P. of St Edmund's College, Ware, England.

the aid of private interpretations, which inevitably resulted in the multiplication of minor sects."

Right here we find one reason why the Puritan was so serious and the Catholic so gay; why a passionate love of civic freedom so moved the heavy heart of the Reformer while it left the Papist comparatively indifferent. The Papist was gay because he considered himself not only an individual but a citizen of the Universe. He felt uncommonly rich as the heritor of all of God's bounty, and uncommonly sociable in the midst of a communion of the saints already begun. If he obeyed laws, they were not those of a foreign power. To him there was no foreign power.

But the Puritan was poor, limited by his own periphery, rich only in the sins of the world, which he insisted upon carrying on his own back. He was most emphatically his brother's keeper, and if meat caused his brother to offend he would eat no more while the world endured—especially meat that had been sacrificed to idols. If this led to legislation exclusively for dyspeptics at the expense of the normal, no matter. There was the text.

He had the Scotch sense of economy so hilariously celebrated by Harry Lauder, but not the Lauder sense of humour. He had an instinctive aversion to incense, candles, ritual, architecture, stained-glass windows, pipe-organs, pomps, and ceremonies. Almost the first word which history records of Puritanism, openly so called, is in connexion with a godly row over the wearing of caps and gowns by the clergy in the street and the use of the surplice before the altar.

Nor was it their possibilities of colour and costliness alone which led to the condemnation of such trappings. No matter how shabby a cassock or *soutane,* it marks the priest. Such a costume may be nothing but a conservatively retained ancient Roman fashion, but if he wears it he is set apart. His cloth becomes the outward symbol of an inner cloak of authority. It savours of Popery even when worn by an Anglican—and Popery the Puritan had learned to hate as one can only hate a foreigner.

The Puritan was quite willing for a setting apart, but it must be of himself. One of the results of a multiplication of sects is the increase of the number of foreigners in the world. The cry for liberty always arises from small nations, from minorities. It is the demand to be released from laws imposed by outsiders.

"The whole world lieth in wickedness; come out of it!" proclaimed the Puritan long before the anticlerical Browning turned the warning into verse. The Papist agreed heartily as to the wickedness of the world, but he did not believe he was going to be damned for enjoying life—not unless he so chose of his own free will. For nobody to be a monk or a nun, yet everybody to assume monastic obligations, seemed to him much like everybody trying to be monks or nuns—an experiment against nature and certain to fail. He felt quite equal to dealing with the world, also with the flesh and the devil. His had become the majority party.

But the Puritan had each a little Calvin in his bosom who thought that damnation was a foregone conclusion for most people. One had to belong to the elect, the minority, to escape; and naturally one spent most of the time trying to make sure that one did belong. "The lack of a consistent theology was less felt because of the great stress laid upon feeling."

The Puritan could make straight enough deductions from given premises. Grant him his premises, and John

Calvin was one of the most logical logicians the world has ever known. But there was no hope in Calvinism unless you *felt* that you came within its narrow saving provisos. Wesley abolished the rigidity of this horror, permitting the once saved to fall from grace and mayhap clamber back again. But emotion was still the only criterion to go by. If a man did not feel saved at a given moment, he felt damned. He was at the mercy of his liver.

No wonder the Puritan's face tended to lengthen. He was lonely and unpopular, and could never be certain of his brother's election even when he felt confident of his own. Robert Browne, leader of the Free Churchmen or Independents, whom I may perhaps be permitted to describe as the first real Simon Puritan, was hated and persecuted not only by the Anglicans but by the Presbyterians.

It was inevitable that a love for civic freedom should glow in the Puritan's heart. In patriotism he found a way of escape from his awful isolation. In becoming a nationalist he could experience the warm confidence which is born of marching shoulder to shoulder. Nationalism was also a ready weapon against Internationalism, and politics promised a substitute for that brotherhood he once had found in the Church. Here was an Individualist who wanted to set up Principalities and Powers. We all do—Powers in our own image.

In England this was difficult. There was the Crown, not only reminding the Puritan that this was not his country in a secular sense, but actually seeking to exercise a religious authority through an anti-Roman Catholic Church established by Act of Parliament. Clearly it was a world to withdraw from.

Now, when the Catholic withdrew from the world, as he frequently did, it was with the idea of coming yet closer to grips with the powers of darkness. He was inclined towards what the modern social scientist calls superstition. When the Puritan thought of withdrawing, he thought of some wilderness from which he might drive the devil bodily in advance. His untamed ego had the unelastic strength of muscles hard-set in one who grits his teeth. The world must be made perfect and less dangerous. He distrusted such things as absolution and indulgences. He found it easier to kill passion than to control it—at least so he thought.

But notwithstanding the continual threat of the Church of England, minor sects multiplied as had been foretold. There came to be Fifth Monarchy Men, Levellers, Diggers, and many other sorts of Puritan, all Protesters but by no means all inclined to wear the same kind of spiritual hat. Indeed, to one sect the hat of another was almost as bad as a red hat.

The Presbyterians decided to consolidate their front, at least against episcopacy, and, meeting at Edinburgh in 1560, adopted the first Book of Discipline—in flat defiance of Luther's dictum against ecclesiastical organizations with any force whatever. But who was Luther? The Presbyterians had their own Calvin. Moreover, in so far as they were Scotch they were canny, and realized that when it comes to coercion it makes considerable difference whose ox is gored. Eighteen years later they adopted the Second Book of Discipline, which so thoroughly established them that they then began to dispense even with Calvin, and so lost their *raison d'être*. To-day you will look a long while before you find a Presbyterian layman who has ever heard of the Book of Discipline, second edition or first, or has the least idea of what Calvin taught except that it was something extremely disagreeable about hell.

Independent Puritans of the Robert Browne stamp never cared for the Book of Discipline even when it was new. Nevertheless, political persecution kept the Puritans somewhat together until the Long Parliament, with its victories over the high-church Anglican party. But worldliness had not yet taught them any common orthodoxy. Not all Presbyterians were Scotch, and there were also Erastians and Independents. Little birds in their nest agree; not Presbyterians, Scotch Presbyterians, Erastians and Independents.

Generally speaking, the Presbyterian, or right wing, was opposed to regicide, while the Independent, or left, wanted no compromise. Cromwell, an Independent himself, waited until Charles I was safely dead, and then came forward with a force which made the Independent position strictly regular. So was Robert Browne triumphant—until the Restoration, when the Puritan disappeared as an important factor in English politics. To-day, if you are a Protestant Englishman, you will be either Church or Chapel. If you are Church, you may be High or Low, or even Broad, and still be in society. If you are Chapel, you are a Dissenter, and might as well be a Catholic or a Scotchman.

2. THE *MAYFLOWER*

So Puritanism, in its broader sense begining as a Catholic schism, ended narrowly by becoming an Anglican schism, and might have ceased to be of moment had it not been for the little congregation of Scrooby, in Nottinghamshire, led by John Robinson.

This was not the "John P. Robinson he" who, according to Lowell, said: "They didn't know everything down in Judee." Our John thought that they did, and claimed to be one of the few who shared that knowledge. He first moved his congregation to Holland, which is on the way there, and then decided to found a New Judea in what was vaguely known as "Virginia." There was again a ship chartered, this time the *Speedwell,* which did not speed well at all and should have been christened the *Colander*. It managed to leak its way from Delftshaven to Southampton, where the passengers crowded into the smaller but less perforated *Mayflower*. This steered for lands belonging to certain London merchants and situated somewhere between the Hudson and the Delaware, and consequently arrived at Massachusetts Bay, December 20, 1620. Some say that the captain was bribed by the Dutch to lose his way, but in any case the voyage was symbolical, prophetic. For it has always been characteristic of the Puritan that he never reaches the particular port for which he sets out.

Thus, quite recently he thought to abolish intemperance, and succeeded only in driving the American people from honest liquor to dishonest synthetic hooch. He sought to save the Plymouth germ-plasm from contaminating "scum" imported from Southern Europe, and succeeded in substituting a stream of criminals and stowaways for open-and-aboveboard arrivals at Ellis Island —and incidentally in inducing a vast Negro trek from south to north, east and west, to supply the labour shortage which bootlegged foreigners were not quite able to fill. More recently still, he helped to establish a bad government in Mexico. The result? Still another unforeseen port. Mexicans, unable to endure conditions at home, are pouring by millions into the United States and preparing yet further to dilute the white corpuscles of our blood—this time with a rich red Indian strain. The Puritan no doubt will survive it. He is the sort of leaven a very little of which leavens the whole lump. His real danger comes from his own yeast, as we shall see.

But first let us return to the *Mayflower,* with its human cargo of one hundred and two passengers—"seventy-four English Puritans and twenty-eight women," as one chronicler quaintly puts it. Even this plasm was soon watered by immigration of a wealthier and more educated type. Thus the Plymouth Colony, which was Congregationalist, suffered absorption—but not extinction—by the Massachusetts Bay Settlement, which was Presbyterian. Other Puritans of course arrived later, but their name was not legion. Very often their name was not even Puritan. Increasingly they became Irish, Italian, Jew, Greek, Russian, and what not—a class we have been taught to regard collectively as our "inferiors." There were also Senegambians brought over in chains to till the cotton fields of Dixie. And all these have increased and multiplied into a nation of more than a hundred million people.

Has the Puritan lost ground? Not a bit of it. He—and more especially she—dictates our thoughts, our dietary and our social customs. The Puritan speaks of the United States as *his* country, and none dares to say him nay. It *is* his country. That the Spaniard, the French, and the Dutch also founded early colonies—in some instances even earlier colonies—may be a matter of history, but it is not a matter of paramount political or moral importance. They turned Puritan in proportion as they survived. The Cavaliers of Jamestown, Virginia, were outnumbered by indentured servants of sterner stuff from the start. Hard by landed the *Ark* and the *Dove,* but what promised to be Ararat turned out to be Baltimore, Maryland, whose streets are but little more shaded by the olive branch than are the streets of Boston. If any change has come over the spirit of the United States, it has come from the Puritan. Aye, if a wooden horse has at last been smuggled into Troy, the natives first gave it the O.K. of their Individual Judgment—though perhaps they don't even yet know exactly what is inside. There have never been any concessions made to the enemy.

For, as Hudson and Guernsey so candidly observe,[1] "It is of course altogether an error to suppose that the founders of Plymouth and Massachusetts were in any sense apostles of toleration and religious freedom. What they sought in New England was not liberty of opinion but liberty for their own opinions." Robert Granville Caldwell[2] phrases it thus:

"Though the Puritans had come as the result of bitter persecution, they could not afford to be tolerant without introducing the seeds of heresy and sedition. They could not allow an Antinomian or a Baptist or a Quaker to live among them without denying the very certainty of their faith. And from their point of view they were entirely right. Those who disagreed with them had a right to stay away. But they had no right to come among them and harry the Vineyard of the Lord."

Those who disagree have the right to stay away! And this from squatters! Pretty good, I think. Thus do the meek inherit the earth. Or is there still a catch in it somewhere? The "Simple Cobbler of Agawam," one of our

1 "The United States from the Discovery to the End of the World War," by William Henry Hudson and Irwin S. Guernsey, p. 78.

2 "A Short History of the American People," Chap. 2.

early *littérateurs,* foresaw no danger—except that of excessive generosity. "He that is willing to tolerate any religion or discrepant way of religion besides his own, unless it be in matters merely indifferent," the simple one declared, "either doubts his own or is not sincere in it. He that is willing to tolerate any unsound opinion, that his own also may be tolerated, though never so sound, will for a need hang God's Bible at the Devil's Girdle."

Sometimes I wonder what would have happened had the Puritan yielded to this temptation. Plenty was offered him right in the vicinity of Plymouth Rock. The Pokanoket Indians (not having exercised their right to stay away) had been rendered helpless by a providential plague; but 1622 had not come and passed before Thomas Weston, a Londoner, arrived with "sixty lusty men" filled with the monstrous idea of making a Merrie as well as a New England out of the wilderness.

These lusty threescore must needs found the colony ot Wessaguasset, afterwards called Weymouth, only twenty-five miles north of the Rock itself. And on their heels trod Thomas Morton, described as "a pettifogger," and worse, of Clifford's Inn, "who not only introduced the Episcopal service at Wessaguasset"—he tried to rename it Merry Mount!—"which was bad enough," observe Hudson and Guernsey,[3] "but indulged in regular carousals and 'revels and merriment after the old English custome.' When May Day came he even went so far as to set up a Maypole 80 feet high, round which, having been duly stimulated by much 'excellent beare,' the settlers and a number of Indian girls 'frisked together like so many fairies or furies rather.'" Our authors are quoting from "New England Canaan," [4] and show clearly what a nar-

[3] *Op. cit.,* p. 68.
[4] Bk. ii. chap. xiv, in Force's Tracts, vol. iii.

row escape we had. But maypoles, excellent beare, and frisking fairies or furies rather, were never to be ours. When the Puritan took to erecting poles, it was to form a gallows higher than Haman's, a gallows of individual judgment, whereon to hang—himself.

What he feared, however, was not to go forward, but that he should turn back. The Pilgrims and their immediate followers feigned to have washed all taint of Popery from among them; but, after all, their robes were scarlet to a considerable degree. Not only had they adopted that old Catholic Bible (in another translation, of course): they had—some of them—flirted with the by-no-means-sufficiently-non-catholic Church of England, at least to the extent of failing in its extirpation. A man like Roger Williams could not tolerate such semi-free consciences. And so the Puritans of Plymouth, moved by the strong property-sense of trespassers, could not tolerate Williams, but sent him packing to found Rhode Island.

Then there was Anne Hutchinson, who as a danger reduced all Williamses to the plane of lusty fellows and pettifoggers dancing after the old English custome but not meaning any harm. Here was a real menace. Did she not gather about her the first women's club in the land and encourage its members to criticize the sermons that were preached by the male leaders of the flock? She did. And not only that, but she herself preached—the doctrine of the "Inner Light."

This doctrine sought to establish the principle of Individual Interpretation in a state of chemical isolation. As long as one clung to the Bible, one clung to something outside of self. However individual the interpretation, it was necessary to find a text which could be twisted to support it. The Inner Light put Egoland *über alles*. But the time was not ripe. So Anne was promptly voted "a woman not fit for our society" by the more conservative colonists, and after following Roger Williams to the South, she finally wandered to the then Dutch New Rochelle—there to be murdered by Indians for harrying the hunting-grounds of the Great Spirit.

Of such were my ancestors—and very probably the reader's ancestors. Are we not proud of them? We ought to be. Never was there such hard and forbidding virtue since history began. Yet it was virtue; and it had its reward. There was increase; a conquering of the wilderness; and a reflex action reaching back to Europe and turning the Old World upside down.

The Puritan was poor and ignorant. He was an egoist. But he was sincere. If his spiritual baggage did arrive via Rome, it came originally from Bethlehem; and though his worship of individual judgment tended to make him an Ishmael, with his hand against every other man, he managed to do some wonderful team-work in those matters which the Simple Cobbler had described as "merely indifferent." The hostility of the ungodly long kept even his spiritual program from disintegrating altogether, while his political genius at one time promised—or threatened—to dominate the globe.

But of late there is to be heard a voice shouting in our streets: "Mene, Mene, Tekel, Upharsin! John Alden, thy glory hath departed!"

Impuritans have arisen, offering to set us free from the Puritan and all his works. It is high time we took account of these new prophets, spied out their origins, and examined in some detail the mess of pottage which they offer in exchange for our birthright.

CHAPTER II

THOSE WICKED TEN COMMANDMENTS

"THE Decalogue," says Otto Weininger,[1] is the "most immoral book of laws in the universe." Why? Because it "enjoins on obedient followers submission to the powerful will of an exterior influence."

This idea that morality is an imposition, and therefore immoral, is very widespread. Thus, Havelock Ellis [2] declares that "what we call morals is simply blind obedience to words of command . . . of which the significance is hidden."

One would like to object that this is not what "we" call morals, but simply what Havelock Ellis calls morals—that "we" in fact have a very different notion of the term. But it is impossible to read much current ethics without realizing that the Ellis "we" includes a large, influential, and very articulate section of the population. So he is really a spokesman when he goes on: "We still accept, in theory at all events, the Mosaic conception of morality as a code of rigid and inflexible rules, arbitrarily ordained." That is, we accept this as a description of what morality is, and conclude that morality is something bad.

As to those "we" of whom Ellis is the "I," this is cer-

[1] "Sex and Character," authorized translation from the sixth German edition; London, William Heinemann; New York, G. P. Putnam's Sons, chap. xiii, p. 313.

[2] "The Dance of Life," chap. iv.

tainly true. Falsehood creeps in only with the "still accept," which should be "have come to accept." Formerly we were far from accepting morality as either arbitrary or inflexible, or from considering ourselves bound to obedience, blind or otherwise, of a code whose significance was hidden—and by implication non-existent. Naturally, the moment we discovered that we were bound in this way to a code of this sort, we decided that we were *not* bound to it.

But in the days of our bondage we supposed that the code's significance (that is, its meaning) was pretty plain. Or, if "significance" is to be understood in the sense of "consequence," that too seemed clear. The consequence of obedience was our welfare. And how could that be "arbitrary" which was enjoined for our good? Is the family doctor arbitrary when he prescribes a healthful diet?

And as free will was held to be the very basis of moral conduct, where did the "blindness" come in? With our faith, no doubt, though not even here was blindness considered a virtue. We were encouraged to learn all we could about the Physician, it being supposed that knowledge would tend to increase our belief in His wisdom, skill, and good intentions. Sin rather than virtue was held to be blind.

Now sin has become insight. The modern never tires of describing the Decalogue as a "code of rigid and inflexible rules," sans rhyme and minus reason. Inflexible? What do you mean? To find out what Ellis means, we have but to turn to another page in this same chapter, where he commends Aristotle for having remarked in his "Poetics" that if we wish to ascertain whether an act is, or is not, morally right, we must consider not merely the intrinsic quality of the act itself, but the person who does it, the person to whom it is done, the time, the means, and the motive.

"Such an attitude," Ellis goes on, "puts out of court any appeal to rigid moral laws." So a moral law is rigid when it takes into consideration neither the intrinsic quality of the act, the person acting, the person acted upon, the time, the means, nor the motive. Granted. But where can one find a moral law like that? Certainly not in the Ten Commandments.

I say the Ten Commandments, but it is always the Seventh which nowadays is meant. "Thou shalt not commit adultery." Aye, there's the rub. But it seems to me that the intrinsic nature of the act involved is unmistakably set forth. I seem to gather what is meant, though of course, for all I know to the contrary, this language may leave Havelock Ellis in the dark. What leaves me in the dark is the suggestion that any act can be either forbidden or enjoined without its nature being defined. Thou shalt not! Shalt not what? Until there is an answer to this question, there can be no commandment at all.

Let us now attempt to define adultery without considering the person who commits it, the person with whom it is committed, the time, the means, or the motive. It is flatly impossible. As to persons, they must, in the first place, be responsible human beings. And if one be a husband and the other his consenting wife, the intrinsic character of the act hardly falls within the prohibition. The means, I fancy, may be assumed. But how could one say whether the pair were married or not without considering whether the act complained of occurred during the time of such marriage? We must even go beyond that if we be competent casuists. For what is marriage? Is a man who goes through a marriage ceremony with his deceased wife's sister married? He was not, in England, until a few years ago. Can he be lawfully married to his cousin? His sister? His grandmother? Can divorced persons who remarry during each other's lives be regarded as married from an ethical point of view? Is marriage legal and binding between blacks and whites? Between whites and yellow men?—or brown men? And what of the age of consent? What of mental and physical capacity? What of freedom from intimidation or actual coercion? Nor will the moralist be permitted to stop even here, ignoring the motive and holding "arbitrarily" that there can be no wrong done between those whom God is said to have joined together.

So the Law of Moses proves to be a general statement to the effect that man, as a social creature, cannot be a law unto himself. To apply it, one must consider all the circumstances. Casuistry, which is both the science and the art of morals, fairly reeks with regard for the intrinsic nature of acts, the persons who do them, the persons to whom they are done, the time, the means, and the motives.

True, the word "casuistry" has come to mean a system of specious reasoning, for there was a time when some of us were fallen so deeply into ignorance that we were fain to believe that cases of conscience could be settled without the use of intelligence. Our individual interpretations had become our whims, and our whims direct and divine inspirations. We understood—whatever it was we happened to understand. Anybody else attempting to arrive at a different understanding—above all, anybody attempting to defend a different understanding by means of argument—was, *ipso facto,* prompted by Satan. Conscience—my conscience, not yours—was lord of all.

Not so had Newman thought of the Inward Monitor, for in the section on Conscience in his Letter to the Duke of Norfolk, he had said:

"The sense of right and wrong is so delicate, so fitful, so easily puzzled, obscured, perverted, so subtile in its argumentative methods, so impressionable by education, so biased by pride and passion, so unsteady in its course, that in the struggle for existence amid the various exercises and triumphs of the human intellect, the sense is at once the highest of all teachers, yet the least luminous."

According to this, the Inner Light lifted on high by Anne Hutchinson may at times be blinding and amount to an inner darkness. What is to be done?

Well, for one thing, we might call an Experience Meeting, compare one inner light with another, put our heads together, take notes, and keep a record of results. In the course of ages we shall have accumulated considerable information, eliminated a great many individual idiosyncrasies and personal equations, and arrived at that Great Mean which is our fairest image of the truth. And we shall call this a creed, a civilization, a tradition, or a culture. It may even suggest a Revelation to some of us. And it shall be ours—when we have verified its experiments and made them our own.

This is the famous "scientific method" which the Puritan was so quick to adopt in "matters merely indifferent," like planets and atoms. It is a good method. But one should not apply to matters of moment the mere *results* of observations made upon matters indifferent. The new "cosmic rays," which are supposed to flow in from beyond the stars when the electrons of disintegrated matter, radiating through "curved space," meet and reintegrate, may do well enough for astronomers. But beware of the philosopher who uses them to explain the real universe. For they are not "cosmic," but local, and pertain to a little universe which is far from being universal. Their "closed system," which seems to exclude Deity from the scheme of things, is not the whole machine, but merely a little wheel in the shop of the Clockmaker. It seems to go of itself only when we shut our eyes to the winding Hand. Observation should include all the subject-matter involved in the conclusions to be drawn from it. Matters of moment are worthy of being studied themselves.

But in the span of one short life the individual cannot be expected to pioneer the totality of time and space, or even such part of it as is within reach of human experience. If he rejects tradition, he puts himself in the condition of a new-born savage who has yet to learn how to make a fire or to tie a stone to the end of a stick.

Now tradition had said: "The object of the sensuous appetite is the gratification of the senses; the object of the rational appetite is the good of the entire human nature, and consists in the subordination of the lower to the rational faculties and again in the subordination of reason to God, its supreme good and ultimate end. The opposition between appetite and reason is natural in man and not a corruption of human nature. Nor have the inordinate desires (actual concupiscence) or the proneness to them (habitual concupiscence) the nature of sin, though it be true that they are temptations to sin."

That is to say, sexual pleasure is natural to the natural man, and becomes reprehensible only when it begins to stand in the way of some higher development which otherwise might be his. It was no new idea. Nobody claimed any special credit for it. Solomon (notwithstanding his conduct), with his "There is a time for everything under the sun," must have known all about it. Centuries had been spent in noting the consequences flowing from other ways of thinking. They had all been tried. But the Puritan, still childishly horrified by his discovery that men may be lustful, to say nothing of ambitious and cruel, even when dressed up as popes and cardinals, was distrustful of anything and everything which strove to reach him through a mitred source. So Luther, with all the eagerness of an amateur inventor seeking to improve a steam engine by eliminating its "useless" balance-wheel, promptly announced that amorous desire was not only a temptation to evil but was *malum in se,* an evil in itself. And when the Council of Trent declared this view to be erroneous and heretical, since it put a ban on pleasure as such and made propagation lawful only when it was not enjoyed, the Reformationist was doubly sure that Luther was right.

I do not know why the Puritan happened to specialize in the Seventh Commandment the way he did. Perhaps it was because the higher reaches of lust are so sociable, and he was inclined towards solitude. To attempt merely to keep concupiscence in its place impressed him much as High Licence impressed the early Prohibitionist. It was compromising with the devil. Better get rid of the mischief, root and branch, by taking the joy out of it. Better fail altogether than to succeed by half-way measures. Thus we arrive at that impractical idealism which is today the father of so many of our woes. One is reminded of the boy who tried to grab a handful of nuts from a narrow-mouthed jar. Rather than let go of a part of his plunder, he chose to remain for ever with his fist caught in the mouth.

So Ellis must have been listening at some chapel door

when he heard the chinking of those hard phrases which led him to conclude that the Decalogue was arbitrary. The robe of truth, made of the whole piece of cloth and adjustable to all human shoulders, had been cut and sewed into a suit of clothes to fit some individual figure. The personal interpretation of anything makes it a mere hand-me-down for others. It was therefore easy for Ellis and Weininger to convict the wrinkles—and then to pretend to have convicted the cloth.

The Puritan was of course at fault. He had made concupiscence (which once actually meant the yearning of the soul for good) a synonym for crime. He had decided in his own mind who was married and who was not, and had reached his own conclusions as to what sort of sex conduct was proper. His mistake, Newman would tell us, was in ceasing to look outside of himself as well as within, and in limiting his science to indifferent matters. His mistake, according to Weininger and Ellis, was in continuing to look outside of himself at all, even at atoms.

Therefore let us throw aside our garments and enter naked into the Empirical Universe, where every man is his own god, forgetting, if possible, that "empiric" is but another name for "quack." "Man," says Weininger,[3] "is an inflexible empiricist." And this after having remarked:[4] "I have nothing to do with the empirical school," and declaring:[5] "The mind itself is the creator of time and space."

[3] "Sex and Character," p. 244.
[4] *Ibid.*, p. 142.
[5] *Ibid.*, p. 109.

CHAPTER III

HERMES AND APHRODITE

1. OTTO WEININGER

WE have all come under the spell of Otto Weininger, even those of us who have never heard of him, for he was one of those geniuses whose ideas echo far beyond any sound that is made by their names. I have chosen him as the model Impuritan reasoner not because of his intrinsic importance—though his influence, however little acknowledged, has been immense—but because he is so typical, both in his logical processes and his conclusions.

As to his personality, it is something of a mystery to everybody. It is not even known how old he was when, on October 4, 1903, his unhappy candle was snuffed out. Some say he was only 23. Certainly he was very young when he became *Dozent,* or lecturer, at the University of Vienna, and less than twenty when he published *Über die Letzten Dinge,* or "On Things Ultimate." His masterpiece, "Sex and Character," appeared soon afterwards, and he went to Italy to await results.

There appeared to be none, and during the next four months an intellectual malady, described by his friends as "a too grave sense of responsibility," but bearing more the marks of a disappointed love, became acute. He decided that his conjectures as to ultimate things were

at pains to set forth. Sex, we are bidden to understand, is not only a means by which a certain end may be attained (a hateful end, in his estimation), but it is something in itself—that is to say, masculinity is something in itself, and femininity something else again. And this conviction, so dear not only to his school of thought but to his personal rancour, he sought to establish biologically—the most untrustworthy method of establishing ethical truths which has yet been found, but the only one that the modern mind regards as valid. So he begins his book with an appeal to embryology, a description of the parting of the ways.

"In the case of a human embryo of less than five weeks, the sex to which it will afterwards belong cannot be recognized. In the fifth week of fœtal life, processes begin which by the end of the fifth month . . . have turned the genital rudiments, at first alike in the sexes, into one sex [or the other] and have determined the sex of the whole organism." [3]

The mischief, then, is a question of shape. Life is evil. Sexual differentiation is a means to life. Therefore sexual differentiation is evil. If the genital rudiments had but remained alike, no murder would ever take place, and if the sex of the whole organism chances not to be determined very definitely, it will be less murderous to that extent. What endless variations upon this theme are now current!

Our author is also about to assure us that while one of these shapes is evil, the other is good; nor can I any longer conceal the fact that man is to be the hero of this perverted drama, and woman the villain. Man is spirit; woman, but dust. Moreover, spirit is an Allness which

[3] *Ibid.*, pp. 5–6.

proves upon analysis to be akin to Nothingness, while matter is Nothingness curiously like the All.

But before coming to grips with this awesome metaphysic, and since we must demand biology's permission to think, let us glance at real biology, ignoring for a moment the purely imaginary brand which Weininger and his followers have been at pains to set forth.

2. THE PARTING OF THE WAYS

The primitive cell is a very complicated organism. It multiplies by dividing itself into halves, one precisely like the other. Prior to this division, a number of minute bodies called chromosomes from the readiness with which they may be stained so as to show as coloured or chromatic specks under the mircroscope, have also divided, so that half of them go into one division, and half into the other. Within the chromosomes there are supposed to be yet smaller bodies, known as chromomeres, or genes, and it may be assumed that they too divide before the chromosomes divide—though it must be admitted that here we roam in the pure fairy-land of conjecture. What is certain is that the number of chromosomes in each cell of a given species is constant—a circumstance to which those who contend that species are arbitrary distinctions made in a continuous series, with no real gaps or fences to separate neighbour from neighbour, would be wise to pay more attention. In every human body-cell, for example, the chromosomes number forty-eight, while the monkey-cell, according to Professor E. B. Wilson, of Columbia University,[1] boasts fifty-four. We seem to have come down a peg, yet may remember to our comfort that

[1] *Vide* "The Cell in Inheritance and Development."

the trout must get along with twenty-four, the onion and the pig each with a beggarly sixteen. It is by doubling their number by splitting that the chromosomes make it possible for the cell to become two cells, each with its full complement.

All of the lower forms of life multiply in this way, and in this way alone. Most of the cells in our own bodies multiply in this way, and in this way alone. It is not a very good way. After a time it seems to run down. So we find intermediate forms, a little higher than the lowest, using it for a general method but resorting now and then to a special method, an improvement. The cell divides as before, but prefaces the act by a novel enterprise among the chromosomes, termed reduction division.

For reduction division the chromosomes do not split; they separate into two groups, one group at one end of the about-to-be-divided cell, the other in the other. When the cell now shrinks at its equator, cutting itself into hemispheres, each hemisphere finds itself with but half the original number of chromosomes. Such a hemisphere is therefore called a gamete, an incomplete or "marriageable" cell, because before it can go any further it must find and marry itself to another gamete so as to make up the requisite chromosome contingent.

It might unite with its own dissevered half, but it never does. It seeks a far more exciting experience—union with the gamete of different ancestry, even from another body, even (in the case of all higher animals) from a different kind of body. Sex has made its appearance upon the stage of life. Two gametes which will, if brought together, unite and form the nucleus of a new creature, are said to be sexually differentiated.

Near the beginning of things, this difference is not

very apparent. The sexes of the bodo (a microscopic parasite of the cod) seem alike until we come to note their conduct. The bodo multiplies at first by simply dividing. Then lassitude overtakes the colony, and reduction division is called in to act as doctor. The husband cells are identical in appearance with the wife cells, but the one is lazy, the other active. The lazy one is called the female; the hustler the male. Throughout nature generally, lazy gametes tend to get fat, hustlers to stay thin. The evil for which Weininger bade us look stands here revealed as corpulence!

In multicellular animals—that is, colonies of cells more or less unified by a nervous system—most of the cells adhere to the primitive custom of multiplication by simply dividing. These are the soma- or body-cells. The great majority of our own cells are of the soma variety. We have, however, a few rogues which multiply by division only so long as their own multiplication is concerned. Before they undertake the making of a new individual, they undergo reduction division. These specialists in what Weininger knows as crime are called germ-cells.

If the same body furnishes both parties to a germ-cell espousal, we call that body a hermaphrodite, or two-sexed. Sexually it is two bodies in one—an arrangement not to be found, normally, except in very humble forms. What we now have to consider is the distinction between the two bodies which furnish the two sorts of gametes which will unite and fructify. Curiously enough, this distinction resembles that already made between the two sorts of gametes themselves. The body having the lazy marriageable cell (egg, or ovum) tends to get fat and become sedentary. Bodies having hustler marriageable cells (spermatozoa) tend to remain emaciated and lively. In other words, the germ-cells loan some of their own characteristics to those who possess them. Males fly about a great deal and quarrel among themselves. Females collect substance. It might almost be said that, from the very first, man is the beloved vagabond, while the place for women is the home.

But what determines the sex of the new individual born of the union of two sexes, and at what moment in its life-history is this determiner applied?

As to the moment, it differs considerably according to the species. There is a South American armadillo which regularly gives birth to quadruplets formed from a single ovum fertilized by a single spermatozoön—an ovum which then divides into four. As the resulting family may be either males or females, but never both, it is clear that the differentiation was determined not later than the fecundation. On the other hand, there are beings whose sex actually seems to depend upon circumstances occurring after birth.

The barnacle as known to seamen is either a female or a hermaphrodite, stout and sedentary. But it begins life always as a "male." These males swim, and show the genuine wanderlust, the divine discontent of masculinity. But if left to themselves they soon lose their aspirations and settle down, fasten to something fixed, and grow into sluggish womanhood. But sometimes something inspires them to turn aside from this broad road leading to destruction, and this something is invariably a female of their own species who has already turned traitor to her first persuasion and grown a roof over her head. Should a male still young enough not to have lost his manliness come into contact with one of these waiting Delilahs, he succumbs to temptation and enters not only whole-heartedly but literally into the situation, the body of the female, to wit, and there proceeds to perform the functions of a male germ-cell. Here nature consents to play but half of Weininger's game; for though she shows the female threatening to enslave the male, indeed reducing him to a mere parasite, a warning to all, she also shows the bachelor male turning into a female and becoming a mother. Of a truth, celibacy hath its perils.

The biologist Steinach claims that art may come within an ace of changing the sex after birth even in an animal as highly developed as the guinea-pig. As to human beings—artificially produced monstrosities aside—sex seems to be determined at the time of conception. The determiner, however, is in dispute.

Dr. Oscar Riddle, of the Carnegie Institute, holds that sex may be described in terms of energy, a little more or a little less—the *more* being the sign that some such name as John or James is about to be added to the family register, while the *less* will result in the use of the appellation, it may be, of Kate or of Eloïse. Dr. Alexander Graham Bell believed to the day of his death that his experiments upon sheep indicated diet as the *deus ex machina;* females being, if I remember rightly, the painful consequences of semi-starvation. A fat cell, then, is produced by fasting. Gluttony is the Weininger root of all evil.

There is also the X and Y theory, X standing for male and Y for female. X-Y biologists say that in every male germ-cell there are both an X and a Y, and that when the cell divides into gametes the X goes into one and the Y into the other. In every female germ-cell, they say further, there are two Y's but no X's, with the result that there is a Y in each female gamete. In other words, the female is purely feminine, while the male is a house divided against itself. If this be true, then if the Y gamete of a male happens to unite with the gamete of a female (always Y), the result is Y plus Y, or female. But if it be the X gamete of a male which functions, the result will be X plus Y, or male.

All of these theories seem to be approximations, more or less happy, to what may be termed the Theory of the Swollen Chromosome.

For it seems that in some gametes one of these so-easily-to-be-coloured specks is larger than the others; that this giant, in fact, is present in every mother gamete, but in only fifty per cent of father gametes; and, further, that the union of two gametes, each housing a giant, produces a male, while if the father gamete lacks its Titan the result will be feminine. From which it may be concluded that female offspring are always produced by a lack, though feminists are clearly entitled to retort that a lack originating in the father can hardly be called the woman's fault. But we shall never be able to understand how we inherit our sex until we consider heredity in general.

The subject was first given a scientific basis in 1865, when Gregor Mendel, the monk, delivered in the little town of Brünn in what was then Austria a lecture which —though making no great stir at the time—has since been heard around the world. Mendel believed that all our hereditary characteristics could be reduced to pairs of opposites. This implies that our traits can be reduced to units, which he called unit characters. And he was of the opinion that half of these unit characters had the faculty of always being victorious when confronted with the opposite unit. So he named these chronic champions "dominant characters," and their victims "recessive characters."

When chromosomes were discovered, it looked as if the actual vehicles of character transmission had been laid bare. Now we know that their number is entirely insufficient, so it is supposed that the chromomere, or gene, is the actual means by which a trait passes from one generation to another. Such an assumption, however, does nothing to explain that mystery of mysteries which loads a bit of protoplasm with strange powers, as one might put letters in a mail-bag. Physics must throw up its hands at that. Nor will any number of chromomeres account for the orderly distribution of traits, such as in the symmetrical coat-patterns of tigers and zebras, or into those other patterns known as noses, eyes, ears, limbs, etc. Granting that the chromomeres furnish, somehow, the necessary influence, what governs the placement? What power leads the blue-producing influence to manifest itself at precisely the right spot in the pupil of an eye? How does the unit character which is fitted to furnish off the end of a nose manage to get to the end of the nose rather than somewhere else? This is the great problem of living, plastic design.

There is no question as to the way in which Mendel solved this problem in his own mind. He was familiar with the scholastic theory which holds that the forms taken by matter are governed by a more impalpable stuff, called substance; and that back of substance lies something more impalpable still, called spirit, past all accounting for. If the chromomeres supply the bricks, substance furnishes the plan of the building, though we see nothing of this plan until it begins to be filled out with matter.

We of to-day do not like this theory, for it puts us in

the position of not being able to see to the base of things. Some of us even prefer to assume that matter has no existence, that we imagine or dream it. And that leads to the conclusion that the dreamer dreams even the other dreamers, that there are no other dreamers outside of his own consciousness. Now and then there is one who will go so far as to say that even this consciousness is only a figment of his own dream. There is then neither an outside nor an inside, no neighbourhood and no manor house. Egotism thus commits suicide upon the altar of its own logic. The Cartesian formula, "I think, therefore I am," becomes "I don't think, therefore I am not."

To people who reason thus I have for the moment nothing to say. They themselves admit that there are no such people. Suffice it to remark that the chronomeres do not explain the distribution of particulars, but do furnish the possible machinery whereby the material for these particulars is furnished—furnished, too, in double quantity, two bricks for every place for one.

For instance, the influence which acts upon those parts of the organism governing a certain portion of its growth finds itself confronted with another influence, another brick, so to speak, seeking to have its say upon the same matter. And this other say may be quite different. We will call the influence with the more ambitious idea as to proper height the trait of Tallness; and its rival, the trait of Dwarfness. In such a case tallness wins every time. When Mendel crossed tall peas with dwarf peas in the garden of his monastery, the resulting plants were tall—not tallish, but tall, as tall as the tallest. Always.

The recessive trait, however, was only in hiding, for if he took these hybrid talls and dusted them with pollen from their own anthers (or bred them to similar hybrids), some of the ensuing seedlings were dwarfs, showing that dwarfness had been carried over through a tall generation that gave no outward sign of it. Moreover, this cropping-out of the recessive trait took place in the long run in exactly one case out of four.

It would seem that when a germ-cell divides into gametes, a given dominant trait and its opposite recessive tend to avoid each other, so that only one of them normally gets into the same gamete. Only one of these gametes takes part in any one union, since the other must have a different origin. It is thus an even chance whether the gamete thrown aside contains the dominant trait or not, and one chance in four that the dominant is thrown aside by both parents. Only in the latter case does the recessive trait become active in the body of the offspring —for recessive traits never win save by default, when their opposites are absent. This means that half of the second generation of hybrid seedlings were themselves hybrids, tall in appearance but carrying dwarfness as a recessive trait in their germ-cells. Half of the others were pure-bred talls, incapable of producing dwarfs if bred to themselves or their similars. The remaining were pure-bred dwarfs, just as pure as if there had never been tallness introduced into the strain. The law for hybrids, then, is that three out of four will show the dominant trait; and that of these, two will carry the recessive trait. In other words, out of four plants, one will be a pure dwarf, one a pure tall, and two will be hybrids, tall in appearance but with latent dwarfness capable of being transmitted to subsequent generations.

Now, since each one of us—unless indeed we sprang from the head of Jove or from the foam of the sea—has had both a father and a mother, we are always sexually "crossed," and therefore our inherited sex-characters ought to appear in conformity with Mendel's law for hybrids. Assuming that the essential masculine traits are dominant over the feminine, then there will be born three times as many boys as girls. Or assuming that the feminine is dominant, girls will outnumber the boys three to one. But observation shows that the sexes are about equal, numerically at least. The law works beautifully when applied to tallness and dwarfness in peas, to black rabbits and albino rabbits, and to other comparatively simple matters. But if one tries to make it account for the actual proportions in which all features appear throughout creation, difficulties, at first sight insuperable, soon begin to appear.

There is the difficulty, for instance, of discovering an opposite for every trait. The opposite of a black rabbit is a white rabbit. The opposite of a tall pea is a dwarf pea. Very well. But what is the opposite of a pair of blue eyes? It helps if we reduce our supposed units to very small proportions and admit that a great many of them must unite to produce that group which we call a simple feature but which is in reality a compound of many minor features. But the question remains, What is the opposite of blue? I think we should abandon the word "opposite" altogether and use the word "different." Biologically speaking, the opposite of blue is any colour other than blue, any shade in the least different from the one proposed by a given unit-character carrier.

It is in this sense only that the sexes are "opposite." Nor was there ever a greater error than the supposition that sex involves two simple things, substances, entities, or ideas, like an X and a Y. Sex is merely an improved technic which nature introduced into her art of multiplication.

In the lower forms of life, where each cell is submerged in the fluid it feeds on, there reigns eternal youth, threatened only by such catastrophes as might bring general famine; the simple division method was sufficient. The new cells could swing free, and not interfere with each other. But with multicellular creatures there is crowding. Parents surround themselves with their own progeny, which come between them and breakfast. The old cells starve and die, or are maimed and imperfect. Their decay produces toxins, which are gotten rid of with increasing difficulty. When our own body-cells find themselves in this situation, we begin to complain of imperfect metabolism. We grow old. Age is the starvation of disadvantageously placed cells, maimed, it may be, in the crush. So we introduce glands from young animals, and try by every means to stimulate elimination. But artificial rejuvenation is not yet a success, and the great rejuvenator, Voronoff now claims he never said that transplantation would make us actually young again. Perhaps there is something within us besides our cells which becomes weary and starved, and—unable any longer to nourish itself with worldly things—resents all attempts to prolong the situation.

Nature rejuvenates by means of the baby, product not of one parent but of two. By reduction division, resulting in half-cells which needed completion by union with other half-cells, a double source of heredity was secured. There was now less danger of defects being perpetuated, a better chance that a lack in one parent would be supplied by the other.

We do not know how the transition from non-sexual

to sexual propagation was accomplished. It may have been one of those sudden leaps which some scientists call emergences, outcroppings from the hidden depths of things —phenomena not acknowledged by ordinary theories of evolution, though they are quite the most important phenomena on earth. But somehow there was a meeting of two cells, and a struggle between their hereditary factors. It must have been here that the phenomenon of dominance and recessiveness began to manifest itself. The process is very complicated and but imperfectly understood.[2] All I wish to insist upon is that sex entered the scheme of life when two gametes resulting from the reduction division of a single cell were forbidden to undo this work by uniting again and were compelled to go abroad for succour. A difference of some sort was demanded between the parents, were it only a difference in origin.

But in regard to certain differences, nature seems to have wished to preserve some of the weaker characters—weaker, that is, in the hereditary contest—which tend to disappear under the handicap of recessiveness if left to themselves in pure lines of breeding. So she decreed that the weaker character as well as its stronger opponent must always meet in any union to be blessed with fruitfulness. When we say that the weaker character and its stronger opponent are *sexually differentiated,* we merely mean that both are necessary. So if we want to know what sex is, so far as gametes are concerned, the answer is easy. It is any differentiation which will admit of fertility. That is the one and only test. Sex originated in a prohibition forbidding like to mate with like, ordering that in certain particulars the strain must be definitely crossed in every generation.

[2] See Appendix A.

If we agree that these weaker but useful traits are what we now call feminine, then sexual differentiation and the curse of sterility launched at the union of gametes not so differentiated were instituted to preserve femininity and with it those finer and more delicate qualities which might otherwise have been elbowed out of existence. It was not a cross between qualities like tallness and dwarfness which was insisted on, but a cross between those features which first began to manifest themselves as the agility of the spermatozoön and the sedate serenity of the ovum.

Nor was it enough that the soft and lovely recessives be given that one-in-four chance of appearance which would have been theirs if merely introduced into the hereditary stream of every generation and then abandoned to the law of dominant characters. The two sexes were to be put upon an arithmetical level, and for this some circumstance was necessary which would nullify the advantage which dominance gave to the male. It is not possible to say certainly what this circumstance is, but it appears to lie in the nature of the swollen chromosome.

If hybrid tall peas are bred back to a pure dwarf, instead of with one another or with similar hybrids, the seeds will come up on an average of talls and shorts in equal numbers—just the proportions we observe to be preserved between male and female births. It is required, then, to get a *pure-bred* group of the essential recessive or female sex-characters into each generation. But how? Women as well as men have fathers. Are they not, then, sexually hybrid to the same extent as they?

Not necessarily. Let us suppose that the swollen chromosome, which is possessed by all gametes produced by females, contains double the usual number of chromomeres, and that these are all laden with the essential sexual unit-characters of the mother. The male parent furnishes a swollen chromosome only half the time. What if *his* extra chromomeres *also* are bearers of the essential *feminine* characteristics?

In the marriage conflict, then, when the male's out-size chromosome is present, its male chromomeres will meet and dominate an equal number of the mother's female chromomeres relating to corresponding traits and contained in the mother's out-size chromosome. But there remains the mother's surplusage of these same units, and against these the male has nothing to oppose but his own male units (already at grips with their feminine counterparts), and his own extra supply of chromomeres —which happen to be traitorously female. We will say that to dominate one opponent exhausts even the pugnacity of a male-trait chromomere. The excess females are left unconquered, and control the situation.

This is equivalent to saying that boys and girls are born in equal numbers for the reason that all women are pure-bred, sexually speaking, while men are but mongrels and quite as likely to furnish one strain as the other. Weininger, who knew nothing of the swollen chromosome (or of any other), must have been groping for it in his mind when he said: [3] "The female principle is . . . nothing more than sexuality; the male principle is sexual and something more." But he must make woman's pure femininity pure carnality (quite another matter) and assume that man is mongrel because he is not yet quite pure spirit—certainly an ingenious way of trying to get Hermes out of a tight place. But if Nature teaches anything, it is that there is no such thing as the male prin-

[3] *Op. cit.*, p. 90.

ciple, and no such thing as the female principle. The meeting of an ovum and a spermatozoön is the meeting of two armies of innumerable combatants.

3. THOSE WHOM PLASMS HAVE JOINED TOGETHER

Pseudo-scientific philosophers, however, are the last people to give an honest account of that Nature to which they so frequently appeal. So masculinity and femininity, according to Weininger and Company, are two principles, two stuffs, which Weininger himself names arrhenoplasm for the male and thelyplasm for the female. And from these he assumes a third—idioplasm.

"Idioplasm is the bearer of the specific characters. It exists in all the cells of a multicellular animal. . . . I have been led," he says,[1] "to the conception of an arrhenoplasm and a thelyplasm as the modes in which the idioplasms of every bisexual organism may appear. . . . Actually existing protoplasm is to be thought of as moving from an ideal arrhenoplasm through a real or imaginary indifferent condition (true hermaphroditism) towards a protoplasm that approaches, but never actually reaches, an ideal thelyplasm."

Truly an awful collocation of words. But it is evident that he would give idioplasm all the characteristics of protoplasm—that viscid, gummy, and often granular, semi-fluid albuminous substance generally regarded as the physical basis of life. As it exists in cells and is the bearer of specific characters, it must be divisible. Then it is not, thank God, a philosophical entity after all. It is chromatin, the stuff of chromosomes and chromomeres, imagined by a philosopher without the benefit of specific knowledge.

[1] *Ibid.*, p. 16.

And yet it "appears" only in "modes," that is to say, forms, one of which is arrhenoplasm and the other thelyplasm, which are real only when they are mixed the one with the other. In their purity they are abstractions, with names but no local habitations—philosophical entities once more. Is it not clear?

If not, let us try yet other words, and see if we can find out what, if anything, was in Weininger's mind. We will say that he means that ideal arrhenoplasm is spirit in a disembodied form, and therefore non-existent in a material sense. And it is male. Therefore masculinity is disembodied spirit. Then it slowly materializes, becomes sicklied o'er with the pale cast of earth. It is now protoplasm. But this, as it grows more and more of the earth, earthy, approaches pure thelyplasm, pure femininity, though it never reaches it—not in this life. What would happen if it did? Why, it would cease to exist, for we learn on page 293 that "the negation of existence is no other than matter," and that "woman is matter, is nothing." Absolute woman, that is. So he compares her[2] with that "ideal gas" which follows the Boyle-Gay Lussac law made and provided for gases—a law which all actual gases stoutly defy.

Man, then, enters upon the worldly scene by becoming slightly womanish, surrendering his spiritual existence for a material existence which is a sort of non-existence. If he keeps on in this downward road, he turns into a "true" hermaphrodite, that is, one which is psychologically rather than physically bisexed. If he deteriorates further still, he becomes as womanly a woman as can be found. Another step, and the last bit of spirit would be squeezed out of him; he would solidify entirely, and paradoxically

[2] *Ibid.*, p. 7.

vanish in pure non-existence, an ideal woman too bad to be true.

This philosophy is not new. It is merely a perversion of the ancient wisdom which teaches us that matter is the veil of mystery and illusion which hides the face of God—a perversion as old as man's attempt to comprehend the Incomprehensible, to reduce Infinity to finite bounds, to guess the riddle of the Sphinx and to make the Absolute explain itself.

It is not even the first time that it has been sought to make flesh synonymous with the female sex. Theologians, of the sort who try to practise continence without a vocation for it, have always wanted to put it this way. Man, they say in effect, is less sexual the more masculine he is. Sexuality is another name for femininity. These men are lost in their own point of view. They blame the beer for their thirst. "Femaleness," Weininger affirms,[3] "is identical with pairing." So there are not two sexes; there is only one. We are all tarred with the same stick, some more and others less. Thus we differ. But the real tar baby is a lady.

Yet we are warned to be careful to whom we apply the name. At present, it seems, "it is fairly certain that many individuals have their sex assigned to them on account of the existence of the primary male sexual characteristic," even "though there may be delayed *descensus testiculorum,* or epi- or hypo-spadism." [4]

Family doctors ought not to be so cock-sure. Having observed the primary sexual characteristic displayed by the new arrival, they may be paying an undeserved compliment if they proceed at once with the blunt and joyful

[3] *Ibid.,* p. 246.
[4] *Ibid.,* p. 47.

announcement, "It's a boy!" And they run the risk of doing a great wrong if, on the other hand, and at the first glimpse of untoward circumstances, they permit themselves to sigh, "It's only a girl!" They would do better, Weininger suggests, "at least to make certain of a few facts as to the general condition of the body which might serve as guides to the male or female diathesis, such as, for instance, the distance between the great crochanters, the lilac spines, and so forth." [5] And he reminds us of the sexual differences in brains discovered by Bischoff and Rudinger, and of sundry observations which have been made regarding the same in livers, lungs, and spleens.

As matters stand, a child is in danger of being sentenced to wear skirts for life merely because of the chance possession of female genitals, to the great distress of "his" masculine brain, spleen, liver, lungs, crochanters, and lilac spines. "The internal appendages of the sexual glands," we are asked to believe, "may have a sexual significance quite distinct from those of the external." Therefore, in a truly enlightened age, baby would be carefully summed up, and clothed in conformity with the majority of itself. Marriage would not take place between individuals sexually opposite in a crude sense, but between those whose unlikeness was discovered by careful calculations applied to minute particulars. If, crudely speaking, both spouses happened to be men, or both women, so much the better. "I shall show reasons," Weininger promises,[6] "in favour of the possibility that homosexuality is a higher form than heterosexuality."

And what are these reasons? Well, for one of them, homosexuality has been observed in animals. "If bulls are kept apart from cows for a considerable time, homosexual

[5] *Ibid.*, p. 24.
[6] *Ibid.*, p. 66.

acts occur amongst them. . . . Cattle in captivity behave precisely as prisoners and convicts in these matters." [7] And if the example of convicts and cattle be not sufficient, there is the alleged behaviour of the ancient Greeks and of certain notables of later time—upon whom other authors will soon be heard to enlarge.

"Classical scholars," Weininger laments, "have defended Sappho warmly against the implication that there was anything more than mere friendship in her relations with her own sex." And to show what an evil turn said scholars were seeking to do to her fame, he adds: [8] "Homosexuality in a woman is the outcome of her masculinity, and presupposes a higher degree of development."

He also mentions Catherine II of Russia, Queen Christina of Sweden; "the highly gifted although deaf, dumb, and blind Laura Bridgman; George Sand; and a very large number of . . . women and girls . . . partly bisexual, partly homosexual," to say nothing of Madame de Staël, "whose work on Germany is probably the greatest book ever produced by a woman," Madame de Staël being supposed to have been intimate with August Wilhelm Schlegel, "who was a homosexualist"—though how this peculiarity of his applies to the situation we are not told. We are told instead about "the authoress and mathematician, Sonia Kowalevska," who, "like Sappho, had an abnormally scanty growth of hair" [Weininger has already suggested that the hair of the lover plus the hair of the mistress reaches to an ideal length which is constant in all ideal cases, and that the more hair the less brains], and about "the notorious Madame Blavatsky," who was "extremely masculine in her appearance."

[7] *Ibid.*, p. 49.
[8] *Ibid.*, p. 66.

Madame Blavatsky was, as a matter of fact, extremely corpulent. But Weininger is confident of her as an instance in point, having obviously failed to read the record of her notoriously dropsical existence.

With his men he has more difficulty, for though he calls boldly upon the example of King Ludwig II of Bavaria, whose friendship with Wagner he considers "dubious," Franz Liszt, "whose life and compositions were extremely effeminate," is a puzzle, like "the face of the husband of Clara Schumann," which "might have been taken as that of a woman." [9] He does not claim that either Liszt or Schumann was actually irregular, but he does seem to be attributing superiority to these "effeminates." It must be remembered, however, that Weininger despised music.

Music, history, and legend aside, it appears that the homosexual is a superior person because he is more sensitive to the call of his own particular plasms. He is homosexual only in seeming. Oscar Wilde, according to this theory, was a shining example of the uncommon, or exquisite, heterosexual, one whose virtue was delicately poised, whose thelyplasm was not to be deceived by appearances. It is the so-called normal man or woman, with blunted instincts which take no note of the inner significance of delayed *descensus testiculorum* or epi- or hypo-spadism, who is liable to fall headlong into vice.

So does Weininger, this more-than-Puritan, who would have branded as licentious the declaration of St. Paul that it is better to marry than to burn, this self-appointed prosecutor who charges Eros with murder, this pilgrim bound for Spotless Town, pause on his way to pay his

[9] *Ibid.*, p. 67.

respects to those cultural metropolises euphemistically known as Sodom and Gomorrah.

From this twilight of thought, darkly arrived at by conceiving of masculinity and femininity as two impossible chemical opposites which somehow may be mixed together in varying proportions, emerges the intermediate sex, not of things as they are, but of Edward Carpenter; the Urning of Ulrichs and Krafft-Ebing, or Dr. Albert Moll, Dr. Paul Moreau, Cesare Lombroso, M. A. Raffalovich, Auguste Forel, Havelock Ellis, Dr. Magnus Hirschfeld, Dr. Von Römer, and Montegazza. In this same dusk are destined to move the homo-erotics of Proust. And Weininger is not only prepared to drape them in becoming shadows, but to crown them as martyrs urged by the inevitable against the sharp corners of cruel convention. He sounds the refrain, now so constant in the literature of modern gonad worship:

"If we are fine, we are disreputable and cannot help ourselves; nor can the masses comprehend the nobility of our disrepute. We are born with certain plasms which drag us whither they list even if it be in the immortalized direction of Reading Gaol."

That Weininger intends to give his plasms power is evident when he begins to formulate his famous recipe for domestic bliss.

"For true sexual union," he says,[10] "it is necessary that there come together a complete male and a complete female, even though in different cases the masculine and feminine are distributed between the two individuals in different proportions. . . . Were [a man] completely male, his requisite complement [notwithstanding the supposition that he would then be pure spirit] would be a

[10] *Ibid.*, p. 29.

complete female," i.e., a complete nonentity; and vice versa. If, however, "he is composed of a definite inheritance of femaleness, [then] to complete the individual his maleness must be completed to make a union; but so also must his femaleness be completed."

In other language, a man who is, let us say, 90 parts male and 10 parts female, should marry a woman 10 parts male and 90 parts female, since every couple ought to add up 100 parts masculinity and 100 parts femininity when taken together, even though the man's ten per cent of femininity be so concentrated in the pudendum as to make him technically his mother's daughter, and though the ten per cent masculinity of his ideal wife is scattered about among such harmless things as a manly development of the "lanugo," or hair on the upper lip.

Or it may be that the husband's femininity has manifested itself only in an unusual amount of glandular tissue beneath the skin of the breasts, while the "woman" is only a woman generally speaking. The location of the plasms does not signify. What are vulgarly known as sexual organs, whether alike or different, must not be allowed to stand in the way. All that is necessary is that "there come together a complete male and a complete female," arrhenoplasmically and thelyplasmically speaking.

Why? Well, for one thing, there is the specious symmetry of the idea. Then there is the gratuitous assumption that unlike plasms attract each other. Naturally we wish to wed so as to get all the attraction possible. But let us see what happens when we attempt to get it in this particular fashion. Let us see to what extent plasms will explain the potent wiles of the stork.

4. THE WILES OF THE STORK

Biology has, strictly speaking, nothing fundamental to say about wiles, being concerned merely with the attempt to describe the forms and motions of living matter. What this matter is, what are the forces which make it move, not even physics can discover.

As to the influences exerted by moving shapes (exerted, that is, in the consciousness of the individual), they are or should be psychology's concern.

When we speak of sex we usually mean this psychological part of it, sex in consciousness, not sex in form—passion, in short. For it is in the field of awareness that wiles have play. It is in this field, too, that most of our knowledge lies.

Every time we try to trace an experience back through its physical antecedents, we end with nothing in hand but a hypothesis. In the early days of science our hypotheses had the merit of being comparatively consistent in themselves, but it is no longer so. We have discovered so many facts—to say nothing of lies masquerading as facts—that we cannot even imagine explanations (i.e., physical antecedents) to keep pace with the demand. Many believe that we are progressing towards a gradual clearing up of the Great Mystery. Nothing could be further from the case. We are progressing in the direction of increased incomprehensibility. Every new fact which we add to our store, whether we observe it by studying ourselves or the world, makes it just that much more difficult to guess what other facts have gone before. The plot thickens.

Physicists are no longer able, even by turning their wildest fancies loose, to picture so much as an atom capable of performing all the tricks now expected of atoms.

An atom, we are asked to believe, is a nucleus surrounded by electrons. Well and good. But Bertrand Russell, in that recent book of his which he calls "Philosophy," defines an electron as a series of events taking place where it is not. We might as well fall back upon Octavus Roy Cohen, and say that an atom is an accident going somewhere to happen.

And if inadequacy be true of the theory of atoms, how much more it must be true of the theory of cells. Life no doubt accounts for cells, but certainly cells do not account for life. Consequently they do not account for sex, do not explain it even in the humblest sense of the word "explanation." Nevertheless, biologists have accumulated a vast amount of information which, if it does not furnish us with a complete foundation for the truth, at least knocks the foundations from beneath a lot of error. It is imaginary biology, such as Weininger's, which gives plausibility to false philosophy. What are we to do? Accept the imaginary biology and the philosophy which it supports, or cling to what we know perfectly well in the first place, damning as error whatever conflicts with it?

I confess that I am inclined frequently to take the truth for granted, to depend upon reasoning and evidence of a woefully unscientific character, and to accept conclusions tested by centuries of human experience in a world of people in general rather than by moments of experiment in laboratories ruled by specialists. That is to say, I am inclined to give some weight to the kind of evidence and reasoning which guide us in trivial everyday affairs, such as business and deciding who ought and who ought not to be hanged.

The fact is, we know a great deal more about things by and large than we do about things in particular. A sorry state of affairs, but how can it be helped? The gentlemen who have promised to explain the universe from the bottom upwards have not yet finished their task. Meanwhile it seems advisable to carry on. So let us apply the test of common experience to some of Weininger's data—for instance, his two plasms with their alleged attraction for each other.

If the complete male is pure spirit, while a complete female is pure nothingness, how came it that the Absolute did not collapse into Zero in the first place, avoiding all this intermediate coil which we feel compelled to admit has somehow taken place? What could have kept the primordial Allness and Noneness apart? Would not sexual attraction here have attained its ideal maximum? Or if this smacks too much of the Infinite Mystery, how does it happen that masculinity manages to keep itself together at all? Or Femininity? If unlike poles attract, so do like poles repel. One would think that an arrhenoplasmic spleen would abhor an arrhenoplasmic liver, and flatly refuse to live in the same body with it. Such organs, fleeing as if from the wrath to come, seem, however, to have escaped general observation.

Still worse ought to befall if this alleged rush of arrhenoplasm towards thelyplasm, and the supposed dislike of similar plasms for each other, both happen at the same time. Truly, lovers are in a sad predicament. If their spleens be properly different, these will draw them together. But at the same instant intestines of a single persuasion may thrust them apart—and this in spite of the 100 measures of arrhenoplasm and 100 of thelyplasm in the sum of their two bodies.

As for pure males and pure females, one existent and the other non-existent, they will be constrained to behave

like a pair of metallic dummies, the one positively and the other negatively electrified, which clash together without having a thing to say about it. Is this what the poets mean when they tell us that love is blind?

I had not supposed even sweethearts to be quite so dumb as this. I had always fancied that the expression "sexual attraction" was a figure of speech, that the way of a man with a maid was somewhat more devious than the ways of two bundles of iron filings. Instances have at least been reported of men compelled to travel far and to seek their fortunes before they could approach their maids to any purpose. Are these but travellers' tales? And what becomes of the proverb, "Absence makes the heart grow fonder"? Attraction, literally understood, should vary inversely as the square of the distance.

Undaunted by any such difficulties as these, Weininger insists [1] that his "law of sexual attraction gives the long-sought-for explanation of sexual inversion, of sexual inclination towards members of the same sex," and boasts that "such a view is directly opposed to that of those [like Schrenk-Notzig, Kraepelin, and Féré] who hold that sexual inversion is an acquired character." Opposed it certainly is, for Schrenk-Notzig, Kraepelin, and Féré happen in this particular to have told the truth. But this "law" ought to explain inversion, if anything, since that is precisely what it was invented to explain. So Weininger attempts [2] to apply it to "the homosexualist," limiting the word to "that type of sexual invert who prefers very female men or very male women, in accordance with the general law of sexual attractions."

According to this, the homosexualist is one, outwardly

[1] *Ibid.*, p. 45.
[2] *Ibid.*, p. 52.

of either sex, whose individual plasms are nearly balanced. He finds his complement in one whose plasms are also nearly balanced. And it is true that people so balanced would, under the plasmic theory, be precisely those whose apparent sex would most likely be other than their plasmic sex. We would expect a man with a full share of arrhenoplasm to be a man throughout, that if his arrhenoplasm was scarce it would run the greater risk of exhausting itself in the making of the male genitalia, leaving the rest of him thelyplasmic, possibly even to the extent of overbalancing the male particular. A female particular (still granting this law) could be overbalanced in the same way. And so would intermediates, outwardly of one sex and inwardly of another, sometimes be drawn to mates apparently of the same gender. Homosexuality presents no special difficulty.

Yet Weininger, so blind to trouble where it exists, must needs discover it where it is not.

"The pæderast," he goes on, with an air of having left homosexuality aside, "may on the other hand be attracted either by very male men or by very female women, but in the latter case only in so far as he is not pæderastic. Moreover, his inclination for the male sex is stronger than for the female sex, and is more deeply seated in his nature. The origin of pæderasty is a problem in itself, and remains unsolved by this investigation."

Our philosopher is too modest. Omitting to trouble with pæderasts in so far as they are not pæderastic, we shall find that the law of attraction (barring those difficulties which apply also to normal cases) accounts for them very well. Ninety per cent arrhenoplasmics (or 80 per cent, or what you will) seek 90 per cent thelyplasmics, and so on. Homosexuality arises whenever a more than

50 per cent male body happens to find itself encumbered with female genitalia, or when a more than 50 per cent female body is embarrassed with male genitalia—granting that such bodies may be. If we have neither heads nor habits, but are collections of unconnected magnetized details, the law is established, and there is nothing further to be said. Why, then, was Weininger unwilling to apply it to those inverts whom he distinguishes as pæderasts? Why did he go out of his way to define them as those who are attracted both by very female women and by very male men?

It was partly, I think, because he had chanced to turn his attention to real instead of ideal sinners, and observed that they were apt to be not only homosexual but promiscuously vicious. He admired these people and wished to make them super-mannish, and could not imagine how, masculine both in general and in particular, they could still be thelyplasmic enough not to be drawn exclusively to normal women. Under his definition of the pæderast, the plasmic theory does indeed break down. To explain that kind of an abnormal, one is thrown back upon facts—particularly the fact of acquired habit. This fact will explain also another thing which evidently puzzled Weininger—the preference for a passive partner who is not a woman.

Weininger must also have been dimly conscious that his law of sexual attraction contradicted his belief that masculinity is spirit and that sexuality is feminine, which ought to make the virile impotent. Logic also may have informed him that plasms balanced in the same individual would make even such individuals incapable of that dissatisfaction known as passion. Any plasm which they might seek abroad they could find already at home. So the

cold would not only be the male but the effeminate, the betwixt-and-betweens. So did Pelions of confusion pile upon confounded Ossas.

Yet there are two particulars in which the Weininger theory seems at first sight to be supported by biological facts. A region exists wherein sexual attraction, in a direct magnetic, cellular, molecular, or atomic sense, seems to be in operation. Also those secretions of the ductless glands about which we hear so much nowadays—secretions which stimulate or retard the growth of certain organs and are not only thrown into the blood-stream by particular emotions but tend to increase these same emotions when so thrown—do have a certain superficial resemblance to plasms.

Let us consider the glands first. Their secretions, known as autocoids or hormones, differ from the Impuritan plasms primarily by not being reducible to two. They are as various as the organs themselves. But what about those derived more or less immediately from the genitalia?

Steinach, having castrated young male guinea-pigs, grafted in them ovaries from females—and saw his victims develop mammæ and suckle young. This indeed shows the potency of germ-cells in moulding the body-cells. But it riddles the idea that the general bodily disposition is apt to be at variance with its more obvious sexual characteristics, save through acquired habit. Nor do recessive traits, once dominated, lie uneasy and unappeased, ready to break forth at the earliest opportunity. It requires the introduction of foreign hormones, representing traits coming from a different line of heredity, traits which have not been dominated, to produce such insurrection. A dominated trait always waits for a new generation before trying to show itself. As to the hered-

itary factors, some (called suppressors) seem to exist merely for the sake of holding others in check—but the check continues to be effective, at least until artificially removed. Undoubtedly the genes do a part of their work through the hormones.[3]

But the principal difference between hormones and imaginary plasms lies in the fact that real hormones do not attract each other.

Weininger himself notes[4] that "the chief difference [between organic and inorganic attraction] seems to be that, in the case of the attraction between the inorganic substances, strains are set up in the media between the two poles, whilst in the living matter the forces seem confined to the organisms themselves."

Scientists will smile at this resurrection of the old theory of strains in media, which supposes that the apple falls because of the pull of something very much like a piece of elastic between itself and the ground. But this need not concern us, since Weininger admits that in *living* matter the forces of attraction "seem confined to the organisms themselves."

Again we have a bit of truth. A boy sees the apple. It makes his mouth water. But it does not lift him off his feet. He goes and gets a ladder, for it is the Lord's day, and he is afraid that climbing the tree might spoil his Sunday clothes. In other words, he acts through his nervous system. There does not appear to be any apple-plasm in the ladder. But here we bid good-bye to our precious law of sexual attraction, which was founded upon the assumption that there is a direct pull between all cells of unlike character. Gone is the reason for thinking that

[3] See Appendix B.
[4] *Op. cit.*, p. 40.

an excessively masculine man should mate with an excessively feminine woman, the virago with the effeminate even if said effeminate be also female. Vanished is the need to complete the sum of hidden plasms without regard to apparent sex. The point is of excessive importance —or would be if philosophy could return to its ancient dignity as the guardian of good conduct.

Nevertheless, as has already been indicated, there is a region where Weininger's law of direct attraction seems actually to work.

"It would be extremely interesting," he remarks,[5] "to make observations as to whether the larger, heavier and less active egg-cells exert a special attraction on the smaller and more active spermatozoa, while those egg-cells with less food-yolk attract more strongly the larger and less active spermatozoa."

These observations have been made, and it has at least been shown that there is an attraction between ova and spermatozoa in general. "The male cells of ferns [according to the experiments of Wilhelm Pfeffer] are attracted not only by the malic acid secreted naturally by the archegonia, but by synthetically prepared malic acid, whilst the male cells of mosses are attracted either by the natural acid of the female cells or by acid prepared from cane sugar." [6] Moreover, "according to Falkenberg, the spermatozoa in moving towards the ova are able to overcome opposing forces to a certain degree." That is to say, the attraction is real and direct, though effective only through an infinitesimal amount of space.

But here direct approach is the way to function. Ova and spermatozoa (at least the latter) are loose. They

[5] *Ibid.*, p. 36.
[6] *Ibid.*, p. 39.

behave like individuals. *And the impulse of individuals is always an impulse to function—to function as individuals!*

So the boy desired to function as a boy eating an apple. Boys have many other desires, because they are linked up by their nerves with a great number of organs, each one of which is inclined more or less constantly to function in its own peculiar way. If no opportunity be given to a particular organ to play its rôle, the boy is apt to hear from it. He feels a nervous disturbance, and unless there be other demands upon his time (in which case energy will be withdrawn from the organ, leaving it a prey to innocuous desuetude), he as likely as not proceeds to still the clamour—if of his stomach, by giving it something to digest. But he does not rub his dinner against his belly. That would go far towards satisfying attraction, but it would not enable his stomach to function.

Now ova and spermatozoa are not subject to such a variety of urges as are boys. When they find themselves brought very, very close together, they know of but one thing to do—unite. Even in boys there are moments when one possibility seems to be the only benign possibility in the universe. Ova and spermatozoa are always thus single-minded, and, once they have been introduced one to the other by the functioning of other organs, they do indeed behave as if an elastic band stretched between them.

As for bisexual tugs between other sorts of cells, they are illusions. Lips seek lips, we say, yet John does not kiss a screen even if Mary be behind it—not unless he knows she is there. Nor do lovers embrace because of local strains and stresses either in the particles of their arms or in the media between them. A man may be drawn towards the wax figure of a woman if he mistakes it for flesh and blood, and even if he does not if it sufficiently stimulates his imagination. Weininger would force us to believe that there was thelyplasm in the wax. But the truth is that desire in human beings acts through consciousness, opinions to the contrary being engendered by the fact that we are not always able to give our desire a name.

Schopenhauer has said that "the organs of generation are objectified desire." Yes; but whose desire, and for what? Was he thinking of the prospective parents, and of them as longing to be fruitful and multiply? Did he attribute this creative anxiety to a preëxisting soul anxious to become incarnate? Or was this desire supposed to be a purpose or a thought in the mind of God? All of these interpretations are possible, and some of them are rather more than pretty. It is an old notion to picture souls as budding from a parent Deity and venturing (or being thrust) into separate existence through the ways of matter as little birds are thrust (or venture) from their nest into the ways of the air. I am also mindful that Schopenhauer also wrote: "For the whole world, with all its phenomena, is the objectivity of the One invisible will." But I am very much afraid that he entertained the vague idea that the organs in question came into being in obedience to an individual desire to experience sensation.

Think of the desire for sensation externalizing itself in male and female genitalia provided with ducts for ova on the one hand and for spermatozoa on the other! Shortsighted desire. Unless it wished to benefit by sensations quite different and of a less agreeable order than those which the context suggests, desire might better have externalized itself in that newly discovered luteal hormone which has been hailed as the harbinger of sterility within the reach of all. No, the organs of generation are anything but what desire would have desired. They are the objectified possibility of fecundity.

Weininger scoffs [7] at "the ancient theories as to the influence of the 'unsatisfied womb' in the female, or of the '*semen retentum*' in men." But the ancients were close to the truth, and it is to these influences which the individual is inclined to yield. If an organ functions, he is satisfied, so far as that particular is concerned. But it makes no immediate difference to him whether the gametes function or not, gametes reaching consciousness only through the organs which contain them, not at all in their own act of fructification.

What, then, is sex in the individual? We have seen that in the gametes it is a differentiation which gives fecundity to union—that, and nothing else. In the strict sense, then, sex belongs only to germ-cells. Such cells, once elaborated, may be brought together artificially without the intervention of any other organs. The result is fruitful, too, often enough—witness our fish-hatcheries. Artificial spermatization is practicable to a certain extent even with the human species. But common usage describes as sexual a great mass of peculiarities belonging to soma- or body-cells, and calls some of them primary and others secondary. How shall we determine which are sexual and which are not, which primary or secondary, which masculine and which feminine?

Let us say that any character is masculine which belongs to spermatozoa, or has become associated in our minds in any way with bodies which habitually bear spermatozoa; that it is feminine if it belongs to ova, or is mentally or emotionally linked in our minds with ova-

[7] *Ibid.*, pp. 87–88.

bearing bodies. It will be primary if it is, generally speaking, essential to the fruitful bringing together of gametes, and secondary if it merely tends to further such unions.

Some characters, even though not primarily sexual, have come to be regarded as very definitely male: some as very definitely female; while others remain sexually vague, and others still are lacking in all sexual association whatever. At the same time, it is evident that any characteristic may acquire such associations. In many countries the tobacco habit was for a long while a masculine characteristic (it still is in so far as the smoking of cigars is concerned), while corsets and bustles suggested the "weaker" sex. But snuff-taking was never peculiarly masculine, and quite recently short hair has lost most of its masculine suggestiveness.

Some sex-characters, especially the primary, seem to be definitely hereditary, especially in the higher forms of life, while some of the secondary are acquired. These are often habits rather than structures. But whether they be constant habits, like the strutting of the turkey gobbler, or mere modes, like the fashions of the *Rue de la Paix,* they remain sexual so long as they continue to be associated with sexual passion, and male or female so long as they are associated with only one of the two types of cell whose union will result in a new creature. Everywhere and always, differentiation is sexual only when it tends towards fruitfulness.

It was this which misled Schopenhauer into thinking of the genitalia as if they had been *created* by desire. He confused desire with the probable outcome of desire. But nothing could be further from the truth than to say that lovers are drawn towards each other primarily by the desire for children. Instinct—a thing not directly observable under the microscope but plainly indicated in its effects—may, if uncorrupted, urge satisfaction to take a certain definite and fruitful route. And associations tend to limit satisfaction more or less to routes which have become habitual, and this even in cases where a novel route is deliberately selected. For the novelty is but apparent, and masks a constant habit of seeking for strangeness.

But instinct says nothing about possible consequences, and works just as well, or better, when they are totally unknown. The sexual instinct, of course, like any other, not only yields an immediate satisfaction but obeys a purpose which is super-individual. But when an impulse, because of knowledge and experience, comes to be exercised through desire for its ultimate results, or with a desire to avoid such results, it has ceased to be instinctive and has become rational. And if this rationalizing has been poorly or short-sightedly done, without considering some of its own consequences, we call it irrational, not meaning that there has been no reasoning, but that the reasoning was false and defective.

To conclude, then, this long but necessary excursion into biology, there is no such thing as a stuff which sex is made of; nor are there two stuffs, one of which can be called masculinity and the other femininity. All such stuffs are stuff and nonsense. Sex is a crafty method by means of which nature manipulates a great host of particulars.

5. THOSE THRICE WICKED WOMEN

Gellett Burgess, in a recent brochure,[1] complains of women because of what he terms their "Varm." Their

[1] "Why Men Hate Women."

Charm he seems to find no longer noticeable. Weininger, on the other hand, grants them Charm, but considers them varmints on that very account.

"The condition of sexual excitement is the supreme moment of a woman's life," he laments on page 88 of "Sex and Characters." "If a woman were asked what she meant by her 'ego,' she would certainly think of her body. Her superficies, that is the woman's ego" (p. 201). In other words, her ego is her skin. "Women, in spite of what Schiller has said, have no dignity, and the word 'lady' was invented to supply this defect. . . . A woman extends her claims equally [!] to all men on earth" (p. 203).

"Men who give up their clubs and societies after marriage, soon rejoin them" (p. 205). This looks like a glimpse of Varm. But "whenever a man enters a place where a woman is, and she observes him, or hears his step or even only guesses he is near, she becomes another person. Her expression and her pose change with incredible swiftness; she 'arranges her fringes' and her bodice, and rises, or pretends to be engaged in her work. She is full of a half-shameless, half-nervous expectation. In many cases one is only in doubt as to whether she is blushing for her shameless laugh, or laughing over her shameless blush" (pp. 106–107). Evidently we are back to Charm, but remain ungrateful. As a misogynist, Burgess must now confess himself an amateur.

"The female . . . is credulous, uncritical, and quite unable to understand Protestantism" (p. 207). Anne Hutchinson seems to have lived in vain—or did her criticism of sermons send a ripple of protest clear to Vienna? "Christians are Catholics or Protestants before they are baptized." Or, as Sir William Gilbert once expressed it:

"Every little boy or gal
Who's born into this world alive
Is either a little lib-er-al
Or a little con-ser-va-tive."

"It has been exhaustively proved that the female is soulless and possessed of neither ego [i.e., superficies!] nor individuality, personality nor freedom, character nor will" (p. 207). True, "most women . . . delight to hear discussions on their souls," but "they know, so far as they can be said to *know* anything, that the whole thing is a swindle" (pp. 211–212). Exit Luther, enter Allah!

"Amongst the fathers of the Church, Tertullian and Origen certainly had a very low opinion of woman, and St. Augustine, except for his relations with his mother, seems to have shared their view" (p. 187). So did St. Paul, for that matter. All held a very low opinion of woman—and of unregenerate man as well.

But Weininger is indignant when he remembers that Schopenhauer's "depreciation of women in his philosophical work 'On Woman,' has frequently been attributed to the circumstance that a beautiful Venetian girl, in whose company he was, fell in love with the extremely handsome personal appearance of Byron; as if a low opinion of women were not more likely to come to him who had had the best and not the worst fortune with them." This is from Chapter XI.

Beautiful Venetian girl, indeed! "A nude woman may be beautiful in details, but the general effect is not beautiful; she inevitably creates the feeling that she is looking for something, and this induces disinclination rather than desire in the spectator. The sight of an upright female form, in the nude, makes most patent her purposelessness."

Euphues also preferred drapery, for he wrote: "When once [women] be robbed of their robes, then will they appear so odious, so ugly, so monstrous, that thou wilt rather think them serpents than saints, and so like to hags that thou wilt fear rather to be enchanted than enamoured."

Weininger felt that "in the recumbent position this feeling [that woman is ugly] is greatly diminished." Not that in the "details of her body" she can be regarded as "wholly beautiful, not even if she is a flawless, perfect type of her sex. The genitalia are the chief difficulty in the way of regarding her as theoretically beautiful" (p. 241). So, as "most men theoretically respect women, but practically they thoroughly despise them," it follows that "this method should be reversed" (p. 339). Women, then, are practically beautiful after all, but must be theoretically despised.

Woman even "resents any attempt to require from her that her thoughts should be logical," and "may be regarded as logically insane" (p. 149). In fine, "the further we go in the analysis of woman's claims to esteem,"—since it appears that she claims what she resents having required of her —"the more we must deny her of what is lofty and noble" (p. 243). Therefore, "woman is neither high-minded, low-minded, strong-minded nor weak-minded. She is the opposite of all these. Mind cannot be predicated of her at all; she is mindless" (p. 253).

"Every simple, clear, plastic perception, and every distinct idea before it [can] be put into words, passes through a stage of indistinctness" (p. 94). That is to say, there is a stage during which the two things that Avenarius called respectively "element" and "character," the thing thought of and what is thought about it, remain confused. Claiming that "it is necessary to coin a name for those minds to which the duality of element and character become appreciable at no stage of the process," Weininger proposes "the word Henid." This word he derives on page 101 from the Greek, and not, as one might suppose, from the barnyard, nor does he apply it to minds after all, but to thoughts. If your sense-organs are stimulated by "green, blue, cold, warm, soft, hard, sweet, bitter," or any other Avenarius element and the stimulation impresses you as having the "character" of "pleasant, unpleasant, surprising, expected, novel, indifferent, recognized, known, actual, doubtful," or what not, and if you are nevertheless uncertain about both the character and the element, uncertain as to what it is that you sense and uncertain as to how it impresses you, then you know what Weininger thinks a woman does when she thinks that she is thinking. A hen-id is merely a hen-idea.

"The female expects from man the clarification of her data, the interpreting of her henids." This capacity for interpreting them "is almost a tertiary sexual character of the male, and certainly it acts on the female as such." But, as we learn in Chapter VI, pages 148 *et seq.*, "man never has a conception in the purely logical form, for he is a psychological being." He gets his information through his senses. So it would seem that he is in much the same predicament as woman. I fear that when he clarifies his female's data by explaining things, he sometimes pulls the long bow. But, thank heaven, it works. I have been guilty of suspecting that woman's listening attitude was mere flattery, but evidently I was wrong. She is held spellbound by this tertiary sexual character in the male, even when he is telling her what her own opinions are.

But let him that understandeth take heed lest he fall, for

"nothing is so despicable as a man become a female" (see Chapter XII), and even a trace of femininity is sufficient to make him fail in his high calling. "Only the most male youths are addicted to masturbation" (p. 87). Woman, of course, has no high calling. She "has no evidence of the identity of the subject-matter of thought at different times." [2] "Such a creature in the extreme case would be unable to control her memory for even the moment of time required to say that A will still be A in the next moment, [or] to pronounce judgment on the identity, A equals A." That is, a woman in the extreme case (which is to say, an extremely womanly woman) would be unable to recognize the fact that a cat is a cat or a spade a spade, still less to believe that a chicken now will still be a chicken at some future time. She is obsessed with the henid that it will then be on its way towards becoming a tough old fowl unfit to broil—a fowl to be coped with only in a fricassee.

Is the woman wrong? Weininger admits that there is something to be said for her point of view. If one reasons like a psychological being, that is, like a being imprisoned in a body immersed in time and space, one is compelled to recognize the fact that A is never A more than once. A moment or so is required even to think the thought, and during that moment A has changed. And as even man is a psychological being, not even he, one would fancy, could take oath that A was anything other than B.

But what Weininger is trying to say is that there is a truth above and beyond space and time, an eternal truth which does not change, and that man somehow is capable now and then of getting a glimpse of it—to which I most heartily agree. Not even the simplest propositions of

[2] *Vide* chap. iv, pp. 148 *et seq.*

Euclid are true unless we conceive of things as at rest. It is not true that the interior angles of a triangle are equal to two right angles if the lines of the triangle wiggle continually. And a material triangle does wiggle. There is indeed no such thing as a material triangle, since there is no such thing as a material line. So we conceive of an abstract triangle, something quite independent of matter and the senses, and the very fact that we can think of such a thing proves that we have some contact with the Changeless. Weininger is quite right in supposing that man is not altogether a psychological being.

Of course, "psychological" is an absurd word to use in the sense here intended. Rightly considered, a psychological being is one with a psyche, or soul. But the word has come to mean not soul but body. When Weininger denies that a woman knows A to be A, perhaps he also is thinking "psychologically," in the modern sense—with his body rather than with his mind.

"But has woman no meaning at all? . . . Has she a mission, or is her existence an accident and an absurdity?" (p. 253). Heaven forbid! "Match-making is essentially the phenomenon of all others which gives us the key to the nature of woman" (p. 295). And "not all [man's] erotic incense would have obscured her real nature but for one factor. I have now," says Weininger (p. 260), "to explain this factor which has veiled from man the true nature of woman. . . . I mean her absolute duplicity." This factor being granted, "it is quite wrong to say that women lie. That would imply that they sometimes speak the truth" (p. 274). Therefore, "no one has a right to forbid things to a woman because they are 'unwomanly'; neither should any man be so mean as to talk of his unfaithful wife's doings as if they were his affair" (p. 339).

Naturally, henids and logical insanity have their privileges.

"Men who have none or very little of the instinct of brutality developed in them have no influence [on women]. Since woman desires coitus and not love, she proves that she wishes to be humiliated and not worshipped" (p. 336). Only cave-men need hope. "If [man] is going to treat [woman] as she wishes, he must have intercourse with her, for she desires it; he must beat her, for she likes to be hurt" (p. 337). "The qualities that appeal to a woman are the signs of developed sexuality; those that repel her are the qualities of the higher mind" (p. 250) —and this notwithstanding her anxiety to have her henids clarified. So, "very few men have the courage to acknowledge their chastity" (p. 332).

"Coitus is the price man has to pay to women," however unwillingly, "and although it is true that women may be more than content with such recompense for the worst form of slavery, man has no right to take part in such conduct, simply because he also is morally damaged by it" (p. 343).

We have already seen how "sexual union . . . is allied to murder" because of its capacity of slaying non-existence and giving it a local habitation and a name. We are now to be told that even when woman murders herself—consummation so devoutly to be wished under the Weininger hypothesis—she spoils everything by having a wrong motive. "The last and absolute proof of the thoroughly negative character of woman's life, of her complete want of a higher existence, is derived from the way in which women commit suicide" (p. 286). She does it just to show off—that appears to be the trouble. Nor does her trail of crime end even here. It is continued by her unsuicidal married sisters.

"A good mother, with the greatest peace of mind and content, will slaughter fowl after fowl for her family" (p. 224). It is here, possibly, that Weininger finds his justification that the prostitute, "not as a person, but as a phenomenon," is more estimable than the mother. Prostitutes do not always have families for whose benefits fowls have to be sacrificed.

"It may well be asked if women," even prostitutes, "are really to be considered human beings at all, or if [this] theory does not unite them with plants and animals?" And he answers: "As a matter of fact, women are sisters of the flowers, and are in close relationship with animals. But they are human beings," of a sort, he hastens to assure us. "Even the absolute woman"—though she is pure non-existence—"is still the complement of man. . . . Animals are mere individuals; women are persons, although they are not personalities. . . . An appearance of discriminative power, though not the reality; language, though not conversation; memory, though it has no continuity or unity of consciousness . . . must all be attributed to them. They possess counterfeits of everything masculine" (pp. 290–291).

They can even counterfeit sympathy. But "it is very short-sighted of any one to consider the nurse as a proof of the sympathy of women, because it really implies the opposite. A man could never stand the sight of the sufferings of the sick; he would suffer so intensely that he would be completely upset and incapable of lengthy attendance. . . . Any one who has watched nursing sisters is astounded at their equanimity and 'sweetness' even in the presence of the most terrible death throes. . . . A man would want to assuage the pain and ward off death; in a word, he could want to help" (p. 198). Not so the nursing sister. She does not want to help. Sympathy is a male character. "Men of genius usually avoid death beds" (p. 129)—even their own as long as possible. And "man's sympathy is the principle of individuality blushing for itself" (p. 199). It blushes, I gather, because it cannot help, its extreme individuality requiring its isolation from painful scenes.

Yet in one particular women are impressionable if not sympathetic. Take the maternal type, for instance. "All her life, through all her body, she is being impregnated. In this fact lies the explanation of the 'impression' which," in Weininger's opinion, is "indubitable, although it is denied by men of science and physicians" (p. 232)—the impression in question being the birth-mark imposed upon the child by something seen by the pregnant mother. He even includes certain character-traits among these impressions, and coins the words "telegony" and "germinal infection" to explain them. Thus "the actual father has to share his paternity with perhaps other men and many other things [such as tables and chairs] which have impressed the mother" (p. 233). "The woman is impregnated not only through the genital tract, but through every fibre of her being. All life makes an impression on her and throws its image on her child. This universality, in the purely physical sphere, is analogous to genius" (p. 233). In the not purely physical sphere, "there is no female genius, and there can never be one" (p. 189).

Nor can there be a scientific genius, even male. "If it were possible for one single man to have achieved all the scientific discoveries that have ever been made . . . he would not be entitled to the denomination of genius" (p. 170). Scientists, you see, have refused to admit the reality of telegony, of germinal infection, of the paternal function of furniture.

And yet "there are no men . . . who are altogether bad; and there is no woman of whom that could truly be said" (p. 252). "Man must endeavour to get [woman] to abandon her immoral designs on him. Women must really and truly and spontaneously relinquish coitus. That undoubtedly means that woman, as woman, must disappear, and until that has come to pass there is no possibility of establishing the kingdom of God on earth."

Meanwhile, "woman can appear everything and deny everything, but in reality she is never anything. Women have neither this nor that characteristic; their peculiarity consists in having no characteristics at all" (p. 294). "The woman of the highest standard is immeasurably beneath the man of the lowest standard"—see Chapter XIII. And so "this book" of Weininger's "may be considered as the greatest honour ever paid to woman" (p. 339).

CHAPTER IV

CHRIST AND THE FOREST

THE modern, irreligious world is usually described as Pagan, and often it so describes itself—the implication being that we are on our way back to the glory that was Greece and the grandeur that was Rome. Even Wyndham Lewis, whose writings are one turgid denial that we are thither bound, thinks that we might better be.

"I prefer," he says,[1] "the chaste wisdom of the Chinese or the Greek to that hot, tawny brand of superlative fanaticism coming from the parched deserts of the ancient East, with its ineradicable abstractness. I am for the physical world."

He is for the physical world because he is a painter before he is a philosopher. He prefers things chaste to hot and tawny, and demands that they hold their pose at least long enough to have their pictures taken. "Tawny," in his vocabulary, comes straight from the coats of lions—beasts chaste enough in actuality, but long since identified, metaphorically, with passions in the heart of man. Restless, too, at times. Mr. Lewis would have them stuffed or—better yet—reduced to definite areas of gamboge on changeless canvas. Therefore he is for abstractions, after all, especially for that static abstraction known as space—the pictorial. What he objects to are superlative, fanat-

[1] "Time and Western Man," p. 113.

ical, and ineradicable abstractions, the Absolute, the mysticism of transcendental mathematics and of India, quite beyond the reach of oils and camel's-hair brushes. In short, Mr. Lewis loves form, definition, the very qualities most conspicuously absent from his all-too-tawny literary masterpieces. As for the physical world which is experienced as emotion, as change, he thrills to it, yet damns it heartily, calling it harsh names, such as "time-illusion" and "music"—his pet synonym for "abominable."

Beyond a doubt Mr. Lewis has been smitten by a great truth, by a sense of spirit beyond matter, of changelessness beyond all change. Through these fitful surfaces he catches glimpses of a steady light, and, instead of losing his sanity in an abyss of effulgence, he means to use his artist's prerogative in the creation of a little world, a framed world, a draughtsman's world, sufficiently moveless to be a witness of that light. And not only does he refuse to have anything to do with those "musical" philosophers who regard life as a cosmic flow proceeding Bergsonianwise out of time into the spaceless space of Einstein: he flatly turns his back upon such of the unmusical as hold the real universe to be its picture, i.e., their own inwards in a static state of congestion. He prefers chaste wisdom either to unchaste foolishness or to arid foolishness. Wise and refreshing Lewis!

But, with all his belief in objective reality, he seems to trust no eyes but his own. Machete in hand, he wanders like a pioneer through the intellectual world—as if it were a region hitherto unexplored. But, let him lay about him never so lustily amidst the cacti, naturally he cannot all alone furnish us with a very clear map. It would indeed have been a miracle could a single pair of eyeballs have penetrated to the depths of every clump, or even to that depth which is permitted to all eyes taken collectively. Inevitably his merely individual vision at times becomes clouded—usually with indignation, but occasionally even with enthusiasm.

Thus, in "Paleface" [2] we find him hailing as "entirely true" a passage from D. H. Lawrence's "Mornings in Mexico" [3] wherein it is said: "The consciousness of one branch of humanity is the annihilation of the consciousness of another branch."

So? What, then, becomes of the chaste wisdom of the Chinese and the Greek? Is even foreign *chastity* noxious for Western nostrils to inhale? And then, as if it were not sufficiently surprising for him to have approved of Lawrence even once, he makes it twice by describing him as "exceedingly sound" in holding that "the life of the [Mexican] Indian, his stream of conscious being, is just death to the White Man," because "a race has a soul (or 'consciousness,' or whatever you like to call it) that . . . is vulnerable and of vital importance."

Of course this is all very true if by "consciousness" is meant racial pride, local customs, and the like. It is even true that one man's meat is another man's poison—if its poison is all that he can absorb. But the idea that either strong men or babes flourish upon the poison which happens to be concealed in their diet—that their stomachs have so little in common that nothing can be said to be wholesome to all—is going rather far.

Mr. Lewis, in fact, seems to create almost too many enemies, not only for the Mexican but for Western man. Already the latter had one in the tawny, superlative, fanat-

[2] *Vide* "The Enemy," no. 2, pp. 33 *et seq.*
[3] "Mornings in Mexico," pp. 105 *et seq.*

ical, ineradicable abstractness coming from the parched deserts of India; and the theory now includes the chaste consciousness of China and Greece, together with this soul, "or whatever you like to call it," of Old Mexico. And there will be still another in every alien "consciousness" which the tribes of earth can furnish.

With each page Lewis adds to the number of our foes. If we survive the everything-moves philosophy of the new mathematics, we then encounter "the elimination of individual ambition involved in the phenomenon of Trust or Corporation"; the "suicidal White War"; the "shattering tremors conveyed to us by the recent gigantic revolution in Russia"; and Heaven knows what besides. I am willing to admit that ours is a parlous case; that the situation offers an amazing variety of calamities. But we ought to have some friend somewhere, and there should be at least a mark by which we might distinguish friend from foe. The Lewis imagination presents a picture bristling with hostile bayonets. What it does not do is to reveal any common impulse back of them all. We want to get our hands on the opposing Napoleon. I find it impossible to believe that he is a compound either of alien races or of foreign geography.

He is no man, either. So let us assume that he is a Proteus capable of taking many forms, a spirit, a soul, a " 'consciousness,' or whatever you like to call it." We shall find then that it is something as dangerous to the Mexican as to the Yankee or the European, to the Yellow man as to the Red, to the Brown or Black as to the White, and that the danger threatened in ancient times just as it does to-day. It has been called the Danger of the Forest. Lewis lumps it with the Danger of the Desert. But the two are distinct, and not even akin save in their deathless enmity to chaste wisdom, whether of the Chinese, the Greek, the Russian, or the Hottentot.

Failure to understand the Forest is responsible for the confused impression which antiquity seems to have made upon the human mind. We go to Greece, for example, seeking ideals of discipline, restraint, order; for the acme of subtle symmetry in architecture; for a deep sense of contained spirituality; for lofty instances of pure friendship. We go also for Dionysiac revels, for sensuality masquerading as mysticism, and for the very devil and all.

This last is what we usually do, and then almost immediately we make a wonderful discovery. The Greeks were great, *and* they were Pagan. They were healthy, *and* they had no sex inhibitions. Conclusion, "and" means "because." Yet a single glance at history ought to show us that Paganism in this sense was fatal to Greece, making it impossible at last for her to retain either her health or her power. Must we go on for ever forgetting that she has fallen? That to-day she is a welter of misery stirred by cheap politicians and skimmed over by tourists? What destroyed her? Why, the Forest and the great god Pan. What saved her, so long as she was saved, was Christ.

It is time that everybody dropped the idea that Christianity began with the Christian Era. If it ever existed at all, it always was. If anybody ever had a real inspiration, then the inspirations of the ancient Pagans were real inspirations. Their intuitions did not discover something similar to Christ, but Christ Himself.

I am speaking, of course, of Christ as the Logos, the Word, the Light which shineth in darkness, the same that was in the beginning with God and without which was not anything made that was made. As to the Mystery of the Incarnation, that is something far beyond the scope of this book. All I wish here to insist upon is that not one of the Three Persons of the Trinity can be imagined as entering upon the stage sometime after the curtain went up. Apart from the historical scenes involved, apart from the dates of the promulgation of certain doctrines in certain forms of language, man, if he has ever been within the influence of these Persons, has never been without it.

Christianity professes to deal with certain spiritual entities. You may deny their reality if you like—but if you do you deny the reality of religion altogether. It becomes a mere system of ethics shot with emotion, fear, superstition—nothing to burn incense to or especially admire. And where, in that case, its ethics, or any ethics, come from or find force or justification, nobody has ever been able to say.

Many attempts have been made to found a morality similar to Christian morality upon "enlightened selfishness," upon the greatest good of the greatest number, upon hedonism or the immediate pursuit of pleasure. It has been said that it pays to be good, and that everybody will be happier if everybody behaves. But if I am not devoted to anything outside of myself, how are you going to make me behave? I may admit that the individual flourishes when the party or class to which he belongs flourishes as well. But it is a tedious process, this of benefiting a whole group, or race, or species. In practice I shall always be seeking a short cut, a special privilege, a little more than my share of the general happiness. And you, my dear sir or madam, may go hang. If I remain content to take potluck with you all, if my selfishness is so enlightened that I cannot be happy if you are not, cannot bear to be rich while you are poor, then I submit that I have ceased to be selfish. To have enlarged the self until it includes others is to have crossed precisely the line which separates Me from Us.

And how can there be an Us without a *Tertium Quid?* People may be united only by what they have in common. Common despair may lead to nothing better than two tarantulas fighting in a bottle, but, moved by a common hope, men will march shoulder to shoulder through fire and water.

Someone has defined modernism as the abandonment of Christian faith coupled with an unwillingness to take the logical consequences. Well, let us take the logical consequences and see what happens. Let us say that we will feed only upon "facts," and that our great fact is the existence not of the spiritual but of the material world. But the only kind of matter which will stand thus upon its own legs is moving-picture matter. We do not see the stars, but merely images on the retina. We do not see even these images, but are made aware of them in the form of the disturbances which they set up in the optic nerve, in brain tissues. And from the brain we trace them to consciousness. There is no physical world. There is only consciousness—my consciousness. As an egoist, I know nothing about yours except as another phase of my own.

But what becomes of even my consciousness if physical fact be the only safe thing to pin faith to? Consciousness is not a physical fact. Physical facts are forms of behaviour, things seen, felt, or heard. Can these things make a consciousness? Not unless matter be conscious, and if it be it is not matter. A consciousness of this sort would be God. Am I, then, this God? Did I create not only myself but you? I think it very unlikely, especially since

I understand myself very imperfectly and you scarcely at all. And yet I can be nothing less if I exist (it goes against even my consciousness to say that I do not) and nothing else exists except my awareness.

I am thus forced to recognize the reality of a spiritual world, superior not only to matter but to me. And I am going to define Christianity as the truth about that world, whatever the truth may be—which is precisely the way Christianity defines itself. There simply must be a religion of that sort, however much it may differ from our ideas of actual religion, and we must call it something.

It follows that the fatal thing in Paganism, in Orientalism, in the Mexican Indian or any other "consciousness," was and is its unchristian element, its error, the mixture of the devil which got into its worship of God. Apart from that, the Greeks and all other ancient peoples had a genuine God-worship—imperfect but genuine. And what makes foreign cultures so fatal to us is the fact that we go to them only for their evils, their lusts, cruelties, unrealities, mystifications, irrationalities, and diseases. If you must go to Greece, or China, or India, or anywhere else, why, in the name of all that is sane, not go for something good?

If you can find this good much better nearer home, better still. But if it is the devil—and I don't care what you mean by the word, whether a personal imp or the sum of unrighteousness—if the devil is the gentleman you want, it makes no difference where you seek him. Difficult as he is to recognize, he is not at all difficult to find. And when found at his worst, he is a mind, an ego lost within itself. A very arid devil. And it was this teetotaller that Mr. Lewis not only found but recognized in the tawny, superlative, fanatical, and ineradicable abstractness of the parched desert. But for the moment I am more interested in a more amiable fiend—a devil drunk and raving in the woods, one who impales us upon the fleshly horn of the matter-and-mind dilemma.

He is the Danger of the Forest; the threat which the lower presents to the higher; the hatred of the body for the mind; the threat of the flesh against the spirit; the eternal enmity of Pan for Pallas Athena. Nature—nothing more, nothing less.

We have come to worship nature, and by a trick of words have made it seem quite a rational thing to do. It is a very simple trick. You have only to understand by nature something which is not nature. Read your own higher aspirations into the landscape, and the landscape becomes friendly and beneficent. How sweet is the countryside as it basks in the slant sunshine of a tranquil Sunday afternoon! Are there not sermons in stones and what-nots in running brooks? So who would not rather stay outside the church and listen to the homilies of the farms?

But this is not nature. It is something tamed and enriched by human courage, toil, and sacrifice, much sweat and not a little blood. Disgraced, too, by considerable cowardice, avarice. Even so it remains cruel to itself, and real nature is cruel to all things. It requires very little knowledge of natural history to convert the country landscape into an eternal Verdun where nation rises against nation, creature against creature, plant against plant; where the very crystals of the stones struggle one with another. We may dream beneficence even into the untamed, into oceans and mountains. But the sea remains a shambles, and there is agony straining at the rocks.

Nature is not kind save to that which conquers it. To

make it anything but a struggle for the survival of the fiercest, we need to loan it something from ourselves—something supernaturally gentle. If we have no store of any such thing, our delight in out-of-doors may be merely a delight in the spectacle of suffering.

The struggle, the suffering, accomplishes something, of course. It tries the sinews even of stones and trees. But it is not good in itself. Our only legitimate source of pleasure is the triumph over pain and death shown by everything which manages to keep itself alive. Evidence of this triumph we call beauty.

Unfortunately, that which survives is not always the best. Ice crystals may survive the flowers. Here is another shadow upon the fields—the peril which accompanies advancement in the scale of being. Hence there are many grades of beauty, and to the eye which has learned to love one sort another sort becomes hideous. But it always gives us a particular satisfaction when we recognize the higher being in the act of winning out. "We can but love the highest when we see it," and know it for what it is.

But nature-worship too often means an admiration for the base, mistaken for the fine. It may be a very inspiring thing for a blade of grass to contemplate a grasshopper; but for man, grasshoppers make unlovely gods. You look to nature only to see therein a manifestation of the Highest of All? Very well, if you look as deeply as that. But Pantheism does not look as deeply as that. It stops short. And that is why, though a very excellent thing for one who does not know of anything better, it is quite a different thing for anybody who does. I should greatly admire a dog who was a Pantheist. He would be a brave beast, more noble even than that mountain which Vachel

Lindsay has immortalized as Rising Wolf. A mountain trying to be a wolf is a sublime mountain. A man trying to be a wolf is a degenerate.

So the glorious Forest of Pan is an enemy of that which is best in us—and it always was an enemy. Paganism itself contained a nobler thing. Not only were there "the breasts of the nymph in the brake": there were the breasts of the Goddess of Right Reason symbolized in stone by Phidias and set up in a temple upon the Acropolis. And when Greece lost this nobler thing, she fell. Neither Bacchus nor Dionysus could save her, for, without Pallas Athena, Venus herself becomes a mere slut—even something worse. No, the great god Pan is not dead. What is dead is Hellas.

She was never either wholly bad or wholly good. But her good was our good, and her evil our evil. There is but one good, a preference for the better; and but one evil, a preference for the worse. How could it be otherwise? One's position upon a slope is hardly as important as one's motion there. To climb and to fall are different things, and one may do either from any position.

Now, if it be true that the Mexican is beneath us (I am far from granting that it is necessarily and always so), then his culture, if we adopted it, would in a measure kill us. But our culture would be good for him—unless our culture be a merely destructive agency. But then how could you call such an agency a higher culture? There is nothing particularly moral in a big gun, or in a charge of high explosive dropped from an airplane upon the poor. But a higher morality would undoubtedly be good for a Mexican, or for anybody else who would breathe its spirit rather than adopt dead forms or have them thrust upon him. What happens to the weaker races when brought in contact with the stronger is that the weaker are destroyed by a higher degree of immorality, of ruthlessness—an invasion of Pan, of Forest mist—nowadays quite likely to be smoky vapours from forests of steel and stone. It may be an aggressive immorality, a military frightfulness. Or it may be something evil absorbed more or less willingly —and so much the worse.

As Thomas Aquinas said, centuries ago:[4] "A thing may be a hindrance to virtue in two ways: first, as regards the ordinary degree of virtue, and as to this, nothing but sin is an obstacle to virtue; secondly, as regards the perfect degree of virtue, and as to this, virtue may be hindered by that which is not a sin but a lesser good."

Which I take to mean that there is a point below which misconduct cannot be said to have anything in it which could be considered good for anybody, but that above this there are things which might be relatively admirable for the less high though not good enough for the better.

And now I think we may safely venture into the Forest, or at least cast an eye upon some specimens of its flora and fauna that have been dragged out by modern explorers and recommended to us as improving additions which we ought to make to our personal herbaria and zoos.

[4] *Summa Theologica,* q. 153, art. 2.

CHAPTER V

AN INVITATION TO THE DANCE

I. JUNGLE BOOKS

EDWARD CARPENTER goes to the Grecian Forest hunting for prestige for his Intermediate Sex. It was not enough that these born-so-and-can't-help-it Urnings should be given existence: they must be given coats of arms and crests such as were borne by the mighty men of old.

Taken by itself, the anthology of famous friendships which Carpenter has published under the title "Iolaüs," is a pleasant performance, and the worst that can be said of it is that the author's attitude towards his material is slightly ambiguous. Unfortunately, he has written other books. More unfortunately still, there are other authors from whom it is impossible to disassociate him altogether. One cannot pretend to be unaware of the motive for bringing the stories of all these illustrious lovers together. The world waits for someone with quite another motive to do the work all over again, and then what a different picture we shall have!

The real Iolaüs, you will remember, was charioteer to Hercules, and master and man were great cronies. *Ergo,* it is argued in some quarters, they were no better than they might have been. *Ergo* again, they were better still. Wherever Hercules sits is the head of the table. Descendants of his lineage must take precedence even over the children of the Crusaders or of earldoms dating from the Norman Conquest. We should be careful, then, to make plain our meaning before we say that hero and charioteer were lovers.

And after Hercules there come Achilles and Patroclus —*"Achille,"* as Dante sings, *"che per amore al fine combatteo,"* who at the last was brought to fight by love. There is at least no doubt of Dante's beautiful intent. But how few Dantes we have!

"At Sparta," says Carpenter,[1] eminently satisfactory in his grasp of the fact that in the heroic ages friendship was an institution, "the lover was called Eispanêlos, the inspirer, and the younger beloved [was called] Aites, the hearer." A similar distinction seems to have been made throughout Greece—not always without confusion, for, as Plato reminds us in the "Symposium," Æschylus made the mistake of describing Patroclus as the love of Achilles. Patroclus, being the elder, was the lover.

These two rôles were preserved likewise by the members of the Theban Band, those famous warriors who fought, each within sight of his love or his lover, preferring death rather than to see scorn or disappointment in the loving or beloved eyes. So Plutarch, telling how Cleomachus fought and won in the sight of his inspirer, pauses to accuse Homer himself of ignorance of proper warfare, since (as Carpenter puts it) "he drew up the Achæans in order of battle in tribes and clans, and did not put lover and love together." It ought to be evident by this time, the chaste nature of the inspiration and devotion involved.

But even Socrates is often sought to be enlisted in the

1 "The Intermediate Sex," p. 71.

Urning campaign, not to say claimed as the prize recruit. It seems to be taken for granted that, having been made to drink hemlock for his alleged corrupting of youth, he must have been gloriously guilty. What makes the whole thing excessively bewildering is the fact that Socrates to all intents and purposes never existed. In the flesh he seems to have been so insignificant that we certainly never should have heard of him through anything which he ever did of himself. The only records tending to show that he lived at all date fifty years after his death.

"It was on the stage . . . that we seem to find the shadow of the real Socrates," says Havelock Ellis, justly enough.[2] "But he was not the Socrates of the dramatic dialogues of Plato, or even of Xenophon; he was a minor Sophist, an inferior Diogenes, yet a remarkable figure, arresting and disturbing, whose idiosyncrasies were quite perceptible to the crowd."

Ellis likens him to Chidley, the philosophic Australian tramp, "who might have entered modern history just as Socrates entered ancient history," only that there was lacking an imaginative genius to put him there. The first biographies of Plato did not begin to be written until four hundred years after Plato's death—that was the chance which enthroned Socrates as Plato's teacher. In reality he was essentially Plato's invention—an invention chiming in with the inventions of Xenophon and the dramatists. And a most noble invention it was. The attempt to twist it into a high example of vice is sheer folly.

Carpenter, it is but just to say, avoids this particular mistake. "Socrates," he says,[3] "describes [or is made to

[2] *Vide* "The Dance of Life," chap. iii.
[3] "Iolaüs," p. 47.

describe in the 'Phædrus'] the passion of love between man and boy as a 'mania,' not different in quality from that which inspires poets. He declares that the true object of a noble life can only be attained by passionate friends, bound together in the chains of close yet temperate comradeship, seeking always to advance in knowledge, self-restraint, and intellectual illumination." Carpenter quotes also from the speech of Socrates in this same "Phædrus," wherein it is said: "Fate, which has ordained that there shall be no friendship among the evil, has also ordained that there shall ever be friendship among the good."

This is almost the earthly communion of saints. So why not drop the attempt to borrow from these examples of temperate comradeship a glamour to cast over the modern and intemperate invert? Carpenter does not often commit himself to this futile sort of romancing—not in so many words. But he does it continually by indirection and by an atmosphere filled with purple implications.

In a civilization like the Greek, where no women except the *hetæræ* were educated, any intellectual interest naturally tended to draw men towards men—as it does to a certain degree even to-day. That some of the Greeks were moved malewards by quite another interest cannot be denied. It must be confessed, too, that propinquity, however brought about and whether between sexual similars or dissimilars, offers an opportunity which the flesh is not always slow to take advantage of. But this is no reason for interpreting friendship as a sublimation of vice. One might as well argue that, because marriage occasionally leads to homicide, only a nicely restrained homicidal impulse can give charm to domestic existence.

How far removed from carnality these famous historical companionships actually were may be shown from the authors cited in "Iolaüs" itself.

"Fraternity in arms," J. A. Symonds reminds us,[4] "played for the Greek race the same part as the idealization of women for the knighthood of feudal Europe. . . . The chivalry of Hellas found its motive force in friendship rather than in the love of women; and the motive force of all chivalry is a generous, soul-exalting, unselfish passion."

That is to say, sexual love, whether of men or women, has nothing to do with it. The affair is between human beings, and is not erotic. What matters the maleness or femaleness of an eros who is crowded off the stage?

Thus, Müller, in his "History of the Antiquities of the Doric Race," [5] says that "it appears to have been the practice for every youth of good character to have his lover, and on the other hand every well-educated man was bound by custom to be the lover of some youth. . . . The connexion was recognized by the state." Clearly, then, the connexion was that of tutor and pupil. No state not anxious for its own destruction ever recognized a sinister relation except as a crime.

According to Hahn,[6] the Dorian customs of comradeship still flourish in Albania to-day as in ancient times, and these "loves" are, "with few exceptions, as pure as sunshine and the highest and noblest affections that the human heart can entertain."

"Such friendships [passionate friendships between men] of course occur in all nations and at all times," adds G. Lowes Dickinson,[7] "but among the Greeks they

[4] "Studies of the Greek Poets," vol. i, p. 97.
[5] Bk. iv, chap. 4, par. 6.
[6] *Albanesische Studien,* vol. i, p. 166.
[7] "The Greek View of Life," p. 167.

were . . . an institution. Their ideal was the development and education of the younger by the older man." "Passionate," therefore, is a misleading word to apply to them, though it is the word which Dickinson unfortunately uses. That it was at least a sexless passion becomes still more obvious when he continues:[8] "Some of the best of [the Greeks] set the love of man for man far above that of man for woman. The one, they maintained, was primarily of the spirit, the other primarily of the flesh." And since they did maintain this, the setting of the one above the other was inevitable.

Carpenter, however, is stricken with astonishment. "Nothing," he says,[9] "is more surprising to the modern than to find Plato speaking, page after page, of Love as the safeguard of states and the tutoress of philosophy, and then to discover that what we call love, i.e., the love between man and woman, is not meant at all . . . but only the love between men, . . . what we should call romantic friendship; it is an absorbing passion, but it is held in strong control."

It would have been much more surprising, I think, had we found Plato meaning anything else, but of course we are free to marvel at the change which time has wrought in the significance of words, and the difficulties of translating them from Greek to English. Translators, I fear, take a positive delight in creating a wrong impression with their "loves" and "passions." But not even literalness accounts for Carpenter. For him, romantic friendship is passion held in strong control, immundity held in check, the stale Freudian fallacy of sex as the nigger in every woodpile.

[8] *Ibid.*, p. 172.
[9] "Iolaüs," p. 42.

But we are only pretending to be in the Forest here. There is a slight fog, but it soon clears itself away, leaving everything as fresh and wholesome as a Midwestern Prairie. The morality of these classic instances is above reproach.

So Carpenter and his ilk, whose name is legion, take us to another purported thicket—quite unclassical this time. And what do we find? Why, that among the Arab tribes "every Sheikh" has his body-guard of young men, "whom he instructs and educates"; that "among the Benyani" the elders teach the young men what is known as "Bonzai," or the duties of manhood and citizenship; that among the Bengali coolies two youths or two girls will exchange flowers in token of perpetual alliance; that the Balonda, inhabitants of Londa Land among the southern tributaries of the Congo, have a "most remarkable" custom of cementing friendships with a ritual called "Kasendi"; and that Livingston discovered friendship fairly rampant among the Manganjas and other tribes of the Zambesi. For that matter, he might have discovered it among dogs and horses, Tammany tigers, and suburbanites along the Bronx.

Herman Melville contributes his bit, and in "Omoo" [10] we read of "the really curious way in which all the Polynesians are in the habit of making bosom friends at the shortest possible notice." And it seems that "although among a people like the Tahitians, vitiated as they are by sophisticating influences, this custom has in most cases degenerated into a merely mercenary relation,"—mercenary, not libidinous—"it nevertheless had its origin in a fine and in some instances heroic sentiment."

"There is great emulation [in Germany] among the

[10] Chap. 39, p. 154.

companions as to which shall possess the highest place in the favour of their chief," was long ago the testimony of Tacitus.[11] And even St. Augustine had his friend, for he says:[12]

"In those years when I first began to teach in my native town, I had made a friend, one who, through having the same interests, was very dear to me, one of my own age, and, like me, in the first flower of youth." They were not even differentiated by years. It was an attraction between similars. Where were Monsieur-Madame Arrhenoplasm and Thelyplasm?

S. Buckingham, author of "Travels in Assyria, Media and Persia,"[13] unable to emulate St. Augustine himself, knows at least of an Augustinian instance. He one day heard his guide, a dervish, say that he "loved the son of his friend Elias." Buckingham "shrank back from the confession as a man would recoil from a serpent on which he has unexpectedly trodden." But this hysteria was premature. "In answer to enquiries naturally suggested by the subject," the dervish "declared he would rather suffer death than do the slightest harm to so pure, so innocent, so heavenly a creature." Whereupon the only partly tranquillized traveller "took the greatest pains to ascertain by a severe and minute investigation, how far it might be possible to doubt of the purity of the passion by which this Afghan dervish was possessed, and whether it deserved to be classed with that described as prevailing among the Greeks." Results were more than satisfactory.

Even Ernst Haeckel gets into this anthology because of a passage in his "A Visit to Ceylon," where he tells of

[11] *Vide Germania.*
[12] "Confessions," bk. 4, chap. iv.
[13] Second edition, vol. i, p. 159.

his friendship for his Rodiya serving-boy at Belligam, near Galle. The boy was named Gamameda, and was only a pariah. The mutual attachment appears to have been very strong, but capable of scandalizing only such as were wounded by Tennyson's poem, *In Memoriam* (of Arthur Hallam).

Must we, then, look askance at the history of Wagner and Ludwig II? At Emerson's "Essay on Love"? At Montaigne's on "Friendship"? At Thoreau's references to friendship in "On the Concord River"? At the twin lives of Beaumont and Fletcher? Say ill things of Sir Philip Sidney and Hubert Languet? Wonder why the name Charles occurs in Browning's poem beginning, "I wish that when you died last May"? Grimace over the loves of Amis and Amil in mediæval France? Damn Damon and Pythias? Blaspheme the memory of David and Jonathan? Shudder (or gloat, as the case may be) because Michelangelo's sonnets seem not to have been written to a lady's eyebrow? Or sigh, "The less Shakespeare he!" over the first 126 of certain sonnets greater still? If so, then we shall cry, "Aha!" at Suffolk and York in "Henry V," and at Antonio and Bassanio in "The Merchant of Venice." We shall even leer at that beloved disciple who lay upon the breast of his Lord. And all the world shall become not a stage but a pigsty, apologies being due to the pigs.

Carpenter by no means insists upon all this evil—not in "Iolaüs." Carpenter is of no importance, anyway, save as the popularizer of Weininger, Karl Heinrich Ulrichs, R. von Krafft-Ebing, and their brothers in literature. But our memory of his "Intermediate Sex," informs us for whose brows he weaves his friendship's garland. Not that such a mild-spoken and most gentle man could mean any harm. But ah, some of the chestnuts which he takes out of the fire! Witness this one, culled from Dr. Jaeger's *Die Entdeckung der Seele,* page 168:

"Among the homosexuals there is found the *most* remarkable class of men, namely, those whom I call supervirile. These men stand, by virtue of the special variation of their soul-material, just as much above Man, as the normal sex man does above Woman. Such an individual is able to bewitch men by his soul aroma, as they—though passively—bewitch him." The *most* remarkable men, then, are homosexual, and they act through a special soul-scent. The plasms of Weininger have been promoted to superectoplasms which thrill the spiritual world of sodomy. "That there are distinctions and gradations of Soul-material in relation to Sex—that the inner psychical affections and affinities shade off and graduate, in a vast number of instances, most subtly from male to female, and not always in obvious correspondence with the outer bodily sex—is a thing evident enough to anyone who considers the subject." So Carpenter comments.[14] Homosexual Soul-material!

"The defect of the male Uranian or Urning," he goes on,[15] "is not sensuality but rather sentimentality. The lower, more ordinary types of Urning are often terribly sentimental; the superior types strangely, almost incredibly emotional; but neither as a rule . . . are so sensual as the average normal man." The homosexual soul-material, therefore, must be less sensual, though more emotional, than the heterosexual. It is more soulful, and yet it is super-virile! It requires less sensuality (though still more emotion) to drive in the face of nature and against cus-

[14] "The Intermediate Sex," p. 10.
[15] *Ibid.*, p. 13.

tom than is needed to bring about a normal and approved relationship.

Krafft-Ebing may now be permitted to put in a word:[16] "How deep are congenital sex-inversion roots may be gathered from the fact that the pleasure-dream of the male Urning has to do with male persons, and of the female with females." This, of course, is no proof of *congenital* inversion, but merely a sample of how these philosophers reason. Can one dream only of the innate? Are acquired habits excluded from the land of Nod? Krafft-Ebing, however, insists that there is involved "an hereditary neuropathetic or psychopathetic tendency, . . . a *neuro-psychopathische Blastung*."[17] He afterwards abandons the notion that it is pathological, which causes Carpenter to remark:[18]

"It is an obvious criticism on this that there are few people in modern life who could be pronounced absolutely free from such a *Blastung!*" One touch of *Blastung* makes the whole world kin. And it is not even *neuro-psychopathisch,* but normal. "The question," Carpenter heedlessly goes on, is not "whether the [inverted] instinct is capable of morbid and extravagant manifestation, . . . but whether it is capable of a healthy and sane expression. And this," he concludes, "it has abundantly shown itself to be."

What, now, is a "sane expression" of inversion? If this sanity is non-sexual, the whole theory of the Urning as a sex falls to the ground, and Carpenter had no right to suggest that all these flowers culled during his pleasant holiday excursion through the fields were in reality

[16] From "P. S.," seventh edition, p. 228.
[17] *Vide ibid.*, p. 190.
[18] *Op. cit.*, p. 60.

growing in the shade. Why, then, flatter an evil place by crediting it with growths so utterly foreign to its native fungi? Why even hint that the famous loves of which the world is so proud were Forest affairs?

2. HAVELOCK ELLIS AND NOSE-RING PHILOSOPHY

On February 2, 1859, and therefore "eight months before the publication of 'The Origin of Species,'" Susannah Mary Wheatley Ellis, wife of a British sea captain, gave birth to a boy. "It was a successful, normal delivery," says Houston Peterson, the boy's subsequent biographer,[1] "although forceps were required because of the infant's large head."

It was some weeks before the father, who was in an Australian port, even heard the news, and more than a year before he saw the youngster, who by this time had been christened Havelock. It was the mother who began and continued the education of the little stranger, helping him to form the afferent and efferent legs of his reflex arcs. She seems to have been a typical Puritan, endowed from her girlhood years with a deep sense of the sinfulness of pleasure.

"At seventeen," says Peterson, "this growing seriousness crystallized in her conversion to Evangelicalism, from which she was never diverted. In the tradition of John Wesley, she felt deeply the need of redemption . . . and was quite indifferent to the rationalistic elements in religion. She lived soberly, if not ascetically. She dressed very simply, without any particular style. . . . Her convictions forbade the theatre, and alcoholic beverage was

[1] *Vide* "Havelock Ellis, Philosopher of Love," by Houston Peterson, p. 3.

not served at her board. . . . She disliked jewelry, and thought ear-rings as barbaric as nose-rings."

Such notions are perhaps not the most healthy mental diet imaginable for a boy, and Havelock was a very clever boy. His large head craved to have something in it. It abhorred the vacuum created by the absence of rationalistic elements. He began to discover virtues in nose-rings, stylish clothes, the theatre, and alcoholic beverages—nose-rings more especially. He became sceptical. "The Origin of Species" had not been published in vain.

It was the usual cranial house-cleaning which accompanies puberty in all but the mentally inert. And then he underwent what Peterson calls "conversion," which in this case was the "harmonization" of a lot of individual notions, individual judgment acting as a pedal base and serving, after the manner of pedal bases, to make the harmony sound more harmonious than it really was.

The phenomena of reaction are curious. There is a great upsetting and an intolerable deal of dust; but when the dust has settled, the fundamentals invariably remain. The "harmonization," we find, has been done with those same old reflex arcs. So this harmonic philosophy merely inverted the maternal *cantus firmus*. In other words, Havelock's house-cleaning was not very thorough, a matter of brooms and furniture rather than carpentry and masonry. Straight-backed chairs and haircloth sofas were set aside to make room for—well, for grass mats and various eclectic museum pieces. But house-building was not on the program. When all was over, Ellis could be described as "a sort of mystic," who had readopted religion as a sort of "emotion," with even fewer rationalistic elements than are to be found in the teachings of Wesley.

He loved to reason, but had joined the modern move-

~ HAVELOCK ELLIS ~
"Let joy be unconfined!"

ment to make it unreasonable. The thing that mattered was instinct, intuition, the way you happen to feel. So a creed must say nothing about God, but a great deal about and in praise of savagery—as Ellis understood savagery. Sweet are the uses of head-hunting—seen from a distance. Thus, having raised a splendid set of aboriginal whiskers, he entered upon his literary career moved by a passionate hatred of all laws and customs tending to put the slightest restraint upon impulse, the sex impulse more especially. Precisely his mother's attitude towards spiritual things applied to things in general.

To-day, his beard having turned white, he looks like what he is—a gentle, soft-hearted, and not very hard-headed old patriarch, still a "sort of mystic," who believes that God, however vague, is good, and that man, once he frees himself from laws, not very much worse. To say that Ellis' passions have burned themselves out is to misstate the case. Passion in this sense he never had to any virulent degree. His desire was always rather to see others eat than to do trencher work at the banquet himself.

The one great romance of his life was his apparently quite Platonic friendship for that asthmatic, neurasthenic genius, Olive Schreiner. This rogue whose opinion of the law comes from hating to feel the halter draw is a rogue only in an academic sense, with never a real crime in his dossier. He has been a theorist, who never could quite understand why men fight. Erudite to the last degree, but in an unanalytical fashion, he lacks the ruthlessness of the thoroughgoing philosopher. Here is a dilettante, with a tolerant intestine but no great powers of assimilation. A sentimentalist, in short—and by sentimentality I mean emotionality unjustified by thought.

When the publication of his first book on sex resulted in the arrest in London of a dealer who had disposed of three copies, Ellis took his wife and went for a vacation —to Morocco. The dealer, in exchange for a suspended sentence, pleaded guilty of handling obscene literature. Who can blame either of them? He who writes and runs away may live to write another day. Nevertheless, it is not of such stuff that heroes are made.

Not heroes of the common sort. But no doubt there is a certain valour in discretion, a mental heroism which disdains mere physical courage and the applause of the unthinking, and dares to incur disgrace while keeping its skin whole. Along these lines, the courage of Havelock Ellis is beyond praise. No man of our times has done more to dissipate the odium which once threatened to stifle all sensible discourse about sex. It is largely to him that the belly owes its restoration to verbalized thought, and the overtaxed stomach its reduction as a descriptive epithet to its natural limits in the abdominal area.

That the good work should stop here was perhaps too much to have expected. Inevitably the reactionary becomes a partisan of whatever disorder he has himself introduced into the old home. Ellis has skilfully epitomized the sex-writers of the day, but always with a fair word for perversity in proportion as it was perverse. Advertising himself as a "reconciler of irreconcilables," his method is to make the good do all the reconciling so that evil shall not be incommoded. Anything that is fishy he swallows—hook, line, and sinker.

A certain decrying of mental balance seems to be part of our inheritance. The flesh is the only evil, or else it is the only good. We were brought up to regard the rendering unto Cæsar the things which are Cæsar's as trafficking with the devil. In moral matters, any tendency towards that just proportion which is the essence of truth we denounce as "compromise," a word having a disreputable implication which begs every question into which it intrudes itself. And yet, an unbalanced mind is an insane mind. Ellis preserves his sanity by keeping the hold dark, thus managing to carry a lot of sound ballast forbidden by his charter-party, without being in the least aware that he is dishonest with himself.

Quite lately he has suffered apotheosis. His best work won him harsh words from high quarters, but the moment he became a *littérateur,* lay theologian, and prose-poet, there was a general acclaim. Others abide our question, not Ellis. At the moment it is considered a positive breach of good manners to make so much as a motion towards raking him over the coals.

Nor can it be denied that his main philosophical slogan —Life is a Dance—has such a charm that it seems a pity to disturb it by enquiring into any meaning which it may be supposed to have. I am myself so taken with the phrase that for a long time I could hardly bring myself to quarrel with it, no matter what context happened to surround it. The dance of life! Are these not words to conjure with? What metaphor could better express the loveliness of balance and proportion? Rhythm, and the reign of law—the two expressions are synonymous. But Ellis achieved the miracle of conceiving of the dance as lawlessness.

"The philosophic Hipparchia and her husband must not nowadays consummate their marriage in public, and our modern philosophers meekly agree that philosophy is to

[7] *Ibid.,* p. 102.

have nothing to do with life," he complains.[2] A marriage consummated otherwhere than in public is not "life." When the individual has to shape his steps so as to avoid trampling upon the sensibilities of others, life gives up the ghost.

"Even if we are not ourselves dancers, but merely spectators of the dance, we are still—according to that Lippsian doctrine of *Einfühlung* or 'empathy,' by Groos termed 'the play of inner imitation,' which here at all events we may accept as true—feeling ourselves in the dancer who is manifesting and expressing the latent impulse of our own being." [3] Spouses seeking privacy rob our empathy of its play-hour. *Einfühlung* should unite us all in what someone has called "a continuous plasmodium."

But at the same time and on the other hand and notwithstanding, unless our play-hour is taken away, unless our sexual impulses are denied expression, both vicarious and personal, we do not, he says, progress.

"The ascending zoölogical series have been developed out of the impulse of repressed organic sexual desire striving to manifest itself ever more urgently in the struggle to overcome the coyness of the female." [4] That long-sought force which lies behind evolution stands at last revealed as thwarted sexuality! Thus, the ant-eater, through repressed sexual desire and confronted with the coyness of the female, wished himself into a man. If the female had been approachable, the male would have been content to remain an ant-eater. But we strive to please, and ascent

[2] "The Dance of Life," p. 74.
[3] *Ibid.*, pp. 60 *et seq.*
[4] *Ibid.*, pp. 100–101.

in the zoölogical series is our reward. Man not being coy, woman is left unstriving and far behind. I do not see how she advanced at all. She must have been dragged. The rural lover, painfully struggling into high collar and tie to win favour from his sweetheart, must then turn around and force her to spend some time on her own personal appearance.

But "the boy or girl [girls have somehow got into the running] who first becomes conscious of the mental stimulus" which is at work "is unaware of the instinct it springs from, and may even disregard as unimportant its specific physiological manifestations." [5] The boy, however, does not, it would seem, continue long in his disregarding. "When he has ceased to be a child and puberty is approaching, another question [not quite apart, I should say, from the why and wherefore of that strange necessity for sprucing up] is apt to arise in the boy's mind: What is a woman like?" He may solve the problem as to its specific physiological manifestations, but otherwise, I fancy, it is likely to puzzle him to the end. And as he persists in hankering for admiration from this inexplicable creature, the zoölogical series continues to ascend. Still striving to please, he finally becomes a superman.

Nevertheless, this impulse to please another is "auto-erotic," a mere love of self. "It is impossible to say what finest elements in art, in morals, in civilization generally, may not really be rooted in an auto-erotic impulse." [6] "The lower forms of art, such as myth-making, standing near to dreams, and the higher forms, such as the drama, philosophy, and the founding of religions, near to psycho-

[5] *Ibid.*, pp. 95 *et seq.*
[6] *Ibid.*, chap. iii.

neurosis," all possess "the sublimated life-force which has its root in some modification of sexual energy." [7] So auto-eroticism, sometimes manifested in masturbation, may at other times be sublimated into that lower form of art known as myth-making, which stands near to dreams, and then again may turn its hand to such higher forms as play-writing, philosophy, and the founding of religions, which stand near to psycho-neurosis, or quasi-insanity.

However, "as the accumulated experiences of civilization have been preserved and handed on from generation to generation [alas, and alack the day!] this free and vital play of the instinct has been largely paralysed." See page 218. But on page 216, the vital play in question is described as "an illegitimate confusion." One is at least glad that confusion may occasionally be illegitimate.

Oh, what a tangled web we weave when first we begin to use such words as "sex" and "sublimation" without taking the trouble to find out what we mean by them! Leaving the zoölogical series momentarily to shift for itself, how much easier it would have been to account for the desire for personal improvement without dragging sex into it! Call it pride; or even love, for once in a way. We might, I think, also leave the word "erotic" out of that urge to discover and to depict the divine harmony and beauty of things which leads to the highest art. Let the urge pick up sex on its way, if it will, later to drop it. But it is unreasonable to ask sex to pick up the urge. Ellis has never even tried to wean himself from his reactionary habit of always describing this, that, and the other as a "sublimation" of the "sexual."

But the sexual instinct is life-force already specialized in a particular channel, and obviously it can remain sexual only while it remains in that channel, only while it continues to concern itself in some way with that physical passion which tends towards the propagation of the species. If it gets into some other channel and ceases to be physical desire, it ceases to be sexual. Therefore art, philosophy, and religion are sexual sublimations if they are aphrodisiacs, and not otherwise. Pornographic things (and I am not stopping here either to praise or to blame them) may of course call themselves art, philosophy, religion. But non-pornographic things are clearly sublimations not of sexuality but of a life-force which has not run into the sexual groove, or has escaped from it.

The point is all-important. To miss it is to miss everything. To speak of the non-sexual as a sublimation of the sexual is like saying that north is a sublimated south. But you cannot take a southerly route and convert it into a northerly route without robbing it of all—yes, all, all, all—its southerliness. Only direction in general may become a specific direction, and still be included in its original definition. Sublimation is a going forward, leaving old landmarks behind. But all these Impuritans cling to a fixed milestone, crown it with garlands, and think it is carrying them somewhere.

Ellis does not consider himself a preacher of lawlessness, but the only law which he acknowledges to be just is the inner law of the self, "the impulse of our own being." Such phrases have a pleasant sound. But the very word "law" implies that it is something apart from that which obeys it. Even a "natural law," which is nothing but a description of the way in which things have been observed to behave, implies something apart—unless the jump of a kangaroo be indeed the kangaroo. The impulse of our own being proves to be not quite our own, and the attempt to prove the contrary breaks down before it can start. It has nothing to start from. Of course a higher self may impose laws upon a lower, and the lower may learn not only obedience but willing obedience—through what may be termed a mystical union with its Lord. Indeed, until we have consented to be governed, we are not good citizens of any commonwealth, either of the body or the spirit. But to Ellis an impulse, once disciplined, represents a total loss to the race.

"Our own affirmations are always the best," he declares in the preface to "Affirmations." "Let us but be sure that they are ours." It is not necessary, then, to make sure they are the best, or even good. It is taken for granted that all our geese are swans. "It is as undignified to think another man's philosophy as to wear another man's cast-off clothes. Only the poor in spirit or in purse can find any satisfaction in doing either." Is there no philosophy, then, but cast-off philosophy? Or must we wear rags forever so as not to imitate the well-dressed? Are there no such things as tailors of the spirit? How are we to go through this famous dance of life? Naked, evidently.

3. THE DANCE OF DEATH

"Dancing and building are the two primary and essential arts. The art of dancing stands at the source of all the arts that express themselves first in the human person. The art of building, or architecture, is the beginning of all the arts that lie outside of the person." [1]

Dancing is egotistical, then, not tribal. It has its birth in the first person singular. "It is even possible that, in earlier than human times, dancing and architecture may

[1] *Ibid.*, p. 1.

have been the result of the same impulse. The nest of birds is the chief early form of building, and Edmund Selous has suggested [2] that the nest may first have arisen as an accidental result of the ecstatic sexual dance of birds." [3] So even building is fundamentally individualistic and erotic. Fancy a hangbird's nest resulting accidentally from the shivers preliminary to copulation!

"The joyous beat of the feet of children, the cosmic play of philosophers' thoughts, rise and fall according to the same laws of rhythm," [4] that is, a sexual rhythm. Sexual desire, having externalized itself in genitalia at the bidding of Schopenhauer, now at the bidding of Ellis externalizes itself still further in dancing, thus producing the basilica of St. Peter.

"The significance of dancing, in the wide sense, lies in the fact that it is simply an intimate concrete appeal of a general rhythm, that rhythm which marks not only life but the universe, if one may still be allowed so to name the sum of the cosmic influences that reach us." [5] Why this doubt of the propriety of calling the universe a universe? Why, because it may imply that the universe exists, that its influences really reach us. Ellis believes, as a matter of fact, that the only influences there are proceed *from* us, and that the universe is the result. We dance it into being. It is the great hangbird's nest woven of our bodies weltering in their own cosmic rut. "Matter is a fiction, just as the fundamental ideas with which the sciences generally operate are mostly fictitious." [6] "Matter . . . is merely a substance we have ourselves invented

[2] *Vide The Zoölogist,* Dec., 1901.
[3] *Vide* "The Dance of Life," note at beginning of chap. i.
[4] *Ibid.*
[5] *Ibid.,* p. 34.
[6] *Ibid.,* p. 89.

to account for our sensations."[7] And at the same time, of course, our self is something we have invented to account for the universe. "The atom," he says, quoting Boscovitch, "is a hypostatized nothing."[8]

"We are beginning to realize that there are no metaphysical formulas to suit all men, but that every man must be the artist of his own philosophy."[9] "The problem which Vaihinger [Hans Vaihinger, in "The Philosophy of As If"] set out to solve was this: How comes it about that with consciously false ideas we yet reach conclusions that are in harmony with Nature and appeal to us as Truth? That we do so is obvious. . . . In mathematics it is notorious that we start from absurdities to reach a realm of law, and our whole conception of the nature of the world is based on a foundation which we believe to have no existence."[10]

At last here is a realm of law that Ellis approves of. We have only to start with absurdities which we believe to have no existence.

"Berkeley, in attacking the defective conceptions of the mathematicians, failed to see that it was by means of, and not in spite of, these logically defective conceptions that they attained logically valuable results."[11] That is, by starting with a falsehood, non-Berkeleian mathematicians are able logically to arrive at a conclusion in harmony with nature. Using this same "logic," I might argue that, since the moon is made of green cheese, it therefore is not. And yet "even a cheese-mite, one imagines, could only with difficulty attain an adequate metaphysical conception

[7] *Ibid.*, p. 213.
[8] *Ibid.*, p. 89.
[9] *Ibid.*, p. 218.
[10] *Ibid.*, p. 83.
[11] *Ibid.*, p. 87.

of a cheese."[12] Least of all, a cheese-mite, I should say.

But it appears that the cheese-mite has invented the cheese to account for his thrills. And we world-mites have for the same reason invented the world. Naturally, therefore, we are beginning to realize that there are "no metaphysical formulas to suit all men." If I invent matter, I will also invent my own formulas, if you please; nor will I suffer any interference with cosmic play of my philosophic thoughts. Vaihinger's feat of beginning with consciously false ideas and arriving at conclusions which are in harmony with Nature is explained. Nature is merely *what appeals to us* (or to Vaihinger) as the truth. The pragmatism of William James in a nutshell—a fictitious nutshell, of course.

The attack here goes to the very roots of logic and reason. Whatever we think we think, is logical and reasonable, since our fictitious thoughts create the fictitious facts as well as the laws of the fictitious universe in which we dwell. We even use logic to prove that there is no such thing as logic. Under such circumstances it would be difficult to trip. It is not only Ellis who is speaking. No one can pick up a magazine to-day without coming upon similarly melodious words.

Is there any non-fictional, honest-to-God truth in all this? Certainly. We do start with ideas which we know to be *imperfect,* and arrive at laws which we know to be but approximations in a universe which we know we do not fully understand. But to put it this way is to remain within the despised "realm" of common sense. And what is common sense?

According to Ellis,[13] "what we call common sense

[12] *Ibid.,* preface, p. viii.
[13] *Ibid.,* p. 218.

is really a hardened mass of dead metaphysics."

No, Mr. Ellis, that is not what we call common sense. What we call common sense is the accumulated knowledge and wisdom of the ages—not dead knowledge, but living and true knowledge. Do dead things survive? Is this your understanding of the doctrine of the survival of the fittest as set forth in that "Origin of Species" published but eight short months after you were born?

But as an empiricist it is impossible that you should ever arrive at a knowledge of common sense, since it is the sense you have in common with others. With the best of others. For the more common it is to the race, the more able it must have been to resist the tooth of time and the test of experience. So it is not something which it is at all easy to get at. If a man isolates himself, cuts himself off from the main channels of tradition, how is he to know what men have thought and tried and sifted and finally preserved as most true and useful? He only knows what he himself thinks, or what his narrow neighbourhood thinks. Education and culture, and a certain humbleness of mind, are required to make one familiar with the great tradition which is truly the common sense of mankind. And this is Authority, not the antagonist but the correlative of the highest individuality, not that Authority whose symbol is a clenched fist and whose real name is Tyranny, but that kindly authority which waits to be importuned, whose symbol is a helping hand.

And you, Mr. Ellis, do not like it, chiefly because it refuses to encourage you in saying, "The cosmos is chaos, the chaos is I, and I am my interstitial glands." So you call it dead. But there are no dead. Of the totally dead, if such there could be, we would have no knowledge, not even a memory. Is common sense really as dead as that?

But let us on with the dance. "In actual fact, is life essentially an art?" Ellis asks.[14] "Let us look at the matter more closely, and see what life is like, as people have lived it. . . . The whole conception of art has been so narrowed and debased among us that . . . the use of the word in its large and natural sense seems either unintelligible or eccentric."

Good! We are back to "actual" fact, and are no longer to be unintelligible or even eccentric. So let us make the attempt to embrace this large and natural sense of the word "art" with as little debasement as possible.

"We may take, for instance, that remarkable phenomenon called Napoleon. . . . To condemn him is to condemn Man, who made him as he was."

Then Napoleon, for one, did not make himself. He seems not to have been a person, but a phenomenon, a word which my dictionary defines as "an appearance, especially one of unusual occurrence." And this unusual appearance was made by Man. To condemn Napoleon would be to condemn his creator, which would be intolerable.

"Napoleon observed, 'I love power. But it is as an artist that I love it.' " That justifies everything, as fiddling justified Nero. But "it is always possible to dispute about individuals, even when so happy an illustration chances to come before us." The phenomenon has become an individual on our hands, making dispute possible. Dispute, evidently, is not wanted. So Ellis drops Napoleon without saying anything more about him, and takes, "almost at random, the example of a primitive people," about whom it seems there can be no dispute, "the Loyalty Islanders," to wit.

These indisputables inhabit certain blessed bits of land

[14] *Ibid.*, pp. 6 *et seq.*

surrounded by water lying east of New Caledonia, in a southern latitude about equal to that of Egypt in the north, that for half a century have belonged to France. Islands and people have both been vividly described by Emma Hadfield, a missioner's wife, in a book called "Among the Natives of the Loyalty Group," published in 1920.

"The basis of their culture," says Ellis, leaning on Mrs. Hadfield for his facts, "is artistic. . . . Therefore it is natural for them to regard rhythm and grace in all the actions of life, and almost a matter of instinct to cultivate beauty in all social relationships. . . . No clothing is worn until the age of twenty-five or thirty. . . . The people have sweet and musical voices. . . . In one of these islands, Uvea, so great is the eloquence of the people that they employ oratory to catch fish." Precisely what we use it for in the United States. But "for a primitive people the art of life is necessarily in large part concerned with eating."

So it is to their cuisine that we must turn if we would learn, though I might remark, in passing, that formerly there reigned an "implicit trust, and goods were left about without fear of theft, which was rare and punishable by death." One ceases to wonder why it was rare. It looks, too, since a penal code was established, that at one time the islanders had accumulated quite a hard mass of dead metaphysics. But let us not be drawn aside into speculation.

"The Lifuans [inhabitants of Lifu, another island of this same group] are fond of food, but much etiquette is practised in eating. The food must be conveyed to the mouth gracefully, daintily, leisurely." To which Mrs. Hadfield adds: "In the matter of food and eating, they might put many of our countrymen to shame." Ellis resumes: "In old days the Lifuans were occasionally cannibals, not, it would seem, either from necessity or any ritual reason, but because, like some peoples elsewhere, they liked it. . . . If a man had twenty or thirty wives and a large family, it would be quite correct if, now and then, he cooked one of his own children. . . . The child would be cooked whole, wrapped in banana or cocoanut leaves. The social inconveniences of this practice have now been recognized. But they still fail to find anything offensive or repulsive in a corpse.

"To vermin," also, "they seem to have but little objection, but otherwise they have a strong love of cleanliness. . . . The idea of using manure in agricultural operations seems to them disgusting. Being divided into small tribes, each with its own autocratic chief, war was sometimes inevitable." However, it "was attended by much etiquette. . . . As soon as half-a-dozen fighters were put out of action on one side, the chief of that side would give the command to cease fighting. . . . An indemnity was then paid by the conquerors"—to the side which had voluntarily quit. "This whole Lifuan art of living has, however, been undermined by the arrival of Christianity with its usual accompaniments. The Lifuans are substituting European vices for their own virtues. Their simplicity and confidence are passing away."

Is it not pitiable? They no longer make war. They use manure in agriculture. It has been made socially inconvenient for a husband of twenty or thirty wives, granting that he still has them, to feed even now and then upon their numerous progeny. But they are not yet altogether lost. "They still . . . fail to find anything offensive or repulsive about a corpse." They still retain those wonderful table-manners developed by familiarity with little long pig wrapped in banana leaves. Some saving remains of their cannibal birthright linger on. And Havelock Ellis is thrilled. "The Lifuans," he says, furnish an illustration which seems decisive." Decisive of what? Evidently of the proposition that nature, so long as it can escape the curse of Christianity, leads its votaries a dance.

How glorious that dance once was! "Dr. Louis Robinson has pointed out that the 'spasmodic jerking of the chimpanzee's feeble legs,' pounding the partition of his cage, is the crude motion out of which 'the heavenly alchemy of evolution has created the divine movements of Pavlova'; but it must be remembered that the anthropoid apes are offshoots only from the stock that produced Man. . . . It is the more primitive love-dance of insects and birds that seems to reappear among human savages in various parts of the world . . . and in a conventionalized and symbolized form . . . is still danced in civilization to-day."

So Pavlova gets her divine movements not from her cousin the chimpanzee so much as from her cousin's cousins, the birds and the bugs. But why call that alchemy "heavenly" which introduced so much restraint into the art? "On the threshold of the moral world we meet the idea of Freedom." [15] So Pavlova's steps are either more "free" than the spasmodic jerking of the chimpanzee's feeble legs, or else they are less moral.

One thing at least seems clear: The lower is father and mother of the higher, the pint cup gives birth to the ocean; so, naturally, the "higher" is a debasement, and the sea smaller than a mug. "What we consider our highest activities arise out of what we are accustomed to regard

[15] *Ibid.*, p. 91.

as the lowest. That is indeed merely a necessary result of evolution."[16]

Our custom of "considering" the lowest as the lowest is no doubt lamentable. But what about evolution? With Ellis (and a great many other people) it seems to be an unfolding of that which has never been folded, the "development" (magic word!) of the atom into man with nothing behind the atom to account for the stature of man. We had already learned from Boscovitch that the atom is a hypostatized nothing. Everything "comes from" nothing—in which case it necessarily remains nothing. Can you pour out more than has ever been poured in? If Pavlova has progressed, it must have been downwards. She is a degraded insect if she has gone and curbed her primitive spasmodic jerkings with technic—and when I saw her last, that was precisely what she seemed to have done.

Even Ellis, however, insists at times that there has been real progress—nor does he always manifest a proper amount of repugnance to this unfortunate state of things. "The dance," he says,[17] "is the rule of number and of rhythm and of measure and of order, of the controlling influence of form, of the subordination of the parts to the whole." Indeed it is. And "it is Propriety—the whole ceremony of life—in which all harmonious intercourse subsists."[18] "If human feelings, the instincts, . . . are the field that has to be cultivated, [it is] ceremony that ploughs it . . . and discipline that is to weed it."

I agree, but am left wondering how ceremony and discipline happened to arrive on the field out of the primitive

[16] *Ibid.*, p. 95.
[17] *Ibid.*, preface, p. x.
[18] *Ibid.*, p. 22.

hypostatized atomic nullity, self-impregnating parent of the instincts and of the "field" itself.

And now, in spite of that Propriety in which all harmonious intercourse subsists, we are told [19] not only that "all religions . . . have been at the outset . . . in some measure saltatory," but [20] that "religion . . . is a private matter, as love is."

Then religion is dancing at the chimpanzee stage, a spasmodic jerking of weak, undisciplined spiritual legs. And both religion and love are private matters, concerning nobody but the worshipper and the lover. From religion, as from love, no social consequences have ever been observed to flow!

Notwithstanding which, "Jesus . . . proclaimed symbolically a doctrine of heredity which is only to-day beginning to be directly formulated: 'Every tree that bringeth not forth good fruit is hewn down and cast into the fire.' There was no compunction at all in his promulgation of this radical, yet necessary doctrine of the destruction of unfit stocks. . . . The religion of Jesus was the most aristocratic of religions." [21] So that private matter which is religion comes to this: discipline gone mad, compulsory eugenics. Really, Ellis should read the parable of the wheat and the tares.

He prefers a parable of his own: [22] "It is only too familiar a fact how, when the impulse of religion first germinates in the young soul, the ghouls of the Churches rush out of their caverns, seize on the unhappy victim of the divine influence and proceed to assure him that his rapture is, not a natural manifestation, as free as the sun-

[19] *Ibid.*, p. 37.
[20] *Ibid.*, p. 195
[21] *Ibid.*, p. 331.
[22] *Ibid.*, p. 221.

light and as gracious as the unfolding of a rose, but the manifest sign that he has been branded by a supernatural force and fettered for ever to a dead theological creed."

Certainly we would better avoid being branded by ghouls. Branding is the prerogative of the Eugenics Society, whose destruction of unfit stocks was licensed, it seems, by the very Authority which licensed the ghouls.

"The first creators of civilization were making the dance, and the philosopher of a later age, hovering over the dark abyss of insanity, with bleeding feet and muscles strained to the breaking point, still seems to be weaving the maze of the dance." [23] Did this philosopher of a later age try to hover, perchance, too long, and fall over the edge? This would account for the fact that our dance has become a dance upon emptiness. So we hang by the neck, waiting for death, and there does not seem to be long to wait. "When the gods, to ruin a man, first make him mad, they do it, almost invariably, by making him an optimist." [24] Ellis himself is an optimist, since he hopes even for the doing away of poor dancers by the castration of inferior stocks. And yet he says [25] "the place where optimism most flourishes is the lunatic asylum."

I am optimist enough to think that he is unjust to himself; for I believe that, when he is not exercising the terpsichorean art of writing, he is a good neighbour and a sane and kindly man.

[23] *Ibid.*, p. 61.
[24] *Ibid.*, p. 84.
[25] *Ibid.*, p. 83.

CHAPTER VI

THE BUSKINEERS

THE chief objection to the philosophy of As If is that it pretends to be the philosophy of As Is. The modern philosopher may say that he wishes to be regarded as an artist, but he would be by no means content to be regarded as an artist only. Always there is the assumption that these theories of his are realities, as real as nature's own. Even Nietzsche and Schopenhauer become intolerably dull once we read them as out-and-out yarns. Both science and philosophy are, notwithstanding Mr. Ellis, written with the pretension that their premises are true.

There is a class of fiction, however—the fantastically romantic—whose premises are confessedly false. H. G. Wells begins his story of "The Time Machine" by pretending that we can live our days in the ordinary or the reverse order, and at any speed. He does not expect us to believe it, but to grant it "for the sake of argument." After that, all we can ask of him is that his deductions shall be logical, that things shall happen just as they would happen did time's wheel run backwards in sober fact. Indeed, we ask rather less, for it is flatly impossible to imagine all the results of a palpable absurdity. It is enough if the tale is fairly plausible.

Wells, of course, uses his palpable absurdity as a means for bringing upon the stage certain of his social theories, and these he expects us to take seriously. The fantastic romance seldom remains merely fantastic. Inside its sugar coat there is usually a heavy dose of propaganda, and this has all the responsibilities of philosophy. We can no longer grant it for the sake of any argument, however ingenious.

Usually the tale of fantasy goes further even than this, and pretends to a measure of actuality in its sugar coat as well. In "The Black Seal" Arthur Machen assumes that Professor Gregg has discovered a way by which "man can be reduced to the slime from which he came, and be forced to put on the flesh of the reptile and the snake." At once a metaphorical meaning is suggested, an allegory. Probably no fantasy is strictly non-allegorical. We are so steeped in life that we can never get quite away from it. But an allegory is philosophy in fancy dress, and even a jester in cap and bells may be called to account if he assumes to preach. To be absolutely irresponsible is the prerogative only of the utterly meaningless.

At the same time it would be absurd to expect the fiction-writer to be continually toeing the mark. If he begins his novel with the frankly implied statement, "Herewith opens a pack of lies," he should in all conscience be allowed a little licence. The lies must hang together more or less, and if they don't ape truths now and then, or make us smile by their recognizable caricature of falsehoods, a yawn shall be their reward. Nevertheless there is a field where lies may romp, assured that the frown of sensible ethics masks an appreciative wink.

Most of our impulses are evil only when circumstances make them so. Ordinarily there is no harm in eating a good dinner. But if there is only one dinner and several starving people at the board, it becomes another matter. Or the circumstance that I have just dined may convict me of gluttony if I proceed to dine again. Romance, then, may provide an opportunity for the innocent exercise of suppressed impulses by turning them loose in the imagination under imagined circumstances which made their capers quite right and proper. Literature which does this is called the literature of escape.

When we were cave-men we had plenty of opportunities for hunting and fishing. It was often necessary to track down our human enemy and to follow his spoor through the woods. But to-day there are so many people in the world, so many policemen, meat-packers, and salmon-canning factories, that little room is left for our old habits to stretch in. So we read adventure and detective stories. Not many of us would like to be real detectives or real adventurers. We have beome soft. But fancy makes a comparatively faint impression. To partake, in fancy, of a polar expedition merely makes us feel comfortably cool on a hot day in August. We did not actually pine to join the heroic Amundsen in his search for Nobile. Nor, because a tale of the tropics is an agreeable companion in January, are we anxious to be sunstruck or to have the black vomit. It is nice, however, to make believe that we are of this stern stuff which is (presumably) the bone and sinew of explorers.

"But," said the Puritan, "beware of the sins of the imagination! If you exercise your piratical talents in dreams, you will wake to find them strengthened as if by practice. To contemplate fictitious characters walking the plank, to revel in the cutting of fictitious throats, is to prepare yourself for crime. Look at the boys and girls who have gone wrong through reading penny dreadfuls."

Well, let us look at them. How many are there? An urchin brought before the judge for some piece of mischief must be a dull fellow if he can't think to lay the blame upon something, but such self-serving statements ought to be taken with a grain of salt. Statistics show that the opening of a moving-picture theatre in a southern village tends to reduce the number of lynchings in the vicinity. Where speech is free, disgruntled citizens, who might otherwise wreak their vengeance against the government in deeds, frequently take it out in talk. It won't do to bottle us up too tightly. The attempt to prohibit cigarettes often results in stimulating the opium traffic.

At the same time it must be admitted that there are both good and bad specimens of the penny dreadful and its modern counterparts; there are movies and movies. Pernicious incendiary talk exists as well as wholesome free speech. The question arises, where should we draw the line? The Puritan speaks of the sins of the imagination. What are they?

I should say that they are just like any other sins, though walking on much more feeble legs. It is usually a long step between thinking about picking a pocket and actually attempting the feat. And what is sin? For one thing, it is an old-fashioned word, unpleasing to the modern ear. Otherwise, if we are to credit those experts who have most deeply studied the subject, sin is a deliberate choosing of evil in preference to the good, the good and evil in question being both within the sinner's knowledge and capacity. Here is certainly a practical touchstone with which to test the literature of escape. All that can be required of it on moral grounds is that it shall first of all be true to its premises, and then depict as virtue only such actions as would be ethical under the circumstances as given. All other actions should be depicted as vicious.

If I am a freely roving savage, I crave your indulgence if I scalp the white man who seems bent upon sweeping all the tepees of my tribe into his museums, especially if I am only pretending to be savage and only half pretending to scalp. Of course, if I am in that state of mental disequilibrium which makes it impossible for me to distinguish between fiction and fact, such reading may do me harm. Nothing in this world can be made entirely fool-proof. No book worth anybody's reading is fit for everybody's reading. I, for one, am in favour of giving the romancer a very long bow, and only ask that he shoot straight and at fair game.

But there is another archer in our midst, who calls himself not a romancer but a realist. He pretends that his bow and arrow are a real bow and a real arrow, that his game is real game, and his hunting field the field of everyday experience. What about *his* hunting licence?

Strictly speaking, he ought to come under the statutes made and provided for philosophers. But, after all, nobody takes him quite so seriously as that. He is, as a matter of fact, a bit of a humbug, whose realism is a cloak thrown over his romantic figures in hopes of giving them a natural look. Confessed romantics use this cloak as well. It is common property. But while the romanticist admits that it is a cloak, hiding the more unlikely joints of a lot of dolls and lending a certain solidity to otherwise thin air, the realist offers it as the native vestment of creatures of flesh and blood. And this habit makes him a dangerous fellow. His premise is an As If, and he swears that it is an As Is.

However, it is but a convention of the stage, a bit of overemphasis, which should deceive nobody. All novels should be read as romances, and then few bones will be broken. Without exaggeration, there can be no work of art. Let the realist assume, then, that all women are strumpets and all men thieves. If he goes on and draws an honest picture of a world like that, it will be an edifying performance. The trouble comes when he violates the law of romance which says that it shall be true to its premises. He is, you see, under the necessity of being agreeable. Nobody reads a disagreeable book unless moved by some outside consideration, such as a salary, or the idea that it contains valuable information. A world peopled exclusively by blacklegs would be a very disagreeable spectacle for most of us. So the realist is tempted to become that most sinister of romancers, the one who pretends that bad things are good, that one may spend a lifetime industriously doing wrong and be not a whit the worse for it.

This is quite a different thing from discovering fineness in unlikely places, or from showing that there may be a streak or so of decency, or heroism, or loving-kindness, in the most miserable creature alive.

The out-and-out romancer usually side-steps the moral issue as much as possible. The realistic romancer sometimes points a false moral, and drives it home. He not only degrades fact: he degrades ideals. The immoral novel begins by assuming that its characters are people, or fairies, or devils, Robots, or what not, and then proceeds to make them act as if there were something less. It does not so much matter if Robots behave like men, but it matters a lot if men behave like Robots, or worse, and continue to be called gentlemen. The Tin Woodman may be never so human. It is only personification, and a harmless invention. A human being conceived of as wood and tin is a depersonification and altogether pernicious.

To speak of anything in terms of something higher and make it live up to the terms, is an admirable thing to do. But what if that higher something be merely a higher humbug, and in reality not higher but vastly lower than the most lowly truth? Why, then we have the glorification of vice. We have also the goody-goody tale, a disgrace even to its worst blood-and-thunder brothers. It holds up Elsie Dinsmores for admiration when they behave like intolerable prigs. We had at one time such a flood of these volumes—not all as viciously pious as Elsie, it is true—making morality so repulsive to the healthy human sense that nothing less than a revolt could have saved us.

It is this revolt which we must now review—the literature, as it is called, of disillusion. Writers once more have come forward promising to tell us the truth, the essential truth, even about Sunday schools, to say nothing of bedrooms. Well, let them. And, as St. Jerome long since declared, "if an offence come out of the truth, it is better that the offence come out than that the truth be concealed." If the offence consist in showing us how bad we are, it is time we were offended.

But let us make no mistake. The literature of disillusion is, like all other fiction, the literature of escape. It is romance, the world as we think we would like it. If it succeeds in passing itself off as something else, it has become that very objectionable form of history which shirks the responsibility of actually being history. But to those who continue to regard it as fiction, it is something agreeable. For disillusion, when it reaches the pages of stories which are accepted as yarns and nothing more, is already *welcome* disillusion to those who turn the pages at all.

Censors seem to care only for incidents, and insist that

incidents should represent conventionally correct conduct. The viewpoint, the angle of narration, the influence brought to bear upon the reader's sympathies, count for nothing. This is probably why censors are such ridiculous persons. They are moved by the letter, not the spirit. Hidden philosophy, however false and unnatural, is nothing to Mr. Bluepencil.

Now Puritanism was an unnatural philosophy in regard to sex. It did not tell the whole truth. Indeed, it told as little of the truth as possible. Inevitably there arose an art which defied this conspiracy of silence, and laughed at the bowdlerizers. In fiction it became popular to specialize in the forbidden. One began to hear of George Moore, Theodore Dreiser, and a host of others.

But François Mauriac, the French novelist, has recently expressed the belief that the new fiction is the necessary result of "the terrible logic that impels our world, which has lost its God." If this be the case, a novelist, in so far as he is realistic, must of course describe men and women who have lost their God. Mauriac contends that love and devotion are no longer comprehensible, that the novelist must be content to ascribe to his characters only such motives as remain, and this, he believes, makes it necessary to go for plots and the *mise en scène* to "the secret life," by which I understand him to mean the sex life. He also appears to hold that by going far enough in this direction we shall eventually get enough of it, and return to an older way of thinking.

It seems a drastic remedy and to call for novelists who are not themselves lost in the mire which they describe. Such might delineate a godless world with an accuracy that would appal the hardiest, though, if they honestly set about the task, I hardly see why they should continue to call themselves novelists. Why make up as a thespian if you are going to sit upon the bench? Many do, but to me their words are duller than Justice Darling's jokes. I hate to be sold sugar-coated medicine in a candy store, though I admit that there has always to be some touch of the remedial or else of the poisonous in everything. Still, for drastic cathartics it is better to go to a chemist's shop.

As a matter of fact, our novelists are not the aloof physicians of the soul they pretend to be. Those of the Impuritan type have simply ceased to find romance in the current creeds, and have plunged more or less whole-heartedly into that secret life where, Mauriac tells us, salvation is yet to be found—as it were, by a rebound from striking the nadir. Not that they have actually gone quite to such a depth—not many of them. The new movement was in large part a new appeal to experience, and essentially a revivifying retouching of earth. My chief objection is that these romancers dwell too much upon the claim of being realists, as if they had totally laid aside the prerogative of artists. As merry-andrews, they are not too harshly to be condemned—certainly not to be stoned without a hearing.

CHAPTER VII

THE TESAM OF THE CREJ

I. CABELL

IT is to police methods of reform that we owe the particular prominence of James Branch Cabell. Between the day of his birth at Richmond, Virginia, in 1879, and the year 1919, he managed to write eleven books without being discovered either by the public at large or by many critics. But in 1909 came "Jurgen," legal prosecution, and world-wide fame.

This profitable martyrdom had its inevitable effect in turning the indifferent into partisans or foes, and nerved the author to greater efforts. One might as well be hanged for a sheep as for a lamb. "Jurgen" was followed by the bolder "Figures of Earth," published in 1921, and by the boldest "Something about Eve," of 1927.

Cabell is not by nature one who, left alone, would have gone so far out of his way to disturb his fellow beings. Once, just before the war, he engaged in coal mining in West Virginia, but aside from this black business his tendencies were scholarly—so much so that, having taken his degree at William and Mary College, his first move was to get himself appointed teacher of French in that same institution. For hobbies he had genealogy and history, and what chiefly distinguished him from the ordinary professor was a humorous quirk and a tendency not to take things seriously. This led him to commence author with "The Eagle's Shadow," in 1904. He seemed in a fair way to become the mild apostle of a clique, content if now and then he could put a surreptitious rivet in grandfather's neck, but filled for the most part with the spirit of high chivalry so well described in "The Soul of Melicent," otherwise known as "Domnei."

However, like his friend Mark Twain, he had rebellious ideas upon two subjects—the Christian religion as he had come to know it (he still describes himself in "Who's Who" as an Episcopalian), and sex as he saw it in operation among his neighbours. Neither pleased him. So he proceeded to make fun of both—without bothering to go very deeply into the philosophical questions involved.

As he could not be a real high churchman, let alone a Fundamentalist, or quite abandon religion altogether, he adopted that sentimental scepticism which regards Christianity as a most admirable fraud.

As to sex, he noted that every woman is potentially both a mistress and a mother; and that in either capacity she interferes confoundedly with the peace of the poetically minded. If a poet has anything to do with women, he is under the necessity of earning money. Yet the poetic gift itself draws one towards the fair. Here is conflict, the stuff of drama. It is out of this that Cabell has constructed most of his tales.

The Cabellian poet is always young, an introspective of the introvert or schizoid type, which Dr. E. Kretschmer, in "Physique and Character," describes somewhat harshly as "antisocial, congenitally weak-minded," and "gifted with . . . hypersensitive inner capacities for reaction." And his struggles are always dramatized, so that

JAMES BRANCH CABELL

This is the deviltry of our school-days

the story becomes an allegory, with genius cavorting as a White Stallion upon which the poetaster fain would ride to glory. But women lay snares for the rider, as mares do for the beast. The stud becomes only another name for the corral; banns do but a prison make, and mistresses a cage.

This same plot was used in "Goosie," written and published by James Hopper in 1910, six years after "The Eagle's Shadow" but nine years before the Cabell formula was perfected in "Jurgen." Goosie, too, was a poet. He needed no winged Pegasus; he had wings of his own. And a fine time he enjoyed, flying up into heaven trying to break the altitude record—flights so eloquently described that the purple patches their vertigo cast across the pages are unexcelled to this day.

Goosie's wife, as you may remember, was fat and sensible. She trimmed one of Goosie's wings with the scissors, so that instead of soaring off into the unprofitable blue he could only fly round and round in a circus tent and earn a salary, regularly paid by a certain Buffalo Billiam. The whole Cabell story is right here. But there were no trappings of scholarly erudition. What is worse, there was no hint that Goosie's wings were energized by secretions from the interstitial glands. So Hopper remained at large, unadvertised by so much as a threat of jail.

His masterpiece made a little ripple, however. It was even serialized, I think, in the *Saturday Evening Post.* And soon afterwards Inez Haynes Gilmore, now Mrs. Will Irwin, turned the tables by writing "Angel Island," wherein were a great number of winged creatures—all of them female. Girls also, it seems, have fancies which matrimony tends to disappoint. And brute men entrap them, and cut off not only one of their wings but both. Naturally there was more sex in this. But there was little "realism," and the angel girls were—in the illustrations at least—draped in decent strips of seaweed. So once more the censor stayed his hand.

Cabell was more fortunate. To his protest against sex he added a panegyric on sex, thus managing to draw the legal thunderbolt down upon his head. The author of "Angel Island" had thought that domesticity was worth the sacrifice of wings, even if passion was not. Hopper was convinced that freedom from women altogether would be a good literary move—if it could be had. But Cabell felt that women are indispensable even to poets, necessary as provocatrices of emotions which can be turned into verse if the more obvious forms of indulgence be eschewed.

The difficulty is in avoiding conventional social consequences of keeping company. Actually to possess one of these creatures in a humdrum and morally approvable way is fatal, especially in face of the flat impossibility of supporting a wife and family by the writing of sonnets. As to women of the seemingly safe vampirish type, they are likely to turn domestic upon one's hands—and even if they don't, the satisfaction which they offer is unsatisfying, if only because it gives satisfaction and stills our lettered longings. So the only permanent good is an unattainable dream; and dreams, though most unreal, are the one reality. Thus the actual becomes unsubstantial in proportion to its actuality—all of which makes us rather melancholy. *Ergo,* there is something genuine about a nightmare, at least in comparison with a beatific vision.

This is the lyrical whimper which runs through the Cabell books like a refrain, the whimper of the adolescent who discovers that life is not quite what he thought it was. As a babe, he was monarch of all he surveyed. Now there seem to be others demanding their meed of consideration. Art for art's sake is confronted with the h. c. of l. The youthful Ego, which looked forward to love as the final act of self-expression, realizes with horror that it is self-sacrifice. With strong men, with great poets, with those chapel-hacks and *Kapellmeister* who bore the ordinary burdens and their own peculiar ones as well—the true immortals—we here have nothing to do. Cabell is the apologist of the callow and of the jejune.

Yet he is in his way a real poet, of a prose-writing, minor-sort: a born story-teller withal, saved from utter banality by the happy ability of laughing unrancorously at others, if not at himself. I doubt not that some day he will be found in every nursery, and remembered as the inventor of charming fairy-tales. For it is the children who eventually fall heir to such *chefs-d'œuvre,* whose propaganda-features time ignores, makes unintelligible, or simply eliminates editorially. Meanwhile one cannot help being struck by his marvellously Victorian flavour. For Victorians, too, were frequently mildly wicked, and given to crossing the Channel to France or still farther eastward.

Yes, this is the deviltry of our school days, and makes old readers of Fitzgerald and Swinburne feel perfectly at home. Cabell's idea of being salacious is to inform an astonished world that babies are not brought by the stork, neither are they to be found in the cabbage patch—at least that was as far as he went until persecution nerved him to take sterner measures against our modesty. And his idea of being blasphemous was, and still is, to link the name of the Redeemer with the names of Mithras, with the Servian Vii, with Huitzilopochtli, Tamouz, Heracles, Gautama, Krishna, and Dionysus. Surely nothing could be more Victorian than this. Even the spelling is eruditely odd whenever possible. This is wickedness *à la* Frazer and "The Golden Bough," of the parity of religions, of ex-Puritans who think that they have destroyed the foundations of faith when they begin to hint that the earth could not have been created literally in six days.

But at heart Cabell remains as Puritan as John Knox or H. L. Mencken. Individual judgment sets up a straw man. Further individual judgment knocks him down. It is not so much reaction as continued action all in one direction. And when the ground has once been cleared of old beliefs, we begin to wonder if a little education would not be a good thing. So Mencken labours with the moron, begging him to acquire at least some items of that knowledge which has been accumulated since Luther and become enslaved to another "authority," which calls itself Science. So Cabell casts wistful eyes into the past.

He picks up the ancient images, and wonders if they may not still be useful—at least as playthings. He cannot go even as far as Mencken in discarding Christian sentiments. He is far too human to join the Behaviourists in their determination to control the protoplasmic mass and drive it into channels of cold efficiency. Almost all of his figures, even his devils and horrors, are likable. He is sympathetic even towards sirens, even towards domestic women. Indeed, he seems to love them for the very sadness they inflict in one way or another upon the young soul whose pale reveries they disturb.

Cabell is mature only in his literary technic, which is of the most distinguished sort. Some have denied him style—which is like denying beauty to a dear gazelle that just has charmed us with its gentle eye. True, he goes for his models to the earlier centuries, but that is precisely where good models are to be found. The logic of his phrase is beyond criticism, whatever may be said of his argument; nor could his material have been better handled —considering what he means to prove by it—nor his ratiocination more cleverly hidden behind the action. His invention never flags. His humour seldom fails—except in large, implied matters—though once in a while it forsakes the realm of ideal monsters and descends to local politics. In "Figures of Earth" there is a congress of supernatural birds at which, unfortunately, the Eagle is permitted to exclaim: "There is such a thing as being too proud to fight!" And we are frequently told that certain "incantations" are needed to lure the stork from the skies, whereat we blush—not from the exposure of a "secret," but to find our master so provincial.

But not even Homer is always equally interesting, and if Cabell is inclined to be dull except when the sense of being bold excites him to eloquence, the same is true of many other Impuritans.

It was in any case a feat to take the defunct allegory—which men had turned from because they no longer cared for the spiritual things it was wont to express—and give it new popularity, even if this was done by loading it with odds and ends from the nineteenth century's conception of an elder naughtiness. It showed us at least what the trouble was, and what we would have to do to appreciate Dante once more. We still have faith in something, it seems. Very well. Then we will make that the subject of our "Undivine Comedy." And instead of inventing new images, we will revamp the old ones, levying upon the entire past at our need, but giving especial attention to the Middle Ages and to the trappings of that very Faith which we have lost.

So let us hover about the thirteenth century. And for geography, we can find nothing better than that of old Southern France, the land of the Troubadors. Thus not only Christian legends but pagan myths will be available.

2. POETSHOME

Cabell's heroes have usually something to do with Poictesme. A pictorial representation of this country, purporting to be "The Map of Philip Borsdale, *circa* 1679" —a gorgeous map teeming with highly coloured monsters and redrawn with especial reference to the Cabell stories by Frank C. Papé—may be had of any enterprising bookseller. It conforms with fair accuracy to the known typographical features of France just north of the Gulf of Lyons. Broadly speaking, it is Provence.

Here of old sang William IX, Duke of Aquitane and Count—not of Poictesme but of Poitou. Here, more recently, Mistral lived and died. Here, especially between the years 1090 and 1350, flourished the Courtly Lyrics—the *trobar clus,* so wilfully obscure; the *sirventes,* so newsy, topical, and scandalous; the *alba,* or dawn-song of parting lovers; the *vers;* the *canso;* the *ronda.* Its native epics were Girart de Rossilon and Jaufré; its versified romances, the *novas,* such as the well-nigh interminable "Flamena." In prose, it gave birth to the *Breviari d'Amors,* of 1256. Cabell has studied more particularly its later and lesser productions. Most suggestive of all is his possible indebtedness to the Legend of Ulenspiegel, relating to a thirteenth-century heroic vagabond but written and published in the 1860's by Charles de Coster of Flanders—decidedly not a lesser production from a literary point of view.

But I would not advise the reader to risk a headache poring over either this bibliography or this geography—not if he is looking for a key to the "Jurgen" myths. Neither would it be safe to disregard history, legend, and cartography altogether. For we are in the presence of a wag who delights in nothing so much as in sending his followers searching mythologies and gazetteers for things which are not there, and then tempting scepticism to come a cropper over some minor but authentic detail. The whole thing is a hoax. In the midst of made-up substantives and distorted anagrams lurk genuine appellations, pitfalls for the feet of the rash. So it will be well if we watch our step and think of Poictesme simply as the Poet's Home.

Hard by is Philistia, inhabited by the butcher, the baker, and the candlestick-maker, together with those poets of tough fibre capable of facing the world as it is, Michelangelo, Palestrina, *et al.,* winners of common or garden immortality, who have stooped to interpreting the souls of others. The poet of Poictesme interprets only himself. He is an egoist, too fine to succeed in any rough-and-ready way. He finds it easier to pretend, and likes especially to pretend that he is a saviour or a god.

If we begin, as we should begin, with "Figures of Earth," we shall learn how Dom Manuel, the first "Count of Poictesme, . . . came out of the mire" of everyday existence, encountered high adventure, and ended his days gloriously and disappointedly in his seat at Storisende. The book, which appeared in 1922, is dedicated to six other "most gallant champions," viz., Sinclair Lewis, Wilson Follett, Louis Untermeyer, H. L. Mencken,

Hugh Walpole, and Joseph Hergesheimer. The author also seeks to connect his hero with "the Vedic Rudra and the Russian Magarko," to say nothing of Achilles, and the history purports to be taken from *Les Gestes de Manuel,* "mundane stories," supported in the preface by a quotation credited to one "Codman." It is, as Cabell assures us, "a comedy of appearances."

In appearance, Manuel is a swineherd with a squint, which peculiarity reminds his creator of sheet lightning, and reminds me of Bertrand Russell's pretence that men usually attain distinction through some initial error or defect. He works for the Miller, who has married Manuel's practical sister, Math. And all might have gone well had not his mother laid upon him a "geas," or gaseous obligation to "make a figure in the world."

He decides to make it out of March clay, and "this figure he was continually reshaping and realtering." It "stood upon the margin of the pool . . . of Haranton, in the environs of Rathgor not far from the thatched villages of Lower Targamon. . . . And near it were two stones overgrown with moss, and supporting a cross of old worm-eaten wood, which commemorated what had been done there." The perspicacious reader must see already the metaphorical inwardness of this geography.

Manuel is in love with one Suskind. But when a Stranger comes, telling him that the wizard Miramon Lluagor has captured Lady Gisèle, daughter of Count Demetrios, and taken her to the top of Mount Vraidex, Suskind is temporarily forgotten. Here is an adventure of rescue to be undertaken, especially as the Stranger has presented him with "the terrible sword, Flamberge," in a blue scabbard—sharp lightning in addition to the sheet ditto of his squint, with the clear scabbard sky thrown in.

Cabell invents words with a facility greater even than that of Lord Dunsany, and every little vocable has a meaning all its own—in one language or another. No doubt Math was good at mathematics, at least as far as arithmetic. Suskind is evidently of a politely Latin swine kind. (In the Coster epos it is Soetkin, the wife of Claes.) Nobody will need to be told that Vraidex is the hill of Truth. And yet upon it we find this mirror of mind, Lluagor, Lord of the Doubtful Palace and Maker of Dreams.

The climb, however, makes a delightful chapter, for we take it in company with Niafer, "a smallish, flat-faced, dark-haired boy," whom Manuel calls Snip—a marvellously clever boy, who gets past all the guardian snakes of the route by pretending to them that a common egg is a magic egg, a common turtle a magic turtle, and so on. The idea is that "in a world where nothing is certain," and "which lives on what it believes," the worshipper makes the miracle. Even serpents, it seems, have inhibitions that hinder them dreadfully if they permit themselves to be fooled by lies. And yet I wonder. After all, isn't a common egg or a common turtle magical enough?

Miramon proves to be less terrible even than his guardian ophidia. In fact, he is no other than the Stranger himself, who has given the champion the flaming sword in hopes of being slain. Through the door of death he plans to escape from his captive wife. He then expects to come to life again in some other form—like the willing male defendant in an uncontested suit for divorce. You see, Gisèle is a bit of a Xanthippe, and she interferes with the making of dreams, especially salacious ones.

"She takes an active interest in my work," Miramon complains, "and that does not do with a creative artist in any line. She permits me only to design bright, optimistic and edifying dreams."

Manuel sees at once that if he slays the husband he will have the woman on his hands—too dangerous an adventure even for a champion. So he decides to marry Niafer instead—Niafer, who suddenly begins to be the antecedent of feminine pronouns, and remains of the distaff gender throughout the rest of the book. Her name suggests that she may have been a Fainer (alas for the drunken printer who got the letters in the wrong order!), or even fain to appear at first in disguise. But I am terribly afraid that Cabell here yielded not only to his inveterate habit of punning but to the temptation of indulging in an uncomfortable suggestion.

Be that as it may, Manuel and Niafer go down Vraidex, only to meet with Grandfather Death, who says that one or the other of them must now start upon a much longer journey. Manuel heroically decides that it would better be the other, for he has still to make a satisfactory figure in the world. He is anxious to travel everywhither and into the last limits of earth, so that he may see the ends of this world and judge them, and Niafer has already been saying that she would prefer to wait until the roads are better. Under the circumstances, this timely encounter with Death is a calamity which, if rightly directed, may prove a blessing in disguise. For "I am Manuel, and I must follow after my own thinking and my own desire, without considering other people and their notions." In non-figurative language, he deserts his *fiancée* and follows his career—in the manner already made familiar to us by "The Moon and Sixpence." Exit Snip.

Enter Horvendile, who haunts the Cabell epos like a ghost. He might well have been called Neverdie. He is not exactly fate, but he is every hero's inner urge, and eventually he becomes the overlord from whom Manuel holds Poictesme in feudal tenure. He now explains that the way to achieve a desire is to pay the necessary price, which advice is accompanied by a warning: "With the achieving of each desire you will perceive its worth."

"Thus speaking, Horvendile parted the thicket beside the roadway. A beautiful dusk-coloured woman waited there, in a green-blue robe, and on her head was a blue coronet surmounted with green feathers." One reads this passage in all innocence, until a further acquaintance with Cabell makes the meaning appear in retrospect as something perfectly abdominal. Manuel makes a grab and secures a feather, which he takes home to his sister, Math. She promptly burns it, acting on the principle that "a feather is of no use to anybody," not even if it be a feather in the cap of Don Juan. Nevertheless it is from Math that he learns that this particular bit of plumage was moulted by Alianora, the Unattainable Princess, daughter of King Raymond Berenger, of Provence.

Now there was once a real Ramon, surnamed Berenguer, or Berengar, Count of Barcelona, who died in 1245, being the fourth of that line and last of the feudal princes of Provence, his line having ruled since 1112, when fell the princes of Arles. But we need not let that trouble us. We will have to deal chiefly with his daughter. This young lady, it appears, was in the habit of arraying herself in a magic feather boa, or robe, or cloud, which enabled her to travel about in the guise of a swan and to bathe in the pool where strange dreams are engendered. The magic of public plumage. So, though the dead Niafer is "hardly settled down" in her Pagan paradise beyond the veil, and with the deserted Suskind still "wailing . . .

in the twilight," Manuel sets out to discover the worth of this new desire.

The boa, we are told, typifies the mists, and, as Alianora frequents the pool of dreams, it is evident that he only imagines her charms. How is he to reach her in reality? He no longer has her feather. But he finds an ordinary goose feather—it is to be feared that he uses this quill to write a sonnet when he ought to have been doing his chores—wraps it in a bit of red silk from his sister's petticoat, and takes the road for Provence.

But no sooner does he arrive at the territory of the foolish King Helmas of Albania than that silly monarch mistakes the goose feather for a plume from the Shar Ptitza bird, the sharpest of the tits and given to crying, "Fine feathers make fine birds." As this is "a world where nothing is certain," a world "which lives on what it believes," obviously these are the highest words of wisdom, particularly as "wisdom weighs exactly the weight of a feather." And King Helmas, being able to believe that a goose feather is something else, becomes capable of believing in anything, even in the soundness of his own judgment when it moves him to give Manuel 10,000 sequins. Faith, we are told in effect, works miracles, though it be but faith in nonsense. Faith in himself enables Helmas to set up as a Solomon. It is the faith of the faith curists, of the noble company of the late Monsieur Coué.

Manuel makes another figure of earth—this one somewhat like himself and somewhat like the king, loads his knapsack with another *plume d'oie,* and hies him "across the fatal bay of Biscay" to the country of the wicked King Ferdinand.

Ferdinand, too, is certain that a feather half hidden by a bit of silk petticoat is no ordinary feather. Says he:

"I perfectly recognize that feather as the feather which Milcah plucked from the left pinion of the Archangel Oriphiel." And as it has been prophesied that he shall turn from his evil ways at the sight of precisely this relic, he leaves off working in his torture-chamber and proceeds from day to day to get better and better in every way. He becomes a saint—"righteousness is a fine feather in anybody's cap"—and ennobles Manuel with a title, "Count of Poictesme."

But as Ferdinand's goods are not of this world, he fails to state how the promised land may be taken from Duke Asmund—a name which seems intended to suggest the redoubtable ass *d'un monde de prosateurs usurpantes*—at present in possession. Ferdinand, in fact, is not the first publisher ever to indulge in the saintly gesture of accepting a manuscript which he subsequently was unable to sell as a book. Manuel's figure of earth, having Ferdinand for a subject, is not satisfactory, notwithstanding several characteristics of the artist shown in the work. It is time to take French leave.

We arrive in Provence—with another goose feather, of course—only to find that the marmoreal palace of Berenger, King of Arles, is fenced about with silver pikes bearing "the embalmed heads of young men who had wooed the Princess Alianora unsuccessfully." Berenger recognizes the goose feather as one which has actually been lost from his daughter's magic robe. And as its possession was the one thing which he desired in a son-in-law, all goes well—especially as Alianora, who knows more about feathers than most, decides to keep her mouth shut as to any possible substitution; that is, is willing to overlook her lover's infidelities and to let him make her an honest woman.

The princess, now complacent rather than unattainable, even consents to burn her boa, since to continue to fly about beyond the reach of observation and disguised as a swan would obviously be an unwifely thing to do. All she asks is that Manuel permit her to murder her father so that Manuel himself may be king.

The champion demurs. Why should he bother with the affairs of state? He prefers to make a figure of earth in the likeness of Alianora, mingled, as usual, with the likeness of the maker. This figure turns out to be not quite as it should be. Neither is Alianora, now that she is no longer alien in anything but disposition.

"Here lies lust, not love," is the unimpeachable epitaph suggested for the tomb of this intrigue. The King of England wants to marry the ex-swan-girl. Let him. Manuel's desire is now for a certain ring, name of Schamir, which sham is said to have the property of bringing unsatisfactory clay images to life.

This ring is in the Volcanic land of Vel Tyno, in the realm of Audela. We have to do with the "infernal, terrestrial, celestial," and bombastic Bombo—not quite the wicked King Bomba of the Baron Corvo, but sufficiently like him—and with many another fearfulness before we at last encounter Queen Freydis, better known to students of the Norse as Freya, goddess of fire, of passion, and of Friday, whom complete Wagnerites, if any such still be, will recognize as the feminine form of Loki.

She reigns "on the other side of the fire"—and a very pretty conceit it is to say that, whenever there is a rent in the veil which separates us from the beyond, the rent appears as a flame. Cabell makes full use of the symbolist's privilege of allowing his metaphors to glide from meaning to meaning. Only a painfully cut-and-dried and matter-of-fact Bunyan can make his Pilgrim progress consistently both as to philosophy and to allegory, and it certainly should be the figures which yield. Cabell occasionally bends his philosophy, too, but it is to suit his mood rather than his similes. For the most part he is only too consistent—too consistently sexual. Have we not just seen how even his goose feathers, blown occasionally aloft upon refreshingly cool breezes, settle quickly to earth, or scud before the hot gusts of pretended passion?

Queen Freydis ventures out at times upon the nevermoreish plains of Morven, where Manuel traps her with reeds, ribbons, butter, and other gewgaws, and demands her ring. But he hasn't the heart to torture her and make her give it up. That is, he is not the man to maim his genius, now that she has come to him—not for the sake of the public or in accordance with the demands of the commercialized theatre. He will let her go back home first. Nor has she, when finally he burns his hand in her flames, the heart to leave without tending to his hurt. She has become a mortal woman, one with us "little persons that have no authentic life, but only the flickering of a mixed shadow to sustain us" in our brief fretfulness. So she fusses about until it is too late to jump back into the firebush and scratch in what she has lost. Thus love comes to the world—much as it did when Siegfried reached Brunhilde through the guardian flames, though with ingenious and pleasing, if still Wagnerish, variations.

The remarkable thing about these allegories is the pitch at which the stormy interest is maintained. The text, unburdened by the prosaic interpretations which I have laid upon it, is sprightly; and though its inner meaning is sufficiently obvious, once one starts to look for it, there must be thousands of readers who, quite unmindful of what is really being said, merely enjoy the colourful monsters whose literal conduct is presented in a manner at once so lifelike and so gay. As for the less simple, there is always the intellectual pleasure of finding the answer to the rebus, even when they do not care to wallow in the childishness of the author's preoccupation.

Cabell himself seems sometimes to forget that his figures of earth are figures of lust, so absorbed does he become in his happy genius for characterization by incident. But, beneath the veil, the erotic significance is seldom lacking, and often enough one meaning merely serves to veil another. This subtlety does not go so far as it does in the ghazels of Halfiz, where as many as five husks must be torn away before the inwardness of Isq, of Ahad, and of Tarigat is finally revealed. Nevertheless, when we have explored what proves to be the human body, inside and out, disguised as forest, hill, or stream, we not seldom find ourselves handling the tools of the artist in his studio or in his mind, and then witnessing the parody of some religious ritual or turning the leaves of a duly caricatured *Summa Theologica.*

Thus Freydis, who kindly gives life to one of Manuel's figures—it speedily runs away, to return later as the troublesome Sesphra of the Dreams—is not only passion, but inspiration, and at times a sort of unholy ghost. Manuel vacillates between lechery, craftsmanship, and irreligion, inclining at times even to decent domesticity. For, having lost some of his enthusiasm for the artistic calling after noting its effect upon a number of professional image-makers, he brings back Niafer from the dead and marries her—or annuls the divorce, if you prefer. This necessitates his going to work, serving Misery of Earth "during a month of years . . . in a peculiarly irrational part of the forest," and growing older at the rate of a year every day.

The result is that, a daughter, Melicent, having been born, he takes Freydis aside and tells her of "the joy that is in the sight of your children playing happily about your hearth, and developing into honourable men and gracious women, and bringing their children in turn to cluster about your tired old knees as the winter evenings draw in." He speaks of the pleasures connected with "the cosy firelight," when you "smile across the curly heads of these children's children at the dear wrinkled white-haired face of your beloved and time-tested helpmate, and are satisfied, all in all, with your life, and know that, by and large, Heaven has been rather undeservedly kind to you." Yes, art-for-art's sake and body-for-body's-sake Cabell can really write as beautifully and as sensibly as this. And he means it far more than he means the things which have brought him into his lurid prominence.

It is unnecessary to follow the story further, or to tell just how Miramon finally reappears and conquers the poet's home for him by means of various things from the "garrets and dustheaps of Vraidex," things "made for man's worship when earth was younger," things led by a stallion who is none other than Kalki, a favourite horse of the author, here colicky with the divine afflatus and brought to the fore by "dealing unusually with a little fish." To Cabell all is fishy, a mere appearance. He cannot get beyond the philosophy of Mark Twain, who, in "The Mysterious Stranger," explained all by premising that all is a dream—leaving only the dream to be explained when all is said. We gather that Manuel has won literary fame among the common folk by pretending to believe in the objects of their veneration. Goosie's wings have been clipped.

But it will be better now if we wrench ourselves free from the charm of any particular narrative and gather a few incidents together upon the strings of their deeper implications.

3. SOMETHING ABOUT EVIL

"A forced construction is very idle. If readers of The High History of Jurgen do not meddle with the allegory, the allegory will not meddle with them."

This peremptory order, forbidding us to use our brains, and attributed to "E. Noel Codman," appears on the flyleaf of the already too-much-written-about book to which it refers. "John Frederick Lewistam," also on the flyleaf, adds that the volume is "as the world itself, a book wherein each man will find what his nature enables him to see." In all the history of advertising it would be difficult to parallel such effrontery as this. We must not think, and if we do we are convicted in advance of digging all the evil out of ourselves.

Probably "Lewistam" is right. If there were not a little evil in our home, we might not be able to recognize even the devil on the king's highway. But the implication that one sees only what he *wishes* to see, is rather naïve. Anybody who could read "Something about Eve," published in 1927, and find nothing but what he wished to find, would have to be either a zany or else of a nature whose prurience falls under the definition which Havelock Ellis somewhere gives of it, a "perpetual itch to circle around sexual matters, accompanied by a timidity which makes it impossible to come right up to them. . . . A sort of impotent fumbling with women's placket-holes."

Ellis regards these as well-recognized characteristics of the insane, but lunatics certainly have no monopoly of them. Impotent fumbling is by no means confined to the crazy. And it is precisely fumbling of this sort which must be charged against that purported history of our first mother which Cabell describes as "a comedy of fig-leaves."

Stark nakedness may be stark virtue. The frankness of animals gives no offence—pet animals sometimes excepted. But fig-leaves, especially sniggering, wilfully transparent ones, are not likely to interest anybody but a sickly sex-visionary whose impulses have, for some reason or other, been denied their natural and healthy means of expression.

It is a night in April, 1805. Gerald Musgrave (i. e., Mustwrite), of the line of Manuel and of Jurgen, sits in a stuffy library in Lichfield—a Faust come to Dixie. Upon his table lies an unfinished romance of Poictesme. But, "whithersoever a man lives, there will be a thorn-bush near his door." So in comes Glaum of the Haunting Eyes, a "Sylan" from the land of Cream On—or, as Cabell prefers to spell it, Caer Omn. Is this the Cream of the Jest?

Anyway, Glaum is Gerald's "spiritual body" acting "at the command of another author"—doubtless the author of "Jurgen"—and is willing to take over all his double's corporal obligations, including an illicit, long-standing affair with Evelyn Townsend. That is, he will stay in Lichfield and look and act like Gerald, giving that tired romancer a chance to stretch his legs and carry out some of his imaginings—in imagination. If the situation is a little mixed, we must remember that it is hardly fair to look an allegory in the syllogism.

Gerald very considerately warns his other self of some of the penalties he may expect to incur in the change of rôles. The Evelyn Townsend liaison is illegal beyond hope of rupture, and he is of the opinion that "there is no more sensible piece of friendly counsel existent than is the Seventh Commandment." Cabell is always amusing when he satirizes real human weaknesses, and he may be pardoned for remarking: "In American literature of a respectable cast no human being has any excretory functions. . . . At most some tears or a bead or two of perspiration may emanate, but nothing more." The supposed date of this pronouncement is, of course, the year 1805. Since then we have gone far towards making the whole earth that glorious public water-closet which the prophets have foretold, with results partially sanitary, no doubt, though it has been said with reason that one good custom may corrupt the world.

Glaum is afraid of nothing, neither literary handicaps nor obligatory fornication. So Gerald takes the "doubtful road" leading to Antan, "the goal of all the gods of men and of all venturesome persons," though to get there one must face the "Mirror of the Hidden Children"—these being none other than those which Eve, in the Garden of Eden, tried to hide from God because they had not had their faces washed. Since then they have been compelled to hide from men—from ordinary men, that is. Evidently they are the children of the shamefaced imagination. Just as evidently—if "E. Noel Codman" will permit it to be said—Antan is the future, not to mention the past; fame as well as oblivion. And it is in the land of Dreams, transformed into Dersam by means of bitched type.

In dreamland the author—that is, Gerald, whose Mr. Hyde has now rid himself of all traces of Dr. Jekyll—points knowingly to the fig-leaf, that "romance with which human optimism veils the only two eternal and changeless and rather unlovely realities of which any science can be certain."

But Gerald is no Jake, eager for Nigger-Heavenly Harlem's homelike hells. He has burned his candle in the midnight oil. Unlovely realities appeal to him only in dersams. Hardly even there. He seeks to become Lord of the Third Truth—a matter of language, since it is in the keeping of a shadowy somebody known as the Master Philologist. The creative Logos? Hardly! Say rather words, words, words, the windy lords of Als Ob. Consequently he begins his journey by "putting a slight upon Koleos Koleros," goddess of the realm which he has entered, preferring to her Kalki, his calico stallion, who sometimes becomes Pegasus and sometimes does not, all depending upon the horsemanship.

Neither Koleros nor any other Eros can command our hero's services outside of literature. He elects to "pass hastily through this land of quags and underbrush," and to leave this neighbourhood which "has not any name in the reputable speech of men." Ah! Has it not? But he means to travel the "road of the greater myths," and to know the "Great Untruth" which makes men "free."

Not even untruth, however, seems able to free the narrative of Koleos Koleros—or shall we say Kalos Kagathos and Megaloprepes? She hag-rides him through some of the most tediously indiscreet and elaborately anatomical passages in all fiction. Blurred is that "notation of the heart" which Thornton Wilder so rightly describes as "the whole purport of literature." It is indeed difficult not to "meddle with the allegory" here. Cabell fairly rubs our noses in it—and literally so rubs what he describes as "the holy nose of Lytreia." He seems to fear that we shall miss the point. Sneezing has been interrupted—a calamity due to the magic of the Wu. So Gerald promises: "Lytreia shall be rid of her, even though it is necessary that to undo her hoodoo I do with due to-do woo the Wu, too."

At Caer Omn the "three hundred and fifty-odd concubines and seven wives" of the Sylan are lamenting that the sacred mirror before which they were used to pose has lost its ancient magic, and now reflects only what stands before it. Gerald restores its deceptiveness by drawing upon it the triangle of the male and of the female principle, whereupon the dialogue, becoming more and more uterine, seems to feel ashamed of itself, like a drummer who, having launched a smutty story, perceives that he has mistaken his company, yet labours on because he does not know how to stop. But at last Gerald succeeds in stepping through the mirror and imagines himself to be Solomon, who he claims "once quested after oblivion between the thighs of the most beautiful women of Judea and Israel, of Moab and of Ammon, and of Bactria, of Baalbec, and of Babylon," and then "turned to wantoning with boys and with beasts and with the bodies of the dead."

Gerald also sees himself as Ulysses; as Judas, whose infamy is described as "the reply of a very fine poet to Heaven's proffered truce"; as Nero, another "fine poet," since he could get peace of mind "from the satiating of no lust, howsoever delicate or brutal," but hungered only for Agrippina, his mother, whose belly he ripped open "so that he might see the womb in which he had once lain."

~ MARCEL PROUST ~
Inversion was too much for him

One begins to understand Cabell's idea of a poet. But he continues to tell us almost nothing about Eva. Evashera, Evarvan, and many another Evathis and Evathat come and go, but they are all daughters of Lilith, and this "brutish half-magic of the Wu, which maddens men along with all other animals in their rutting season," almost persuades him that he, too, is "only a bundle of cellular matter upon its way to become manure."

Almost, but not quite. He longs to put out of mind "the frailness and the transiency" of his "hold upon being"; and the "nonsensical notion" occurs to him that "forgetfulness may be hired by bringing the epidermis," which masks him, "into superficial contact with the homogenous animal matter in which hides the fox-spirit" of Evaine, whom he finds engaged in destroying modesty by tearing it into bits which she burns in a brazier. But, having given this very fair statement of the philosophy of some of our latest novelists, Cabell is too pre-war to subscribe to it. Gerald crushes the vain Evaine, whose vein, as our author might say, is in vain.

He has already gotten the better of numerous other reminders of Evelyn Townsend, notably Evarvan, whom he puts in her place by talking of those serious things which Victorian ladies used, for the polite flattering of their spouses, to pretend not to understand. She sits at his feet and learns how it happens that a straight line measures the shortest distance between two points; and as she listens she dwindles, reverting to childhood in the effort to become less knowing than he. Then she becomes a mere fœtus, and finally "only two pink figures in the form of a soft throbbing egg and of a creature like a tadpole darting lustfully about it," her parents, ovum and spermatozoön.

But Gerald is not to be convinced, not even when he finds himself before a magic painting, whose subject must ever remain a mystery since he never told anybody what it was. "I know,"—this much he does tell, addressing the picture aforesaid, "I know the two objects which you magnify are not all which exists, and I deny that their never-ending search for each other is the one gesture of life. . . . I very much prefer to believe that I at least am, in one way or another, reserved to take part in some enduring and rather superb performance—somewhere, by and by." We copulate and die, and that is all? Well, perhaps. And then again, perhaps not. One must be broadminded about the matter. "One ought to cherish always, if only as a diverting and inexpensive playing, this pungent notion of being immortal." Which having said, he puts his foot through the canvas. We begin to understand Cabell's idea of art. But, for further light on his idea of religion, it would be better to turn back to "Figures of Earth."

As Cabell is an unbeliever of the Victorian type, he is of course theatrical. Christian sacraments still impress him. He cannot leave them quite alone. So he uses them as spells. And as spells they move him to admiration. Rebels against Puritanism are always thus. On their stage the devil invariably shrinks from a sight of the cross. As invariably, the Devil's Disciple is a wondrously kind fellow, beside whose hearth no woman ever shall weep. For somehow the devil has become mixed up with the Prince of Peace, with Jehovah, or sometimes only with St. Paul.

Sacraments and supernatural things in general were at one time so closely associated with the Catholic Church that believing anti-Catholics could only regard them with mingled feelings. Here were things at once holy and popish. Since then they have been rendered as hateful as possible by that political policy which blames them for every foolish, blind, or cruel act done from the beginning of the Christian era, or before, by any of those human and erring beings who call themselves believers, whether of Church or Chapel. So the rumour has gone forth that kind people are merely Satan's saints, that paganism is merely another name for sweetness and light.

At the same time, paganism has become another name for bitterness and darkness—to those who have decided to give their hearts to what is dark and bitter, or at least permit nothing but bitterness and darkness to be alleged of anything for fear that passion as the chief end of man shall be given a rival and be put to shame.

In the midst of this confusion, Cabell wanders hither and yon. Having named his hero Manuel, he grows bolder and terms him "Manuel the Redeemer"—of Poictesme. And before even this redemption can be accomplished, Miramon must say to him:

"Horvendile informs me that you were duly born in a cave . . . of a virgin mother and of a father who was not human. . . . You have duly performed miracles, such as reviving dead persons, and so on. . . . You have duly sojourned with evil in a desert place, and have there been tempted. . . . These portents have marked your living thus far, just as they formerly distinguished the beginnings of Mithras . . . and all other reputable redeemers." Then Miramon leads Manuel "into a secret place," and there makes him submit "to that which was requisite." What happened "is not certainly known. But this much is known, that Manuel suffered, and afterward passed three days in an underground place, and came forth on the third day." [1]

Do you remember that first figure of clay by the dream-pool of Haranton—that figure which was being continually reshaped and re-altered, which "stood upon the margin of the pool" near "two stones overgrown with moss and supporting a cross of old worm-eaten wood which commemorated what had been done there"? [2] The description sounded innocent enough, and yet it served to combine in one picture the cross and a phallic emblem. We shall be taken back to it.

Meanwhile Manuel, having won to Storisende and prospered worldlily, one day comes to a window of his palace—a window in the Room of Ageus—which happens to be open, now that the room has been suffered to age us enough. So long as he has looked out through the glass, he has seen "a flourishing garden with quivering poplars and Niafer and little Melicent smiling at him, and the child kissing her hand." But as soon as the window is open, what he beholds is vacancy.

"He, leaning out . . . could see that behind the amiable picture was nothingness." And here in this nothingness was "all freedom and all delight . . . all horror and all rebellion," peopled only with those dirty-faced children of Eve already noted, "children . . . unstained by human sin and unredeemed by Christ's dear blood." [3]

It is an attempt to get behind the Fall, to a state of innocence—which the author understands to be a pagan or animal state—that we lose only by having religious

[1] "Figures of Earth," p. 226.
[2] *Ibid.*, chap. i.
[3] *Ibid.*, chap. xxxv.

ideas—what a theologian would call a plea for invincible ignorance. And this innocence, like everything else at Storisende, is nothing whatever.

"That tedious dear nagging woman [Niafer], and that priceless snub-nosed brat [her daughter], may not be real. They may be merely happy and prosaic imaginings, hiding the night which alone is real." For it appears to be admitted that black is somehow genuine, even if white is a sham. But "from the faith of others there is no escape upon this side of the window." And so you can't be yourself, and are nothing. "Youth vaunts windily, but in the end nobody can follow after his own thinking and his own desire. At every turn he is confronted by that which is expected, and obligation follows obligation, and in the long run no champion can be stronger than everybody." Which perhaps is just as well.

But Manuel is afraid that his daughter will have her eyes opened to the true-false state of things. He girds on his sword and rushes out into the darkness, where, besides Eve's dirty children, lurks also Suskind, his first and unknown desire. He hacks her to pieces, and returns.

"Weep, weep for Suskind," then said Lubrican, wailing feebly in the grey and April-scented dusk, "for it was she alone who knew the secret of preserving that dissatisfaction which is divine."

Manuel, then, is at last satisfied with life. Nevertheless, when straightway Death appears—for no man may survive his last desire—he is also so dissatisfied with it that he is willing to go on the long and final journey. This time he even refuses to sacrifice another in his stead. For, as he looks back upon all that he has done, he seems to see "only the strivings of an ape reft of his tail and grown rusty at climbing, who has reeled blunderingly

from mystery to mystery, with pathetic makeshifts, not understanding anything, greedy in all desires, and always honeycombed with poltroonery." If the proof of the pudding is the eating, the Cabell philosophy seems to need no further comment, though it can hardly be denied that here is an eloquent description of despair.

But the end is not yet. What happened when Manuel and Death set out together "is not certainly known," though "there was a lad called Jurgen . . . who came to Storisende in a frenzy of terror very early the next morning with a horrific tale of incredible events witnessed upon Morven."

Certainly known or not, we are presented with the rumour that Manuel eventually came to Lethe, where it was told him: "If you have been yourself you cannot reasonably be punished, but if you have been somebody else you will find that this is not permitted." Whether he passed muster as an original is not said. He merely plunges into the stream and looks back. And, "as his memories vanished, the tall boy incuriously wondered who might be the snub-nosed Stranger that was waiting there with the miller's pigs, and was pointing, as if in mild surprise, towards the two stones overgrown with moss and supporting a cross of old worm-eaten wood."

But we do not wonder. We know very well that Snubnose is Miramon once more. Manuel is back to where he started from. We have the universe of eternally recurrent phenomena of Nietzsche. "This is the preposterous end!" cries Manuel, whose bath in Lethe seems not to have been altogether effective.

Cabell, however, is not content to let bad enough alone. He must go on and write "The Silver Stallion," a parody upon the Acts of the Apostles and upon the history of

the Church down to about the year 1300. It tells how the widowed Niafer succeeds eventually in reforming the country which Manuel had merely redeemed—a Reformation slightly antedated, by poetic licence. She spreads the tale of an Ascension which she pretends has been witnessed by a child. By means of make-believe prophecy, she links the theory of recurrent phenomena with the second coming of Christ. Then she decorates the tomb of her late lord with imitation jewels.

"My Manuel, a whispering tells me, was no more splendid than other men," she informs Jurgen, who has become a pawnbroker.

And Jurgen answers: "Let us wildly imagine the cult of the Redeemer, which now is spread all over our land, to be compact of exaggeration and misunderstanding and to be based virtually on nothing. None the less men are appreciably better because of this Manuel's example and teaching." That is, men are better for having been taught to believe a tale invented to hide the true history of a rogue.

But as one grows old, "one is less certain of everything." Neither Niafer nor Jurgen is certain even of their own unbelief. Christianity, according to their account, "has passed the pragmatic test" and "is a cult that works."

Thus does Cabell reveal his touching trust in the beneficence and efficiency of what he believes to be a lie. He was born too soon to have the courage of his lack of convictions. He wishes to retain Christian sentiment without the beliefs out of which it sprang. A tree is known by its fruits, he says, and the fruits please him. He has the marvellous credulity of the Modernist, who thinks it not unreasonable to assume that a tree will continue to bear after it has been cut off from its roots, or

even after he holds it proved that it never had any.

I sometimes wonder how or what these zero-worshippers intend to teach their young. Do they expect to say: "You must lead a good life according to a high ideal which, I may as well tell you first as last, is based simply and solely upon bosh"? Is that it? I fancy not. Their own children are to be told about the bosh, while they hope that other people's children will be told about the ideals only. Hence all these fine words, this tesam of the crej. Our egoists are planning to live in a world of self-sacrifice—practised by the neighbours.

And yet a spirit of homesickness lingers about the scene. Back in Lichfield, Glaum has become famous by writing a treatise upon "really worth-while ethnographic matters, like the marriage customs of all lands, and the ways of male and female prostitution among the different races, and with the history in each country of pæderasty, of Lesbianism, and of bestiality, and necrophily, and of incest, and of sodomy, and of onanism, and of all the manifestations of the sexual impulse in every era." But Gerald, who has lived for a time upon wholesome terms with Mother Earth, reflects:

"I may well be content, because all that a man may hope for I have had. . . . There was the seeming of a home, and of a woman who loved and tended me, and of a child. I may not speak of my love for these illusions. Now they have perished. But my memories remain, and they are more dear to me than any real things." [4]

But he is not content. Even real pain were better than this.

[4] "Something about Eve," p. 324.

CHAPTER VIII

PILLARS OF SALT

I. PROUST

UPON the face of things, no man would seem to have been less influenced by Puritanism—and hence by any degradation of Puritanism—than was Marcel Proust. His father, a famous physician, was a Catholic, a native of Chartres. His mother, *née* Weil, was a Jewess.

They were the sort of parents who, as the son's biographer expresses it,[1] "were very careful not to let any questions of belief come up between them." That is to say, we have to deal neither with good Jew nor good Catholic. Marcel was baptized, and his early associations were picturesquely Romish; but his youthful mind was innocent either of Moses or St. Peter. So Bergson became his mentor, Anatole France his admirer, and Léon Daudet his friend.

These men are certainly Impuritans, though they belong to that Protestant revolt which still goes on but no longer calls itself Protestantism, and is Puritan in nothing save its dislike of the Vatican and its exaltation of individual judgment, good or bad. It is a less ignorant Puritanism than the one with which we non-Latins are more familiar

[1] *Vide* "Marcel Proust, His Life and Work," by Léon Pierre-Quint, translated by Hamish and Sheila Miles; Knopf, 1927—a book to which I hereby acknowledge my indebtedness for many historical details.

—less ignorant and less moral. Coming into existence late in the historical day, it has skipped the ethical period altogether. To make up for lost time, it substitutes a clean break for a slow estrangement in so far as its relations with Authority are concerned, and so leaps abruptly from full mediævalism into total depravity. Like all rebellions, it finds its justification in the human imperfections of those who should be saints, and its condemnation in the human imperfections of the rebels. Formerly it was chiefly the licentiousness of churchmen which was objected to. Now it is their cold worldliness. For to-day Catholics are almost as Puritanical as are the Fundamentalists.

But a clean break is difficult, and some of the new anti-Catholics still bear the marks of the ancient and lately beloved shackles. A city built in the wilderness must ever be more modern than any would-be City of the Plain, which happens after all to be Paris. So this freshly apostate Impuritanism, though it seeks to outdistance all the isms that romp along the last declivities of the path followed by Protestant haters of Luther, Wyclif, Huss, and Knox, still lags behind. Its modernity is the modernity of Sodom and Gomorrah, not of Harlem. Proust cannot conceive of man as a happy animal, much less as an unfeeling machine.

Anatole France professed not to understand him, saying that one can comprehend one's own generation and the generation immediately following, but not one's intellectual grandchildren. Doubtless this was intended as flattery. Unquestionably it is nonsense. Proust is by no means as futuristic as all that. There is a certain cleanliness about the very latest in philosophy—a spirituality at last decently dead and awaiting resurrection. Even the cult of physical health knows no filth which could not have

been voided by beasts. But Proust is an old heart flowering in its second childhood, an old brain ravaged by cancer—both marvellously articulate.

He was born July 10, 1871, in that house so graphically described in *Le côté de Guermantes,* a house near the Madeleine, on the Boulevard Malesherbes, Paris, in an apartment at the end of a large interior court-yard whose windows looked out upon the Rue de Suresnes. His first summers he spent with his parents at Illiers, near Chartres, where an uncle owned a large estate. Another uncle had a house at Auteuil on the Rue Fontaine, then a Parisian suburb, where was a big garden (now cut in two by the Avenue Mozart) in which the boy used to gather strawberries. Here he met the friend who furnishes the *clé* for the character Bloch—a friend who was to teach him to admire Alfred de Musset, the Bergotte of the novels.

The Auteuil mansion was furnished in lavish style and execrable taste, especial prominence being given to imitation tapestries. Fictionally famous Combray, with its two walks—"Swann's Way," by Méséglise, and the "Guermantes' Way," by the river Vivone—is but an Illiers soaked in this Auteuil, æsthetically so mid-Victorian.

He played on sunny afternoons with a group of children in the Bois de Boulogne and on the Champs-Élysées. There were some girls among them—hence those marvellous pictures which we know as Gilberte and the other *jeunes filles en fleur* of "In a Budding Grove." He never invented in the sense of trying to make things up out of whole cloth. Barring certain philosophies, which he lamentably took from books instead of from observation or experience, he wrote of what he knew, had seen and felt.

And he saw everything which came before his eyes—

with a detail approaching the miraculous. Nor were feelings ever so minutely responsive to microscopic stimuli, or ever so accurately and tortuously described, not as what they might have been, but as what they were; not as they seemed to be on first acquaintance, but as they revealed themselves in later retrospect. With Proust, language forbore its tyranny of conventionalized figures, and permitted a thought to be expressed as in that instant when it is born, when it is as yet unmixed with hearsay, and lies naked in all its integral uniqueness—a ripe thought withal, re-created by maturity, a child seen and understood by its father. Reborn experience, in short, with quick emotions slowly and painstakingly recorded. For once realism and romanticism met in just proportions. For once facts were made to give up their spirit without giving up the ghost, made to reveal those ideal connexions which reduce life and nature to that lesser but more vivid and humanly comprehensible thing which calls itself a work of art.

But, as has already been suggested, Proust was not always an artist. We live in a day when scientists pretend to be both novelists and philosophers, when philosophers pose both as poets and scientists. So it is not to be wondered at that fiction-writers feel constrained to be biologists and philosophers.

It is as a philosopher that Proust exposes his Achilles' heel to the critic. Sex he treated in a falsely romantic fashion. Unquestionably the greatest novelist of his generation, he here fell into propaganda and permitted himself to suppose what he did not know. And it is to the mistakes he made in supposing, that he owes that vast notoriety which has obscured his proper fame.

For the first nine years of his life, no mortal could have

been more happy—nine precious years that sufficed for the accumulation of the material which was to give a core of felicity to seven great novels of despair. And then one day, coming home from the Bois, he was seized with what he himself describes as "a choking fit," first symptom of a frightful asthma which never afterwards was to leave him.

I wish I knew just what happened. It must, I think, have been some great chagrin, for asthma is one of those mysterious complaints which have their origin sometimes in the mind rather than the body. Certainly Proust's contemporaries regarded him as a voluntary invalid, and I do not see how he can be freed of the charge. He was always saying: "I think I shall go and consult Dr. Dubois [the Swiss psychiatrist]. If he cannot cure me, he can at least do something." But he never went. Most of his mature life he spent in bed. Yet he was always able to rise and go out upon any occasion which made it worth his while—such as the opportunity of seeing how the Prince de Sagan really wore his monocle. Asthma became the self-protective ruse of genius.

To begin with, it was useful in securing the undivided attention of his favourite parent. He fell into the habit of getting up for breakfast only after the rest of the family had finished lunch, secure in the knowledge that his mother—a woman of gentle manners, "hair like ebony," and "great lustrous dark eyes" (inherited by the novelist)—would neglect all else to sit by him at the table. His father, who would be gone to attend to his duties as head of the Paris Board of Health, had one son whom he was training to follow in his own footsteps, and meant to form this other into a diplomat. Alas, poor father! He was helpless before a little Marcel supported by a doting mother on one side and by asthma on the other.

Young Proust was undoubtedly burdened with a *"geas"* to make a figure of himself in the world, and he seems always to have known that he wanted to discharge it as a writer. So he consented to enter the Lycée Condorcet—just, as it happened, when Jules Ferry was "putting the reforms of secular instruction into force," when the professors had ceased to wear cassocks, and the pupils no longer were required to say prayers. Proust's health prevented the winning of any prizes, but permitted him to be sporadically "brilliant" and to display a truly remarkable memory by reciting innumerable verses from Mallarmé and Baudelaire. Later, at the Sorbonne, he pretended to consider seriously one career after another, but spared no pains to demonstrate his unfitness to become either a diplomat, a notary, a doctor, or a priest. But he made the acquaintance of Bergson, who by marrying Mademoiselle Newberger afterwards became a family connexion; acquired some knowledge of Spinoza; and showed considerable capacity for botany.

The year 1889 gave him his baccalaureate degree and saw him enrolled in the 76th regiment of infantry at Orléans, a newly passed law having made military service obligatory in France. Still his asthma stood him in good stead, moving Colonel Arvers, the commandant, to make things easy for the delicate recruit. Nor was the time wasted from a literary point of view. The knowledge of strategy acquired at Orléans was used later in the creation of Saint-Loup. He even practised arms on one occasion to the extent of fighting a "French" duel with Jean Lorrain over an article in the *Echo de Paris*.

Long before this, however, the choking spells had brought about a change in the family's summer habits.

Illiers had given place to the seashore, with the result that in the books we have not only Combray, with its "eglantine flowers," its "untamed thickets," its "true wild roses," where one never saw even a dog that "one really did not know at all," but the Grand Hôtel at Balbec, and the little railway whose trains "had contracted a sort of human kindliness" by dint of waiting patiently for stragglers to get aboard.

It is lost labour, however, to look on the map for any of Proust's fictional towns. Like Turner, he knew how to move both hills and dales into new places and strange harmonies. But they are always real hills and dales to begin with, never personified ideas or emotions wandering through an allegorical Poictesme. The Balbec hotel is a genuine hostelry as seen by a poet, though half of it happens to be known to common mortals as the Hôtel des Roches Noires, and half as the Grand Hôtel at Cabourg.

Like all who make the most of a weakness, Proust was partially mastered by his special privilege. Whether his disease was of the imagination or not, it was by no means always an imaginary disease. If it did not actually forbid him to travel, it at least induced a disinclination to travel far. Apart from the trips already noted, there are only a few days spent in Belgium, a few at Geneva, a summer or two at Trouville, and a short sojourn at Venice (in company with his mother and Reynaldo Hahn) to be added to the list. Truly, this was a more than Frenchly narrow, it was an incredibly sedentary life.

In 1901 the Prousts moved to 45 Rue de Courcelles, where the father died in 1903, laving Marcel a fortune which made him independent. Two years later the mother also passed. The son was not only independent, but alone.

There is still in existence a published album of youthful confessions, in the form of a questionnaire, in which may be found the query, "What is your idea of wretchedness?" and Proust's answer, "To be deprived of mamma." And now the worst had happened. Up to the day of his mother's death, he cannot be said ever to have been truly separated from the maternal breast. She was his adoring and adored, and he never loved again. Let Freudians attend. Here was a case of mother-fixation with a vengeance. Yet, though certainly pathological, it remained pure. It had its jealousies, but no suggestion of incest. What it seems to have done was to rob the son of all true delight in sex. He became a solitary.

So he moved to another Paris address, to that famous "retreat," 102 Boulevard Haussmann, retiring to a room which he had had lined with cork to cut it off from all sounds from the outer world. He was but thirty-four. And here he passed almost all the remainder of his days, attended only by his faithful servant, Céleste, wife of Odilon Albarret, a taxicab-driver—incredibly devoted Céleste, deserving in every way the immortalization she was to receive as Françoise, peasant cook of the novels.

The biographer thus describes the scene of this peculiar *ménage:*

"An apartment with the air of being uninhabited. . . . A large drawing-room . . . easy chairs, sofas in gilded wood or upholstered—the furniture of Monsieur and Madame Proust [the deceased parents] crowded together. A portrait of a young dandy of an epoch that now seems distant"—a portrait, in fact, of Marcel Proust at the age of twenty, by Jacques Émile Blanche.

"As a pendant to it on the other side, an Infanta of

Velasquez, haycock-shape. . . . The window was always shut. Marcel Proust could not, without terrible attacks of suffocation, let the scent of the chestnut trees [horse-chestnuts] reach him from the Boulevard. But he adored them none the less, lived with them in imagination, and—as he slept by day and never saw them—he used to ask people in springtime to talk to him of their blossoms. . . . A single lamp on the ceiling cast a feeble glow, its light absorbed by the dull brown cork [of the walls]. In one corner an immense and cumbersome grand piano. On chairs some beautiful books . . . photographs. A dressing-room, its door left open . . . encumbered with large chests of silver plate."

In this gloomy morgue Proust began filling those twenty enormous note-books which posterity, if still under the impression that genius achieves its effects without effort, may well regard with profit. They record the most minute observations ever made of the secular manners and motives of humankind. Were Behaviourism the study of behaviour as it ought to be, the novel which, when the author was well within the shadow of forty, began at last to take shape from these notes, growing from one tome to two, to three, to eight (making 16 volumes in all), would certainly be its bible.

But before thus burying himself, Proust had already made two considerable figures in the world. He had become a dandy and a *littérateur*.

Not, in the opinion of his *confrères,* a serious *homme de lettres,* but a dilettante. Never were *confrères* more mistaken. Here was the true professional, the man at last to whom art was literally all and everything, who considered no labour too great, no sacrifice too appalling, if it led him to the sought-for detail or phrase. The writing man *par excellence*. And he must be dubbed a dabbler, an amateur!

Even when the second volume of his great work had appeared and—thanks to Léon Daudet—had received the Goncourt prize, it was said by a critic in the Paris press that at last the Academy had recognized not only an unknown man but one who would remain unknown to the end of time. Yet Proust already had behind him a long career as author and editor, and had written pages whose significance all but the blind should have seen.

At the age of fifteen he had expressed the impression left upon his mind by the three church-towers of Martinville—expressed it in a passage afterwards introduced into *Pastiches et mélanges,* and later, still unchanged, into *Le côté de chez Swann*—a passage every word of which betrays the master, to be excelled in its kind only by that master himself. His first book, *Les portraits de peintres,* published in 1896, though but a collection of poems and essays, was at least distinguished; and *Les plaisirs,* appearing that same year, was good enough to provoke a preface by Anatole France.

But Paris had made up its literary mind. Proust knew not how to behave as a member of a côterie, or to run true to any form which was prescribed by the politics of letters. He had founded *Le Banquet,* a magazine whose staff were frequenters of the salon of Madame Straus, and he had written for *La Revue Blanche,* organ of the symbolists—and for his first contribution to this had chosen an article, *"Contre l'obscurité,"* in which he pleaded not only for novelty but for intelligibility. Novel and yet clear—what sort of symbolism was this? Let him keep on writing nothings for the *Figaro!*

It was, however, by becoming a man of fashion that he had chiefly offended. Yes, the invalid later to become a recluse had been paradoxically just that. Could any good thing come out of a *boulevardier,* a frequenter of the *salons* of the Faubourg Saint-Germain? The wiseacres thought not.

Unquestionably the cliques of the aristocratic region hampered and dazzled him at first. Not even asthma could keep him away either from a reception or a first night. The *monde* and the theatre became his world. He was so well known at the Ritz that Oliver always treated him as the host, no matter who was giving the dinner.

I do not pretend to understand how this doctor's son wormed his way so far into society—the titled society of that day. But there is the fact—and the worm, at first merely tolerated, dared eventually to spit its venom into the very faces of lords and princes. His father could not understand it either. "Is he really so fascinating?" the man of science would demand.

Those were the days of the Dreyfus case, when the Third Empire was still remembered. Aristocracy was hoping for the return of kings to a world which, as a matter of fact, was approaching the World War. Royalists took themselves seriously, little dreaming that they were so soon to drop into the political nothingness of an *Action Française.* Yet Proust came, saw, and conquered.

In the *salon* of Madeleine Lemaire, the artist, he was permitted to view "the court of lilacs and the studio of roses," and the stage where Mounet-Sully declaimed and Bartlet played *saynètes.* He frequented the *salon* of Madame Aubernon, where Dumas *fils* was the star, where Ibsen's "Doll's House" was first performed—the *bourgeois* and literary "*salon* Verdurin" of the books. He attended the famous "Sundays" at the *salon* of Madame Arman de Caillavet, Avenue Hoche, where Anatole France, who was to "cure" him of his passion for metaphysics, was master of the scene. But it was the *salon* of Madame Straus-Bizet, where he was introduced by a school friend, son of the musician, that did most to teach him those lessons which eventually enabled him to reach the *salon* of the Princess Mathilde, there to mingle with those imperial and royal highnesses which genius afterwards remembered, analysed, and recombined into the almost fabulous Parmes and Guermantes. What was his secret?

Proust at twenty has been described as a man with "large, black, brilliant eyes, with heavy eyelids that drooped slightly to one side; a look of extreme gentleness, fastening a long time on the object it fell upon; a voice still more gentle, breathless a little, and somewhat drawling, verging on affectation, yet always avoiding it. Long hair, black and thick, falling sometimes over his forehead. . . . A continual smile, amusing and inviting, that hesitated and then fixed itself motionless on his lips. His complexion [once fresh and pink] was dull, and in spite of his fine black moustache he gave one the impression of an overgrown child, indolent and over-observant." A man with the manners of a woman, in short; a creature somewhat epicene; a lounge-lizard crossed with a Peeping Tom. Do we not read that he used to conceal himself in Émile Paul's bookshop so as to see "an elegant lady of the aristocracy with whom he was enamoured" go past along the Avenue de Marigny? He would accompany the Princess Mathilde and the Baronne Alphonse de Rothschild to the dressmaker's and—while loudly complaining of poverty—heap them with hothouse flowers. He would say: "Do you not think, madame, that your portrait is really ravishing? Do you know how dreadfully I should be pained if you did not agree with me?" A tame monkey of a man, who loved women's corsets and bustles.

He once asked Madame C. to show him "the little hat with Parma violets" that she had worn when he was a young man. Says she: "Dear Marcel! That is a hat of twenty years ago. I no longer have it."

"Madame Daudet keeps all her hats," he murmurs. "I have seen them."

Just so does the hero of *La prisonnière* discuss old hats with the Princesse de Guermantes.

Yet let those whom he had passed on the way to the top of the tree beware! He had a remarkable talent for *pastiche,* or take-offs, and there was irony always ready to peep out from this apologetic, flattering manner of his. If you were not very great indeed, he would arrive at your reception late, in a cab, after having eaten heartily at home. And as the guests, caught in the act of dispersing, drew round, he would begin to declaim "in an interrogative fashion" and proceed for two or three hours to be "brilliant." That is, he would say: "Do you know whether the Duc de —— stayed on in the boudoir of Madame X the other evening? Could you explain the kiss he gave her in the very middle of the ball? Did someone see through the door?"

We should have called him insufferable, but doubtless those impotent king-makers knew best how they ought to be treated, and respected him accordingly. Proust knew his world. But how he reminds one of a less witty and more theoretical Oscar Wilde, whose crimes were to be committed only on paper.

Beau Brummell is another exquisite to whom Proust

has been compared, a Brummell gone somehow shabby and shoddy in the making. It took him "an incredible time" to button his boots, an operation which he frequently interrupted to hunt for mislaid cuff-links or a "lost shirt-front." Now a shirt-front which can be lost is nothing more or less than a "dickie," and Proust's were always starched, so that their bulging gave him the reputation for a well-developed chest which belonged in reality to his laundress. They were generally of a creamy pink—a shade which, after much trouble, he finally succeeded in obtaining at Caravet's. He wore a heavy pelisse, usually with a button or two lacking, even in the hottest days of summer; a double-breasted waistcoat beneath; "a rose or an orchid in the buttonhole of his frock-coat, tightly waisted yet flowing."

He was "heart-broken," we are told, if this rose of his came from a garden and not from a florist. He wanted its stem to be wrapped in silver paper. Under his turned-over collar, he wore badly tied cravats. His gloves were very light-coloured, with black points, often soiled and crumpled, but he bought them at the Trois Quartiers, because there was where Robert de Montesquiou purchased his. Topping all was a tall hat with a flat brim, and this he invariably placed on the floor beside his chair when making a call. A cane completed the elegant but mussed ensemble—a cane or a sunshade. At Cabourg he was known as "the gentleman with the parasol."

He might have called himself "the gentleman ever remorseful for being better than anybody else." It was his opinion that nothing could compensate the plebeian for being plebeian. When he had paid forty or more francs over and above the price registered by a taxi, he would say: "I am so terribly afraid it is not enough." He would tell a hotel waiter who had brought him a letter: "Here's fifty francs. Oh, but I have kept you talking till one o'clock in the morning. You've no longer any means of getting home. Here's two hundred francs more. And did you not tell me that your mother was on a visit to Paris? You will be wanting to go out with her. That will lead you into various expenses"—and so on without end.

It was really rather fine, this religion of *noblesse oblige* which Proust made out of snobbery. He gives us the entire code in these words:

"Just as the sanguinary instincts of mankind are checked by the laws of the criminal code, so the stern instincts of pride and humility, the foundations of the noble class [humility before inferiors, pride before equals, and servility before superiors] are marked and softened down by the rules of polite conduct. The accomplishment of polite duties [he names among them the obligation of presenting to a royal highness without an instant's delay any person in the room who happens to be unknown to him, and the obligation not to leave before the exalted one's departure] does not enhance the merit of a man of noble birth, for this is based rather on the choice and the importance of his connexions. If you are a duke [politeness] consists in making a *bourgeois* [provided that he knows his place] believe that he is none the less your equal. On the part of the latter it consists in declining to believe in the avalanche of amiable expressions, and in protesting."

Thackeray's "Book of Snobs" is poor stuff in comparison with this. Proust alone saw snobbery to the bottom and laid bare its very heart. But I wonder how Harlem would like it. At the same time, it must be admitted that we have lost something with all our gain. In an age where everyone is as good as the next and even better, few men seem really to believe in their own superiority to the extent of feeling that sense of obligation which once went with it. So doth equality breed a new arrogance, even less lovely than the old.

Upon the death of his mother (she called him "My little Silly" to the end), Proust began gradually to retire from the world. He had lived the plot of the fiction he meant to write. *À la recherche du temps perdu,* though its story reaches back to thirty years before the author's birth, is merely his memoirs pieced out with early family legends concerning Swann, the Jew.

Swann (his real name was Charles Haas) lived long enough for his later life to be impressed on the author's memory, but the tales of his youth were matters of hearsay. Odette de Crécy (fiction's maiden name for Madame Swann) herself began in Proust's experience as "a lady in pink" seen by a child sitting upon an uncle's knee at a café concert. And as the novel grew, there came to be crowded into this one character all that Proust the man had learned about successful *cocottes,* with additional traits borrowed from Madame Laura Heyman, the sculptress. Odette creeps into the drawing-room of the *bourgeois* Verdurins, intrudes (after marriage) into the *salon* of Madame de Villeparisis (the Duchesse de Guermantes immediately leaves the room), and after the war establishes a *salon* of her own, shunned by nobody.

But there is no action to show either this or any other character in its development, only action to indicate developments which have taken place during the long intervals when the character is off the stage. The key to Proust's technic and form is here. Changes are wrought by Time, behind the scenes. Then comes an animated picture, slowly unfolding what has already happened. The method of the theatre.

His figures, and many of his properties, are composites. All music distils into the Venteuil Sonata, first played by Morel (essence of all interpretative musicians) upon the occasion of Swann's falling in love with the fallen woman. It is played again at the moment when Swann realizes that the passion for which he has sacrificed his happiness is dead. Elstir is Monet—and something more. Brichot is not the symbol of pedantry—Proust draws no symbols; he is several pedants reborn into one. Dr. Cottard is Professor Guron, minus some of Guron's traits and plus the traits of a number of others. So with Saint-Loup, who is not only Comte Bertrand de Fénelon, but the Marquis d'Albufera, both of whom Proust met during the *Fête de Fleurs* between the varnishing-day of the annual exhibition of the *Épatants* and the opening of the water-colour show at Georges Petit's.

"The Duc de Guermantes," says Proust himself in an article entitled *"Souvenirs et aperçus,"* in *La Nouvelle Revue Française* for January 1, 1923, "has nothing of the late Marquis de L. in him, but it was with a recollection of the latter that I made him shave in front of his window."

The narrator—the "I" of the novels—has no name, yet he declares himself as Proust by the very fact that, on the single occasion when he steps before the curtain, he says that he never takes a character or an instance from life. This disclaimer is a mere act of caution. With the exception of those unhappily literary philosophies of his, he never took anything from anything but life.

This very important circumstance not only gives his fiction a peculiar value, but enables us to treat it as autobiography. *À la recherche du temps perdu* tells the experience of one who worshipped his mother (expanded into a mother and a grandmother for purposes of convenience and disguise), had choking-fits, frequented society, retired into a retreat (transformed into a "sanitarium"), and finally became a novelist.

And what a novelist! Such trivial material was never before gathered together; a less admirable man has seldom lived. And yet, by its sheer fidelity to itself, this triviality becomes living, and therefore sublime and mysterious.

He laboured in agony to find the "authentic impression" which was his very own—the little gift to himself of that God whom he denied. He knew by instinct that mere memory would accomplish nothing, that dead details raked together make but a pile of rubbish. So he waited always for flashes of another sort of memory, the sort which re-creates the past—what we ordinarily call inspiration, which has the marvellous power of taking incidents and seeing them unite in a new and vital order.

He wrote in bed, holding the paper in one hand—thus dispensing with the "flat surface," the traditional *sine qua non* of authorship. A bottle of ink costing two sous was beside him, with a bad pen in a thin wooden penholder. "He held his sheet of paper in the air," his biographer adds, "without supporting it on a table or even a blotting-pad or a book," and "refused to have a shade fixed on his lamp or to have the table beside his bed cleared."

The almost illegible manuscript would go to the printer, come back in the form of proofs, be revised and sent out again—expanded almost beyond recognition. Again and again. The magic came slowly. One notes that the last two volumes, deprived by the author's failing health of the final touches, are somehow impotent in certain passages. The endless sentences are no longer always mathematically logical. The invoked images and emotions do not always answer as of old to the wand—which begins to falter.

But fame had come from the publication of the earlier volumes, and the wretched Proust tasted a few months of sweetness almost like those of his boyhood days. He received the most distinguished people of his time—compelling them to visit him at night. Summoned to join the colours at the outbreak of the war, he was overjoyed to read that three o'clock in the morning was the hour fixed for him to report—and great was his disgust to discover that the supposed three was really an eight, though his health made the whole matter an empty gesture.

The chamber, in fact, soon became more and more a chamber of horrors. It was never aired, and was always reeking with choking fumigations—enough to have killed an athlete. "Sickness," says Pierre-Quint, "had wrought a deep change. . . . The face had gone pale, the moustache drooped unevenly, the nose was pinched, the cheeks thicker, the eyes more brilliant. He received you, when he was not in bed, in a dark brown dressing-gown . . . wore a pad of cotton-wool over his shirt-collar . . . floss silk gloves on his hands, knitted woollen shoes on his feet."

He would say: "My dear friend, shall I be causing you much inconvenience if I ask you to take the handkerchief out of your jacket? You know I can bear no perfume." He would then ring the bell for Céleste, and order the offending handkerchief removed. "My dear friend," he would continue, "the last time you were so good as to come and see me . . . I was obliged to take the chair you sat in and keep it out in the court-yard for three days; it was impregnated with scent."

Yet news that a *demi-mondaine* somewhere in Paris was giving parties that ended "orgiastically" was enough to send him out to investigate, searching for "material." He drove at times in "a hermetically sealed" carriage, even into the country, and until within six months of his death continued to frequent the Ritz, staying till two A.M.

By now he had lost even the cork room, the house it was in having been sold over his head. A few weeks were spent in the Rue Laurent-Pinchat, in a house once belonging to Réjane. Then came that final "hostile lodging," a gloomy apartment on the fourth floor of 44 Rue Hamelin, where there were children in the flat above. He sent them presents of felt slippers, but quiet was never again to be his—not in this world. The furniture remained unpacked. Frightful disorder reigned everywhere. He began taking veronal and caffeine. He could no longer speak without difficulty, and was forced to scribble even his orders to Céleste, who had become an autocrat.

His brother, Dr. Robert Proust, finally forced his way to the bedside of the dying man, but it was too late. The novelist, on the last night of all, dictated a few notes completing his description of the death of Bergotte. It was the night of November 18, 1922. The bottle of ink upset. Proust was dead.

2. SULPHUR MATCHES

The evil that men do lives after them. Proust's evil consisted chiefly in his theoretical idea of love, in his confused acceptance of what were in effect the imaginary plasms of Weininger.

It is said of Baudelaire that, could he have had his way, he would have published his *Fleurs du mal* as *Les Lesbiennes.* Proust's own title for *À la recherche du temps perdu* was *Sodome et Gomorrhe—Sodome* standing for the spiritual home of his men, *Gomorrhe* being dedicated to his women. Almost all his characters, male or female, are homo-erotic. He paints a world whose rain of fire and brimstone is long overdue.

No doubt there was much justification for this in that sterile Faubourg Saint-Germain whose "honour" had dwindled to a demand for the conviction of an innocent Dreyfus for daring not only to be a Jew but to tell the truth about the army. It was a *milieu* offering many examples of the fact that sexual passion stands ever ready to leap out and fix itself upon any human relationship unprotected by principles, or by ideals of chastity. For propinquity is like the steam in a locomotive engine, driving it in whatever direction it is already pointed, and those whose concupiscence has not been channelized in a normal direction are naturally more or less at the mercy of the winds. But this is no reason for saying that inversion is an "incurable malady," still less for supposing that it is congenital, or for confusing love with lust.

No man can be expected to re-create the world altogether in his own interior image. He must play the historian, and piece it out with fragments from other images. But Proust lacked the critical faculty which would have enabled him to distinguish between true and false inferences in matters beyond his personal habit, even if they came under his eye. And when it came to passing judgment upon the alleged facts which he found in print, he was hopeless. Nine people out of ten know him as the pretended Pepys of the next-door neighbours of Lot—which is the same as saying that nine-tenths of his present reputation is shoddy and destined not to wear.

That time will take the remaining tenth and gnaw upon it in vain, I have not the slightest doubt; for this tenth is no garment of rags, but a living body, which can but grow. To put it in other words, he is an oak which attained to stupendous and lovely proportions in spite of all attempts of mistletoe to strangle it. Some day the world will see the tree. Just at present it is the foreign parasite which most attracts attention.

The root of this parasite sprang, as might have been expected, from a flaw in the native wood. Proust was a solitary. His probable habits one does not like to think of. Yet auto-eroticism has only this in common with homo-eroticism: it viciously avoids nature's saving differentiation. His love for his mother was so intense that it prevented him from looking upon other women in a normal fashion. But here was no life with wings sufficient to keep it *always* above the flesh. Therefore he failed to associate the fleshly excitation with gonochorism at all. And not wishing to fill his fictional world with men altogether like himself, he chose to fill it with Charli, perverts of a drastic and dramatic order. He was enough like them to make the attempt half a success; enough unlike them to make it, unsupported as it was by either science or sound philosophy, half a failure.

He treats inversion everywhere as if the taint were a compulsory, hereditary force. The Guermantes are what they are because of one, Gilbert, their ancient *mauvais sire*. He even attempts to idealize this peculiarity, calling it "a vice which Nature herself has planted in the soul of a child, perhaps by no more than blending the virtues of its father and mother as she might blend the colours of their eyes." This is pure moonshine, and founded upon no well-established truth of human experience. Proust acquired the notion from undigested reading-matter.

Much as I dislike the Behaviourists when they seek to become epistemologists, I am forced to agree with their contention that early education accounts for most of our ways. Whoever has, through some accident in the nursery, had a reflex arc forged between the gonad and a situation upon his own side of life's house, is most unfortunate. But there is no gain in pretending that the calamity befell before birth. The cure, also, may be too long delayed, but that is far from saying that cure was impossible from the moment the false step was taken, or for hinting with Proust that "not always are we somebody's nephew with impunity." Even the psychoanalysts might help us here, for though their doctrine of polymorphous perversion in infancy has been used as the basis of ridiculous conclusions, it is a useful idea if taken to mean that normal conduct arises in part from the grafting of normal restraints upon normal innocence.

But Proust is chiefly concerned with the melodramatic possibilities of the situation. Wanderers from the Cities of the Plain, he tells us, form "a freemasonry far more extensive, more powerful and less suspected than that of the Lodges, for it rests upon an identity of tastes, needs, habits, dangers, apprenticeship, knowledge, traffic, glossary." They constitute, it seems, a sodality "in which the members themselves, who intend not to know one another, recognize one another immediately by natural or conventional, involuntary or deliberate signs which indicate to the beggar in the street one of his congeners in the great nobleman whose carriage door he is shutting; to the father in the suitor for his daughter's hand; to him who has sought healing, absolution, defence, in the doctor, the priest, the barrister to whom he has had recourse; all of them obliged to protect their own secret but having their part in a secret shared with others, which the rest of humanity does not suspect and which means that to them the most wildly improbable tales of adventure seem true, for in this romantic, anachronistic life the ambassador is a bosom friend of the felon; the prince —with a certain independency of action with which his aristocratic breeding has furnished him—on leaving the duchess's party goes off to confer in private with the hooligan; a part suspected where it does not exist, flaunting itself, insolent and unpunished, where its existence is never guessed; numbering its adherents everywhere, among the people, in the army, in the church, in the prison, on the throne; living, in short, at least to a great extent, in a playful and perilous intimacy with the men of the other race, provoking them, playing them by speaking of its vice as of something alien to it; a game that is rendered easy by the blindness or duplicity of the others, a game that may be kept up for years until the day of the scandal, on which these lion-tamers are devoured; until then, obliged to make a secret of their vocabulary, a social constraint, slight in comparison with the inward constraining which their vice, or what is improperly so called [*sic!*], imposes upon them with regard not so much now to others as to themselves, and in such a way that to themselves it does not appear a vice." [1]

This single sentence, so typical of Proust as regards style, affords food for thought, not to say doubt. Here

[1] "The Cities of the Plain," vol. i, pp. 24–25.

we have a vast secret horde to whom later in the same volume [2] he applies that verse of Genesis, "If a man can number the dust of the earth, then shall thy seed also be numbered." Seed, indeed! But no wonder he calls them more powerful than the Freemasons. Were they as a matter of fact even one-half as numerous as he indicates, it is inconceivable that they should ever have permitted laws to be passed against them.

Nevertheless, having depicted this Klan with all the gusto of a Sue describing Jesuits, Proust proceeds to deny that they even constitute that claque whose influence has often been suspected even by the unenthusiastic, and held to be ever ready to boost any likely one of its own to the very pinnacle of contemporary fame. But Proust avers that "whenever a Sodomite fails to secure election, the black balls are, for the most part, cast by other Sodomites, who are anxious to penalize sodomy, having inherited the falsehood that enabled their ancestors to escape from the cursed city." [3]

That is, they blackball in obedience to that inherited fear which made them hide their faces. Fear of what? Fear of being thought to practise "what is improperly called" a vice. Fear, in other words, of being caught with a virtue. One marvels that such a numerous and well-organized band came to care so much for outside public opinion. But what has happened to Proust is that for the moment he has forgotten that he does not believe literally in the Bible story, and so he lets his modern Sodomites be marked with the ancient fear of their psychological ancestors face to face with the angel of God.

Now virtue has known its martyrs who dared to stand

[2] *Ibid.*, p. 45.
[3] *Ibid.*

alone, even to hang upon the cross—not surrounded by the like-minded as numerous as the dust of the earth, but between two thieves and above a howling mob. Nor of lesser martyrs has there been any lack. Why, then—Bible stories aside—this timidity of powerful noblemen, doctors, barristers, beggars, and priests whose numbers alone should give them control of all society? Has there been, after all, some mistake in the counting of noses? Does Proust mean to insinuate that these brains are not up to the average, or that there is here a conscience which doth make cowards of them all notwithstanding the high justice of their cause?

It is a dilemma, certainly, but, instead of attempting to escape from it, he now would make us believe that the hereditarily fearful and ashamed are nevertheless proud of their state.

"They take pleasure in recalling that Socrates was of themselves," which shows at least the power of their imaginations, and they "claim that Jesus [God help us!] was one of them—without reflecting that there were no abnormals when homosexuality was the norm." [4]

Homosexuality, then, was once the "norm." Our forefathers propagated uno-genitally, except for those abnormals whose children make up to-day's embourgeoised conventionals, too dull to have invented secret grips and passwords with which to recognize one another, yet somehow clever enough to have made (a clumsy remedy, I admit) each delinquent an outcast in the eyes of the law.

He even gives the date of this remarkable biological period, the "then" of the text. It was before the appearance of diœcious plants. But that was before sexual differentiation had ever taken place, when propagation was

[4] *Ibid.*, p. 23.

by budding, and long before man walked the earth. To found a homosexual "norm" upon multiplication by sexless division is to commit the final absurdity. And so, by trying to make a lyric out of a lie, and an epic out of a lyric; by turning pseudo-scientist and attempting to herd a multitude of instances, some of them authentic enough, within the provisions of an ill-considered general principle, our novelist comes to grief.

He is, in fine, not a philosopher but a gossip, and the smiling *badinage* of his friend Anatole France has not only robbed him of all belief in systematic thinking but of any capacity to improve his very small talent in that direction.

Yet system is the one thing which Proust cannot let alone. He must always have his "law." Thus, the hero in *Le temps retrouvé,* speaking of his observations upon human character, enquires (p. 177): "Was it not worth more than these gestures that they made, these words which they spoke, their lives, their nature, that I should attempt to describe the curve of it, and from this to disengage its law?"

The answer must be an emphatic *no,* though generalizing is a well-known stratagem of the fiction-writer, a technical trick intended to lend a spurious air of importance to his goods—a showman's ballyhoo, in short. But Proust, super-showman that he is, makes us run the risk of taking it seriously.

There is his precious "general law" that inverts make their wives happy—happier, I gather, than the wives of normal men. And it amounts to this: Such husbands, in the attempt to hide their real kidney from the world, craftily make a great show of affection for women. And in order that there may be no suspicion of the real state of affairs in the minds of any, they behave affectionately not only to their wives but to as many mistresses as possible. And this pretended love for women in general and in particular is the source of the wife's peculiar happiness! Proust puts it thus:

"As to the *genre* of amours that Saint-Loup had inherited [it is always *heredity,* you see!] from Monsieur de Charlus, a husband who is [homosexually] inclined habitually makes his wife happy."

This is the "general law." But the Guermantes manage to make themselves an exception to it, "because those who have this taste wish people to believe that they have on the contrary a taste for women." That is to say, the very family to which Charlus, Saint-Loup, and the other leading protagonists of infamy belong, furnishes the great exception to the law by which infamy is governed. And they are able to achieve this marvel because *"ils s'affichaient avec l'une ou l'autre,"* parade with one woman or another, and so drive their own wives to despair—*"désespéraient le leur."* But this parading of their love of other women is precisely what other inverts are said to do when they make their wives happy. The law and the exception show the same features. The Guermantes overdid the parading—is that the idea?

Saint-Loup not only inherits the family tendency to love in what Italians call "the Greek manner": he loves his wife (Gilberte, *née* Swann) as well. He seems to have "wished for myrrh," which, we are told, "is the desire of Protogenos of twofold sex, who roars like a bull of countless orgies, memorable, unspeakable, descending, joyous to the sacrifice of the Orgirophants." [5]

He "roars" by throwing himself on the floor at his

[5] *Ibid.,* p. 334.

wife's feet, prophesying his own early death. He has affectations of sensibility *"paussées jusqu'à la comédie,"* and continually deceived Gilberte "in a spirit of duplicity which is being perpetually discovered." The situation is still further complicated by the fact that the wife is a Lesbian, and by the circumstance that the husband is the hero's most intimate friend and presented to us as a spotless man of honour, of "indomitable will." [6] He carries to an extreme the blond Guermantes' air of being but a solidified ray of sunlight—*"d'être seulement de l'ensoleillement d'une journée d'or devenue solide."* This gives him a sort of *"plumage,"* so strange that it makes him *"une espèce si rare, si précieuse, qu'on aurait voulu la posséder pour une collection ornithologique."* His antics on entering a drawing-room are such that one wonders if they are not taking place in the Jardin des Plantes, "where the zoölogical specimens are kept." Taken all in all, Saint-Loup is a "bird"—a figure of speech with which I am not disposed to quarrel.

"Les Courvoisier en usaient plus sagement"—they managed their talent more wisely. The young Viscount de Courvoisier believed that himself alone since the origin of the earth was ever tempted by one of his own sort—*"se croyait seul sur la terre être tenté par quelqu'un de son sexe."* He also believed that this *"penchant"* came from the devil—not a bad guess. So he fought against it, espoused a ravishing woman, *"lui fit des enfants."* Then one of his cousins made him acquainted with the fact that this penchant is sufficiently common, "and carried benevolence to the point of conducting him to those places where he might satisfy it." Whereupon Monsieur de Courvoisier, though no longer loving his wife, redoubled

[6] *Le temps retrouvé,* vol. i, p. 214.

his prolific zeal towards her, and the pair came to be cited as having the best *ménage* in Paris. From which I gather, if I gather anything, that his wife was not happy until he ceased loving her and began to find his pleasure elsewhere, leaving her to feast upon his pretence of affection and upon his duty performed.

One did not say as much for the *ménage* of Saint-Loup, because Robert, "instead of contenting himself with inversions" (*au lieu de se contenter de l'inversion*), made his wife half dead with jealousy by his habit, golden bird that he was, of searching "without pleasure" for mistresses.[7]

So, in the case of Saint-Loup, the wife is made happy by being half killed by jealousy, and is made jealous by the fact that her husband is without pleasure in his mistresses. In the case of the Guermantes other than Saint-Loup, the wives are made happy by being exceptions and not made happy. And the wife of Courvoisier is made at first unhappy through her husband's fidelity, and then happy when he becomes dependably sulphurous whenever he is not at home. All of which seems to indicate the "general law" that people are never painfully jealous (though sometimes they may be half dead with jealousy) of rivals not of their own sex, and only then when they are paraded. But as Proust's hero throughout the book is jealous *only* of rivals not of his own sex, the general law becomes somewhat particular and allows itself to be applied solely to women—with what truth I leave it to the reader to decide.

In the words of Kuo Tsun to the "ordinary but not unattractive" Chou,[8] "We perceive that, by a beneficent

[7] *Ibid.*, p. 18.
[8] *Vide* "Kai Lung Unrolls His Mat," by Ernest Bramah.

scheme of spells and counter-charms, when the light goes, darkness gradually appears; and when darkness has run its appointed span, the light is ready again to take its place. What, however, would occur if by some celestial oversight this had not been foreseen, and both light and darkness had been withdrawn together?"

Now we know. There would have remained precisely one of Proust's "laws," confronted by all its instances and exceptions.

3. A LOCOFOCO

The emotional pleasure we get from hearing a statement which we wish were true often blinds us or makes us indifferent to its obvious falsity. In no other way can I account for the tolerance with which Impuritan logic is generally regarded. Thought is a cold conclusion lying at the end of a path. The mind often prefers to halt at the beginning, surrounded only by glowing images.

Proust's genius was intellectual. His best work is wisely malicious—for without malice, that is, without a vision of the unloveliness of natural man—literary immortality is impossible. But when Proust tries to make *bestémmia e il turpiloquio* into something charming and sublime, his rational power leaves him. He becomes ridiculous and sentimental—the inevitable penalty for giving honour where no honour is due.

Sometimes his humour saves him, however, even from his philosophy—as when Palmède, Baron de Charlus, the most noble cock of this most shady walk, struts "in a light travelling-suit which made him appear stouter . . . swaggering through the rooms" of seaside Balbac's Grand Hôtel, "balancing a pursy stomach" with an "almost symbolical" counterweight bulging in the opposite direction.

But too often his cynical inclination deserts him when Palmède is the subject. This brutal, commanding, insolent rooster, with royal blood in his veins and heavy brawn to his bones, was precisely the sort of man that the delicate, base-born novelist must often have liked to fancy himself to be. So the touch grows too indulgent and we laugh in the wrong place—as when he tells us that "the writer ought not to be offended when his inverts [i.e., his readers] give a masculine visage to his heroines," since it is "this peculiarity, *un peu aberrante,* which alone permits" them to enjoy what they read. "If Monsieur de Charlus had not given the face of Morel to the faithless one over whom Musset weeps [in *La Nuit d'Octobre*] he would neither have wept neither would he have understood, since it was only by this narrow and crooked path that he had access to the verities of love." [1]

This is rather too much. And, to make it worse, Proust is not only weighed down with the determination to find some simple and far-reaching law of which his Baron is the puppet: he cannot decide what law to invoke. He is in doubt as to the psychic gender with which the Charlus-psyche should be endowed.

In that scene in *Sodome et Gomorrhe,* prefaced by the saying of Alfred de Vigny that *"la femme aura Gomorrhe et l'homme aura Sodome,"* [2] where Charlus first meets Jupien, the infernal tailor, the Baron crows like a chanticleer, so male that all other creatures in God's barnyard must be regarded as hens in comparison. Here is

[1] *Le temps retrouvé,* vol. ii, p. 70.
[2] *Vide* "The Cities of the Plain," vol. i, chap. i.

the Urning as the supervirile, the excessively arrhenoplasmic man.

Jupien has "thrown up his head, giving a becoming tilt to his body, placed his hand with a grotesque impertinence on his hip." He has lost his habitual "humble, honest expression," and "posed himself with the coquetry which the orchids [in the court-yard of Madame de Villeparisis hard by] might have adopted on the providential arrival of the [pollen-laden] bee."

Is not this Jupien a Carmen among the poultry? Certainly an orchid, however impertinent, must be thought of as passive, be it never so provocative, in regard to bees. "One would have called" the two "a pair of birds, the male and the female, the male seeking to make advances, the female [Jupien] no longer giving any sign of response to these overtures." The tailor retires into his shop, in fact; and Charlus, "humming like a great bumble-bee," disappears in his wake.

To give dignity to the picture—and surely no picture ever needed dignity more—Proust observes that "the laws of the vegetable kingdom are themselves governed by other laws, increasingly exalted," their rule ever extending from plants to bees and up through birds to barons and tailors. Well and good. But what laws have we now? "A true philosophy" means, "in this instance, merely that the arrival of insects, so fertilizing to flowers, is a lesser part of that law of nature which avoids both sterility and degeneracy." So this higher law, which avoids both sterility and degeneracy, is fulfilled when there is "a retired tailor who can stand quivering in ecstasy before a stoutish man of fifty." [3] Fecundity of the soul,

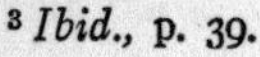
[3] *Ibid.*, p. 39.

doubtless. Insectivorous, certainly. And a male Charlus throughout.

And yet, on page 22, the narrator says that he "had managed to arrive at the conclusion that Monsieur de Charlus looked like a woman," that "he was one"!

"He belonged to that race of beings, less paradoxical than they appear, whose ideal [he means ideal mate, not ideal of self] is manly simply because their temperament is feminine, and who in their life resemble in appearance only the rest of men—a race upon which a curse weighs and which must live amid falsehood and perjury because it knows the world to regard as a punishable and scandalous, as an inadmissible thing, its desire, that which constitutes for every human creature the greatest happiness in life; which must deny its God, since even Christians, when they appear and are arraigned at the bar of justice, must before Christ and in His name defend themselves, as from a calumny, from the charge of what to them is life itself."

Truly, I do not see how any race could be more paradoxical than, according to this, the now masculine, now feminine race of Charlus really is. And they must deny their God in denying their vice, defending themselves from a true charge, even "before Christ and in His name," though we have already been told that He is one of them!

Proust avoids the quasi-scientific terminology of Weininger, yet he has been thinking along precisely the same lines. So he has Weininger's difficulty of conceiving of the active male invert. Yet active male inverts certainly exist. Proust even has one on his hands—this very Charlus, a supervirile if ever there was one.

But Charlus and his like, Proust laments, must needs

"fall in love with precisely that type of man who has nothing feminine about him, who is not an invert and consequently cannot love them in return." The Baron has become a woman again, and the difficulty now is to supply him with an affinity. This affinity is precisely the type which Charlus himself exemplified when he was described as masculine. Proust, blind to the simple fact of perverse habits, stutters and is puzzled and seeks to draw a herring across the trail with the remark that this [unavowedly plasmic] theory will be "subject to some modifications in the sequel." And, as was to be expected, the modifications prove to be no modifications at all—unless we may so term the breaches which solid fact make in the walls of alternating suppositions against which they crash. Again one is forced to the conclusion that there is no such thing as an active male invert—human history to the contrary notwithstanding.

So we are asked to believe that the effeminates' "desire would be for ever insatiable did not their money procure for them real men" or their "imaginations make them take for real men" those inverts "with whom they have associated themselves." Charlus the petticoated has to be satisfied by means of self-deception. Charlus the cock of the walk disappears in obedience to the ukase, "Thou art impossible." But clearly this impossibility, so blessed if it were true, comes from the imagination not of himself but of the author.

Throughout the rest of the work, Charlus remains generally of the distaff persuasion, a lover of suffering like that unfortunate Frenchman who was in the habit, not so many years ago, of walking the streets of the worst quarters of Paris, jingling money in his pockets in hopes of provoking footpads to rob and beat him. He did it once too often, and was beaten to death by roughs who did not know who he was and so failed to realize that they were intended to be the messengers of beauty, not of death. Yes, beauty. For Proust assures us that those who imagine and desire a type which he considers impossible come to understand that "what they have been calling their love (a thing to which, playing upon the word, they have by association annexed all that poetry, painting, music, chivalry, asceticisms have contrived to add to love) springs not from an ideal of beauty which they have chosen but from an incurable malady." [4]

An ideal, you see, which, with all its poetry, painting, and asceticism, has been thrust upon them. It is now a disease again. A little while ago it was something which Nature herself plants in the soul of a child, "perhaps by no more than blending the virtues of its father and mother."

Charlus manages to maintain his ascetic ideals and at the same time to keep on the safe side of death. He contents him with frequenting a *"hôtel louche"* which Jupien presently sets up, a modern dung-mixen, or *"temple de l'impudor,"* where spurious thieves and murderers are always ready to tie the willing victim to his mattress and to lash him with chains until human endurance is almost, but not quite, surpassed. Here he dreams blissfully of "feudal punishments," of *"souterrains moyen-ageux."* His "desire to be chained, to be beaten, concealed within its ugliness," it seems, "a vision as poetic as that longing which other men have to go to Venice or to entertain dancing-girls." [5]

Meanwhile the Baron maintains in society his con-

[4] *Ibid.*, p. 22.
[5] *Le temps retrouvé,* vol. i, p. 200.

tradictory rôle of haughty super-manhood, no longer a masochist, but a sadist pure and simple—as when he insults Madame de Sainte-Euvrette by declaring in her hearing that, to his mind, a party at her house is simply an opportunity for visiting a sewer.

And the lady turns towards him, "as if she were kneeling before her master," showing that she is a social climber who has read Proust's book of etiquette and proved herself worthy of that advancement which subsequently is to be hers. We see now to what degree Soames, in Galsworthy's "Silver Spoon," stamped himself as plebeian and culturally hopeless when he took notice of an insult offered—in her own house, but behind her back—to his daughter by Marjorie Ferror. But Proust has here returned to the field of his own observations, and I do not doubt the accuracy of his description of the sort of thing likely to happen—in that particular field. His snob-philosophy at least hangs together, and he follows it wherever it leads—like a printer following copy out of the window. It is inversion which is too much for him, since he is determined to make it noble, romantic, and artistic, and at the same time congenitally pathologic, scientific, and contemptible.

Charlus becomes understandable enough, once we cease trying to bring him within the purview of an Impuritan-made law and regard him merely as an example of that much simpler law which says that the love of evil is an omnivorous appetite, finding palatable anything which is sufficiently decayed. The bestial is the Baron's meat, and he moves easily from the active to the passive, from the mad joy of inflicting pain to that yet madder seeking for joy which bids him suffer for Satan's sake. He illustrates that very common phenomenon to which psychiatrists are so persistently blind, the tendency of vice to obliterate sex, properly so called, and to substitute for it a sexuality which is merely a carnal excitability, drawing the line at nothing and reaping tumescence from anything, especially that which goes against the conscience.

Conscience in this case may be but an interfering consciousness of what is regarded as decent by the neighbours, and of course its sensitiveness does not resist for ever the callosifying treatment to which it is subjected. But when not even the outrageous can pierce its skin, nothing is left but a flat detumescence, not to be moved even by bodily torture, whether inflicted or endured. We have then the old roué condemned to ennui, an imp no longer able even to snort fire, played out, hopeless, like an extinct crater which seeks in vain once again to devastate the country-side.

The real Charlus was recognized by all Paris as none other than that same Montesquiou who had already served Huysmans as des Esseintes in *À rebours*—a being rather more deserving sympathy than is his fictional double. He was, for one thing, a fairly good poet, and, when told that he ought to publish his verses, exclaimed despairingly: "What good would that do? My reputation as a writer, if I acquired one, could never make me anything but a Montesquiou-beast."

The fictional Charlus is almost equally true to life, in so far as his words and deeds are concerned. The explanations are what is false. We see him finally seated in a carriage in company with Jupien—an old, fat man "with eyes fixed, figure stooped [bowed shoulders], hair and beard entirely white, huddled upon his cushion, making more effort to keep himself half-upright than a child would have required to behave itself" under similar circumstances. Madame de Sainte-Euvrette passes—Madame de Sainte-Euvrette, the once despised. The Baron, reminded by Jupien's whisper that he knows this lady, makes a profound bow. The climber has triumphed. But Proust cannot spare us one last absurdity. He must compare this ignoble ruin to King Lear! [6]

4. LA FEMME AURA GOMORRHE

Proust's unnamed hero, drawn so unmistakably from himself, stands almost unique among his other characters in being a lover only of the opposite sex. The theory that inversion arises when a man has the soul of a woman is here abandoned, for this hero is effeminate and yet no monster. The heroines whom he loves, the delicate petals of "In a Budding Grove," are more feminine still. What makes the abnormality is the fact that they are Lesbians. He can hardly imagine himself as loving anything but a woman. He cannot, or will not, imagine other men as loving them. So the rivals he fears are not men but women. How is one to account for this strange state of things?

The explanation, I think, lies in that unhealthy gynæcian bringing-up to which the male body of Proust was subjected by the domestic situation surrounding his boyhood. His was the intermediate sex, evolved in the only way it is ever evolved, by a pernicious education. He was not so much his mother's lover as her shadow. She had wrapped his heart in a petticoat. Women are jealous of women, not of men—that he could understand. So the lover of Albertine is afraid not of Don Juans but of Mademoiselle Vinteuils.

The complications of the situation, however, were be-

[6] *Ibid.*, p. 226.

yond belief. Thus, the lover of Albertine was in one sense the woman of the pair, and Albertine and her girl friends comparatively male. At the same time they are the most feminine creatures in all literature—necessarily so, since they must serve as mistresses to the softly nurtured narrator of the tale. To have had them unfaithful in the ordinary way, through attachments to Proust's outward similars, would have been too harsh. It would have been like crushing rose-leaves beneath the hoofs of an incredible beast. It would have been like delivering himself over to his bolder brothers, or like giving his rivals an opportunity to drive his inferiority home. Proust could identify himself with the object of his desire, or he could hold himself aloof. And the being which he projected into a given situation could be any part whatever of his highly complex nature.

Thus his toleration of Lesbianism arose in part from his masculinity. The abnormality of the traditional Sappho (the real Sappho is not in question) impresses chiefly women. To a man, the intimacies here involved are less disturbing because he instinctively becomes one of the actors, thus making the intimacies natural. Proust also was able, through the Penelope slant of his eyes, to lessen any masculine horror which he might otherwise have had of men too intimately viewed by men.

And yet another element enters into the situation here. He was a lover of self. Being, crudely speaking, a man, he lived too closely to this man—the only one he deeply knew. So he could, though with some difficulty, think of himself as Charlus. But he could not actually have followed in the steps of the Baron; for it is one thing to dream, and quite another to put a nightmare into practice.

Reality has harsh edges. Reverie softens them as a mist softens a rugged mountain.

The general result of all this was that Proust considered himself free to wander at large in the region of forbidden things. His body was contradicted not by plasms but by mental wont. He could discover unheard-of abominations in a garden of innocent flowers, and innocently flower-like passions in Sodom and Gomorrah. Most often we wonder that we are not more offended. The secret lies in this chameleon heart, infecting us and changing the superficial garments of our gender at its will.

It was this half man, or half woman if you prefer, who created Gilberte, Albertine, Andrée, Mademoiselle Vinteuil, Odette, and all the others of that host of Venus whose images haunt the cork-lined room. The solitary now makes himself as normal as possible. But the "I" (usually implied rather than expressed) which he cast upon the screen of fiction retains its halfness. He cannot quite fancy girls as in love with himself, whether by "self" be understood the hero or the author. That self is, he fears, too little their complement. Hence the ingenious tortures which he devises for his own enduring. He avoids the possibility of normal competition by making the difference between these *jeunes filles* and men of ordinary stamp like that between humming-birds and hippopotami. Lust itself could not bridge such a gulf. Here is something which simply could not happen. But there remains the world of women, in which he can think of no woman as safe. No wonder his style became subtle and involved, that for every event he supplied not one explanation but two, three, five, six, a dozen. He tried to see both sides of the shield, sometimes both sides at once.

This unprecedented state of things enabled him to draw some of the most exquisite figures known to secular letters—above all, this same Albertine, already so often mentioned, a being describable only in his own phrase, the *jeune fille en fleur,* who awakens in the reader such passion as a rose might feel, who, in spite of all the vices her author seeks to endow her with, remains somehow virginal, sweet beyond comparison, charming beyond words; a woman whose womanliness is reduced to child-like proportions, so that while ceasing to be a child she becomes but a fairy to whom all things are permitted simply because we cannot really believe that an earthly speck, let alone depravity, ever sullied her wings.

The grosser fancies, born of Proust's infernal knowledge of himself, are here forborne, or forgotten as soon as uttered, and there emerges somehow an Albertine compact all of fancies that soar—not, indeed, beyond the earth, nor even to that hill-top where Proust worshipped his mother, but to such heights as things created out of the softer side of his loneliness, craving the companionship of that which was softer still, could reach without totally losing their nature. Vice this undoubtedly is, the vice of a Mohammedan reverie, but refining its courtesans into houris which are angels—fallen, it is true, but fallen so little that their very shadows seem luminous.

And yet, because this is truly Inferno and not Paradise, its fairest creatures become but the instruments of pain. Proust's hero, with the keen instinct of one of the damned, puts Albertine under the microscope, so that no possible reason for despair may escape him.

He studies her speech, not for the sake of following her discourse, which is but an innocent prattle, but in order to discover "every alluvial addition originating in soils formerly known to her." He comes to the conclusion that "she must in her short life have received a great many compliments, a great many avowals, and have received them with pleasure, with sensuality." He remembers greeting her first kiss with "a smile of gratitude for the unknown seducer who had wrought so profound a change in her and had so far simplified" his task. But here he but pretends to hardiness. His real apprehension is that this unknown was probably not a man. So he needs must listen with tense anxiety to her slightest word.

She had been used to say, speaking of anything at all: "Is that true? Really?" *"C'est vrai? C'est bien vrai?"* —accompanying the expression with a look of sincere interrogation. But he soon begins to wonder if she has not become so distracted by her secret thoughts—so absent-minded because of them—that she needs to have continual confirmation of the smallest facts about her. The question when she asks it, however, still seems to be accompanied by a slightly coquettish pout, ineradicable trace of its origin. So finally he arrives "at the true solution of this formula," this eternal *"C'est vrai? C'est bien vrai?"* She had begun to use it, he decides, "when first of marriageable age," as a maidenly response to such statements as "You know, I have never seen anyone so pretty as you are!" or "You know, I am very much in love with you!" And now this same *"C'est vrai?"* is no longer of any use to Albertine but as a response when he remarks: "You have been dozing for more than an hour!" Of no use, that is, save as a mask to hide the nefarious thoughts which he thinks must actually, or in all probability at least, occupy her mind.

Proust really pushes matters to this pass? *C'est vrai!*

C'est bien vrai! And when, every now and then, Albertine lets fall some new syllables, alluvial additions originating in soils formerly unknown to her and still unknown to her lover, he cannot rest until he believes himself to have traced them to their muddy source in some evil encounter behind his back which, with all his vigilance, he has been unable to guard against.

Love, it seems, must always obey "its own incomprehensible and fatal laws," and these laws make it but another name for curiosity, denial (not self-denial, but robbery), jealousy, and woe. It is in hopes of profiting by one of these laws that Swann, "by consenting to meet [Odette] only after dinner," tries to make her believe that there are "other pleasures" which he "prefers to that of her company," even to that of "doing a catalpa."

With cunning intent to profit by these same laws, Proust's nameless hero seeks "to give Andrée the impression" that he was "not really in love with her," so that she "would not grow tired" of him, and so that he might be left in a position "to take a joyful and pleasant advantage of her affection." [1] Pleasure at last comes upon the stage—in the form of treachery!

But love itself remains a sad affair. He compares it to soporifics, such as morphine, drugs which are purchased at a "*prix d'or* . . . not by those to whom they give the pleasure of sleep or of a true well-being," but by "those other invalids (perhaps the same individuals, but a little older) whom the medicament does not put to sleep, to whom it brings no voluptuousness, but who, so long as they are without it, are the prey of an agitation which they wish to bring to an end at any cost, even death." [2]

[1] "The Cities of the Plain," vol. ii, p. 360.
[2] *Le temps retrouvé*, vol. i, p. 171.

Swann takes the fatal dose, marries his mistress (Odette), and exclaims: "To think that I have wasted years of my life, that I have longed for death, that the greatest love that I have ever known has been for a woman who did not please me!" [3]

"It is sometimes enough to make us love a woman that she looks on us with contempt . . . while we imagine that she cannot ever be ours; it is enough, also, sometimes that she looks on us kindly . . . while we think of her as almost ours already." [4] Exactly. There are loves and loves. Thus does Proust's keenness of observation lead him finally to enunciate two of his incomprehensible and fatal laws together, so that by cancelling each other they may make room for facts.

And then he enunciates a brand-new law.

"Once we believe that a fellow creature has a share in some unknown existence to which that creature's love for ourselves can win us admission, that is, of all the preliminary conditions which love exacts, the one to which it attaches the most importance." [5] This looks like a good law and a true one. We marry for the sake of getting into society, in hopes of being introduced into some unknown and presumably superior existence, even of placating by means of our adoration the guardian angel of some paradise truly divine.

But the law is not allowed to be applied in this upward direction. This "Open sesame!" we are soon given to understand is pronounced only by the flesh. For "bodily passion, which has been so unjustly decried, compels its victims to display every vestige that is in them of unself-

[3] "Swann's Way," episode "Swann in Love."
[4] *Loc. cit.*
[5] "Swann's Way," vol. i, p. 134.

ishness and generosity, and so effectively that they shine resplendent in the eyes of all beholders." [6]

So? Then why "victims"? Why not "beneficiaries"? Can this unselfish and generous thing truly be called bodily passion? And what does Proust mean when he says, a little later in this same volume: "Love may come into being, love of the most physical order, without any foundation in desire"? I confess myself puzzled by the idea of bodily passion, love of the most physical order, sans desire. I think such love is not of the most physical order. The author seems to be attempting to play the materialist, to say nice things about the flesh and to attribute to the flesh the things of the heart. Desire without the heart is not so much bodily as devilish, and that is why it is so frequently "decried." Not long ago two gilded youths whose unsefish generosity had caused them to shine resplendent as the playful murderers of a comrade came before a jury in Chicago. Really, one should listen to some evidence in the criminal courts before writing too sweetly about the vagaries of lust.

But Proust goes on by saying that in youth "the goal towards which love of necessity tends" is the "linking of hearts"—truly a bodily passion of a highly metaphorical sort. In later years, however, "since we possess its hymn engraved on our hearts in its entirety, there is no need for any woman to repeat the opening lines, potent with the admiration which her beauty inspires, where it sings of our existing henceforth for one another only; we are well enough attuned to that music to be able to take it up and follow our partner without hesitation at the first pause in her voice."

That is, our later mistresses may safely omit the pre-

[6] *Ibid.*, p. 201.

liminaries, that youthful, idealistic, and nonsensical part of the tune, which sings of our existing for one another, and proceed at once—or depend upon us to proceed at once—to the final cadences of selfish pleasure. Many, no doubt, follow this law. But are they to be more admired than our Darbys and Joans, who do not?

Yet this same Proust can rise so high as to say: "We must be in love before we can care that all women are not virtuous, which is to say, before we can be aware of the fact; and we must be in love, too, before we can hope, that is to say, assure ourselves, that some are." [7]

But usually he means no more by his generalizations than does any other novelist. They give atmosphere, that is all—precisely the thing which modern "philosophers" aim at. Everywhere we hear of atmosphere, of art. There is no longer any talk of truth. So we jump from facts to fancies—the more wildly confused, the better. Abandoned is the attempt to have the slightest real knowledge or understanding of anything. Emotion is all that is asked for—emotion, no matter how awakened or what sort of an emotion it may be. Is not emotion enough?

It might be, or at least it might be more satisfying to one's remaining common sense, if it were willing to stand frankly as an emotion and nothing else. But no novelist who does not parade in the borrowed garments of the sage will find himself taken seriously. It does not suffice if the writer is merely wise. He must pretend to have found wisdom's root. If this be foolishness, so much the better—if it can be shown growing systematically.

Less objectionable are those random ruminations with which Proust frequently exercises his faculties without troubling to invoke first principles of any sort. Thus, his

[7] "The Cities of the Plain," vol. i, p. 325.

hero thinks it quite possible that Gilberte, in telling him that the vices of the other girls of the budding grove were mere peccadillos, was trying to hide the fact that she herself, as Albertine had told him, was a lover of women. Or it may have been that Albertine, when she claimed that Gilberte had made *"des propositions,"* wished but "to have a more experienced air" and to enjoy in Paris the "prestige of her perversity," just as at Balbec she had enjoyed the prestige of her virtue. She was (or perhaps was not) like one pretending to have read an author, say Fourrier, or Tolbolsk, of whom one has never heard.

Or Albertine may have learned something from observing Andrée and Mademoiselle Vinteuil, and have used this knowledge as a play-actor uses costumes and paint to make him look like a villain. Then, seeing that her lover's interest in her possible misdeeds was prompted by jealousy, she (instead of taking advantage of the law which makes jealousy the very father and mother of devotion) immediately reversed her tactics, *"fait machine en arrière."*

That is to say, all this may have been so unless it was that Gilberte had lied in the first place. The truth may be anything at all. Proust is merely amusing himself by constructing hypotheses.

No one need take exception to such amiable trifling, which involves no emotions which could not be evoked by a clever puzzle. But, let dance philosophers say what they will, our deeper interests and feelings awaken only when something is asserted as true.

With Proust the assertion usually is of this theory that love is a sorry business. His narrator discovers that he cannot live without Albertine, so he hides her in his town house, where "her rather uncommon charm" was that she went about less like a *jeune fille* than "like a domestic animal, which enters a room, leaves it, is found in the most unexpected places," and passes through any door which happens to be open but never closes anything which happens to be ajar. She behaves, in sum, like a dog or a cat.

Like a cat, too—as he was not actually an ælurophobe—she would make for herself a place upon the foot of his bed without disturbing anyone, though sometimes—and now rather unlike either a cat or a dog—she would "swear that she would rather die" than leave him. And always, everywhere, she is yielding, docile, self-effacing—incredibly so. Not even when she finds Andrée imitating the hero's manner of speech does she make a fuss.

Yet, now that he has her "a prisoner," he "is not the least certain in the world" that he loves her at all. "Love, perhaps, is only the eddies propagated in the soul in the wake of an emotion." That is, the sort of love which he is describing is nervous exhaustion following in the wake of indulgence. So his greatest joy comes from looking out of his window and seeing other and as yet unimprisoned women pass by, *"femmes impossibles à imaginer a priori,"* who have the faculty of making "the street, the city, the world," more desirable, "more worthy to be explored." They give him at the same time "a thirst to be cured, to go forth alone without Albertine, to be free." He half fancies himself leaping after these passers-by, stopping the flight of these faces which offer him a happiness that, "cloistered" in his own chamber, he feels he will "never taste." Albertine, he tells us, "was capable of causing suffering, but not joy." By "suffering alone" subsisted his "weary attachment." [8]

[8] *La prisonnière,* vol. i, pp. 25–26.

Nevertheless, he was "not absolutely indifferent to this sojourn of Albertine." The means which he had taken to separate her from her friends soothes his spirit. She had, he thought, "such force of passivity, such a great faculty for forgetting and for submission, that these [evil] relations [with other women] had," he fancied, "been broken in fact." [9] Anyway, she maintained his heart "in repose, in a semi-immobility," which promised to cure it of its "phobia," even though this calm "was an appeasement of suffering rather than joy." [10] It is really a wonderful sermon which he unconsciously preaches. And then he decides to go to Venice and leave Albertine in the lurch.

But right here, to the reader's unholy delight, Albertine—obeying, no doubt, some subtle "law" of self-preservation—anticipates him. He finds her missing, and a note telling him that he need not look for her. And behold, his *"souffle fut coupé,"* he is struck dumb with amazement, chagrin, and vain regret. Not even the "supreme care" he had always taken not to let Albertine become aware of his love for her, supposing that love her he did, has proved sufficient to bind her to him for ever.

This lover may not be sensitive upon the affectionate side, but he certainly knows when he is wounded in what Dr. William McDougall would call his sentiment of self-regard.

5. PARADISE REGAINED

Proust dimly realizes that the love of which he has been speaking is not worthy of the name. He will try his hand, then, at sublimation.

"If our love is not simply a love for a Gilberte who

[9] *Ibid.*, p. 27.
[10] *Ibid.*, vol. ii, p. 13.

made us suffer so," he tells us,[1] "this is not because it is also love for an Albertine, but because it is a portion of our soul more durable than the divers selves which die successively within us, a portion of our soul which ought, at the cost of no matter how much pain, to detach us from individuals as we know them, so as to reconstitute our unity and give this love, the comprehension of this love, to all, to the Universal Spirit. . . . Each person who makes us suffer should be recognized by us in connexion with that one divinity of which she is but a fragmentary and lovely reflection. . . . As for happiness, it has almost one sole utility—to make sorrow possible. It needs that, in the hours of happiness, we form ties that are very sweet, and very strong in confidence and attachment, so that their rupture shall cause us that so precious laceration which calls itself sorrow. . . . And as one understands that suffering is the best thing that one may encounter in life, one thinks without terror—almost as of a deliverance—of death."

This beautiful passage has a pious sound. We form attachments for the sake of the agony of their rupture, and suffer the agony that it may wean us from earthly things and lead us to devote ourselves to the Universal Spirit. Unquestionably there is here some lingering realization of the existence of that joy beyond all pain which comes when the lesser things of life have been sacrificed to the greater. But beware of Greeks bearing gifts. Proust has bound himself too tightly to the small ever again to be free to give his heart to the great. He is but playing with words, trying to pretend that one may lose a thing and still have it—worse, that one may renounce and still retain.

[1] *Le temps retrouvé,* vol. ii, p. 51.

His Universal Spirit is no spirit, merely the composite of lovely reflections, of the fleshly sweetness of innumerable Albertines. That portion of our soul "more durable than the divers selves" has no real durability. True, he says somewhere that "death is the chrysalis stage of life," but says it only as one might echo some phrase for its prettiness, without thinking to be committed to its implications. His real idea of immortality is repeatedly expressed in such passages as the following:

"As for myself, I say that the cruel law of art is that people die, and that we die ourselves in exhausting all suffering so that there may come up not the herb of oblivion but the life eternal, the sprightly herb of fruitful works, upon which the generations will feed gaily without care for those who sleep beneath their *déjeuner sur l'herbe*."[2]

What he has in mind, then, is not the immortality of the soul, but that wan delusion of the artist, the so-called "immortality" of a book! And it is for this vain dream that we are to endure "that so precious laceration which calls itself sorrow"—for this and for some refined and exquisite tumescence. We have won only to a more politely furnished room in Jupien's hotel, and might almost as well have stayed with Charlus to be beaten into excitement with chains of the cruder sort.

But it would be unfair to leave Proust here. Let us take him in the person of his hero, in Paris, upon the eve of a certain strange experience. It is winter, and he—his hero, that is—has come home cold and exhausted. His mother offers him tea, a thing which he did not ordinarily take.

"She sent out," he says, "for one of those short, plump

[2] *Ibid.*, p. 248.

little cakes called *petites madeleines,* which look as though they had been moulded in the fluted scallop of a pilgrim's shell." And so, "mechanically, wearily," after this dull day which had brought nothing but "the prospect of a depressing horror," he raises to his lips a spoonful of tea in which he had soaked a bit of one of these little scallop-shells of pastry, "so richly sensual under its severe, religious folds."

What happens? "No sooner had the warm liquid, and the crumbs with it, touched my palate," he goes breathlessly on, "than a shudder ran through my whole body, and I stopped, intent upon the extraordinary changes that were taking place. An exquisite pleasure had invaded my senses, but with no suggestion of its origin. And at once the vicissitudes of life had become indifferent, its disasters innocuous, its brevity illusory. . . . I had ceased to feel mediocre, accidental, mortal.

"I retrace my thoughts to the moment at which I drank the first spoonful. . . . I find the same state, illuminated by no fresh light. I compel my mind to make one further effort to follow and recapture once again the fleeting sensation. . . . I stop my ears and inhibit all attention to the sounds which come from the next room. Feeling that my mind is growing fatigued, I compel it for a change to enjoy that distraction which I have just denied it, to think of other things, to rest and refresh itself.

"And then for the second time I clear an empty space in front of it. I place in position before my mind's eye the still recent taste of that first mouthful, and I feel something start within me, something that has been embedded like an anchor at a great depth; I do not yet know what it is, but I can feel it mounting slowly; I can measure the resistance, I can hear the echo of great spaces traversed."

Abruptly, he fathoms the mystery. He has refound the trail to his lost youth, the innocence which underlay his corruption. It lives again in a new sort of memory which re-creates the past in all its reality. "The taste was that of the little crumb of *madeleine,"* which "on Sunday mornings at Combray" his Aunt Léonie used to give him when we went to her to say good-bye before going to mass—the *madeleine* which she used to dip "first in her own cup of real or of lime-flower tea."

It was as if a panel had opened in a solid wall. The opacity of matter is conquered. Soon his whole childhood begins to unroll before his eyes. He recalls how he has had faint visions of this sort before, upon going to bed early and then coming half awake some little time later, with "only the most rudimentary sense of existence," more "destitute of human qualities than the cave-dweller," but filled with memories not yet of the place in which he happened to be, but of various other places where once he had lived. And then it would always seem as if a rope were let down from heaven to draw him up "out of the abyss of not-being." He would have glimpses of Combray, of "the little parlour, the dining-room, the alluring shadows of the path, the hall, the bedroom, seen always at the evening hour, isolated from all surroundings, as though all Combray had consisted of but two floors joined by a slender staircase, and as though there had been no time there but seven o'clock at night."

But the *madeleine* is yet more potent than these half-waking dreams. It not only opens a panel, it flings down the wall, letting in a flood of the long-distant past, of things broken, scattered, still, alone, fragile, but vital, substantial, persistent, faithful, like souls waiting and hoping for their moment amid the ruins of all the rest, bearing unfalteringly upon this tiny and almost impalpable drop of their essence imprisoned in the taste and smell of things, "the vast structure of recollection." [3]

And so the novel [4] begins, with this recaptured life, with a certain night when, "because of company," the child must go to bed without his mother's kiss.

"I must set forth without viaticum; must climb each step of the staircase against my heart, climbing in opposition to my heart's desire—which was to return to my mother, since she had not, by her kiss, given my heart leave to accompany me forth."

I have brutally abbreviated this most lovely prelude to a masterpiece, but even so the *madeleine* seems to have evoked not only new life but a new Proust—the real Proust, purged of all his moral diseases, rid of his theories, a novelist such as the world may not soon hope to see again.

"That hateful staircase gave out a smell of varnish which had to some extent absorbed, made definite and fixed, the special quality of sorrow, more cruel, perhaps, now than ever, because—when it assumed this olfactory guise—intelligence was powerless to resist it."

[3] *Vide* "Swann's Way," "The Overture."

[4] *À la recherche du temps perdu* ("Remembrance of Things Past"), in eight volumes, as follows: (1) *Du côté de chez Swann,* 1913; (2) *À l'ombre des jeunes filles en fleur,* Goncourt prize, 1918; (3) *Le côté de Guermantes,* 1919; (4) *Le côté de Guermantes,* pt. ii, together with *Sodome et Gomorrhe,* pt. i, 1921; (5) *Sodome et Gomorrhe,* pt. ii, 1922; (6) *La prisonnière,* 1924; (7) *Albertine disparue;* (8) *Le temps retrouvé.* With the exception of the last three volumes, which as yet are to be had only in French, the series, translated by C. K. Scott-Moncrieff, has been published in English under the following titles. "Swann's Way," "In a Budding Grove," "The Guermantes' Way" (in two parts), and "The Cities of the Plain."

And so the tale unfolds, each part introduced by one of these flashlight experiences following some trivial, unforeseen touch upon the senses. In *Le temps retrouvé,* for instance, on his way to his final call upon the Guermantes, the hero is forced by a passing vehicle to step to one side and to put his foot upon a paving-stone which is lower than the others. And immediately—

"All discouragement vanished before the same felicity which, at divers epochs of my life, had given me the vision of trees that I had thought to recognize during some *promenade en voiture* about Balbec; the sight of the bell-towers of Martinville; the savour of a *madeleine* dipped in an infusion of tea; and all those other sensations of which I have spoken, and that the last works of Vinteuil [composer of the oft-mentioned sonata] had seemed to synthesize."

This time he is transported to Venice, the unequal pavement having brought to his mind that of the basilica of Saint Mark's. And as the author has promised in the first volume sometime to reveal the source of the joy which such experiences always give him, he now proceeds to do so. Their secret, he says, lies in the fact that these memories are "outside of time." In them "the past imposes itself upon the present."

"The being in me which then tasted this impression," he continues, "tasted in it that which the ancient day and the present have in common, that which they had of the extra-temporal," and the self which tasted "was that real self, the same now as yesterday."

What shall we say of this philosophy as philosophy? As a literary conceit, an expedient for putting a narrative effectively before the reader, it is beyond praise—though

Proust, I think, rather overworked it. But has it any parallel in actual human experience?

Of course everybody knows of those moments when life seems double, running for the second time over an old track—that little shiver which nineteenth-century psychologists used quaintly to explain by the now exploded theory that they were caused by the two lobes of the brain functioning in duplicate but not quite simultaneously. Proust, in fact, frequently compares his flashes to these twice lived moments. He must have something to distinguish them from ordinary memories. But from what flows from them we can see plainly that they are nothing of what he tries to make them out to be. Few things are less vivid than those impressions we have of living the same instant for the second time. The past, with all its sights, sounds, scents, and feelings, does not come back to us then. No book could be written by gazing through such half-open panels as these.

No, the Proust flashlight experience is really a flash of inspiration, and, if expressed in this homely and old-fashioned language, is intelligible enough. What he had when he tasted the *madeleine* or stepped upon the uneven pavement was an idea. There was no stepping outside of time. That is merely inverted Bergson. What did happen, evidently, was that strange, new assembling of ancient impressions into an intelligible and logical pattern, giving at last a meaning to what had been but a series of incidents. That the understanding of them was due to something extra-temporal, to the stirring of that self which is not plural but unique, I have not a doubt in the world. Perhaps this is the explanation which Proust was groping after but was prevented, by his lack of real belief in the

Great Spirit whom he occasionally invoked, from ever clearly putting into words.

As to the joy which came to him—and of course again I mean his hero, for though Proust must have known such moments, it is not to be supposed that they arrived with exactly the trappings which in his fiction he chose to drape them—this joy was probably but that romantic ecstasy which no one who has lived beyond a short span of years fails to feel when brooding over other days. There is, after all, a thrill in being young.

And to Proust these other days were especially precious. He had the nostalgia of the invalid for lost health, of the apostate for the denied Master. He was a Peter dreaming that he was living again before the cock crew. But he could never return in truth, only in fancy. He reached as far as art, that sense of the inner divinity of things which sometimes leads to a sense of the divinity of life. That latter sense, however, he failed to achieve, so persistently did he cling to the illusion that the shadow is more real than the substance, the inspired more real than the inspirer, deceived by the notion that because matter remains opaque when looked upon by blinded, everyday eyes, the divinity seen by eyes at times more full of light is by these eyes created. He remains to the end the great sick man of the novel.

As such—and with incredible skill, it must be admitted—he flings his hero for one last scene into the Guermantes' library, where he must wait for the conclusion of a number on the musical program before entering the *grand salon.* An old servant offers him an orange. He eats, and wipes his lips with a napkin.

"And immediately, like a personage in 'The Arabian Nights' who, without knowing it, has performed precisely the rite which makes appear, visible to him alone, a docile genie ready to transport him to a distance, a new vision of azure passed before my eyes. I thought that the domestic was going to open the window upon the beach [a window in this mansion on the Champs-Élysées which seems to look out upon Balbec]; that all invited me to descend, to promenade along the dike of the high sea. The napkin which I had taken to wipe my mouth had precisely the sort of roughness and starchiness of one which I had [used] before the window that first day of my arrival at Balbec. And now, in this library of the hotel of the Guermantes, it unfolded, shaking from its creases the plumage of an ocean, green and blue like the tail of a peacock."

Other experiences of the same sort fall thick and fast. But the musical number is ended. It is the hero's last return to the world after a long exile. He approaches the threshold beyond which his old friends await him—and he thinks that a masquerade is in progress.

"For a moment," he says, "I did not understand why I hesitated to recognize the master of the house, the guests. Each one seemed to be made up, powdered, in a way which changed them completely. The Prince seemed to have rigged himself out to represent one of the 'Ages of Life.'

"Most extraordinary of all was my personal enemy, Monsieur d'Argencourt, the real hit of the matinée. Not only in place of his hair, once hardly grey, was he muffled in an extraordinary beard of an incredible whiteness, but, besides, there were so many little material changes serving here to lessen, there to enlarge his person, and even more to change his apparent character, his personality, that he had become an old beggar who no longer inspired any respect—this man of whom the solemnity, the harsh starchiness, was still present in my memory. And he gave to his character of old spendthrift such an air of truth that his legs did not cease for a moment to tremble nor the relaxed features of his face, habitually so proud, to smile with foolish beatitude. Pushed to such a degree, the art of disguise became something more—a real transformation.

"But I did not congratulate Monsieur d'Argencourt for having offered a spectacle which seemed to extend the limits of the possible transformation of the human body, because the same difficulty that I had experienced in giving the right name to these faces about me seemed to be shared by all those who perceived my own."

It was no masquerade, no optical illusion. What he saw was his friends grown old, the spectacle of persons "situated at the end of the deforming vista of Time."

CHAPTER IX

THE MEANING OF MENCKEN

THE philosophers heretofore considered are for the most part afflicted with the idea that nothing is real but their imaginings. Before passing on to realists superficially of a sterner sort, it might be well to say a few words about one whose grasp of reality is genuine, practical rather than theoretical.

For years the name of H. L. Mencken was used throughout American to frighten children with. His *Smart Set* scandalized the populace by hinting that sex-differentiation was not confined to clothes, nor caresses to kisses. The hinting was done in a rather sticky way and with the smirk of a bad conscience, but one could not have expected innocent outspokenness in the periodicals of a country which still pretended to respect Anthony Comstock. And yet *The Smart Set* was so little smart and so totally set that it barred even such expressions as "She then went home with him." I know, for I once tried to get it to print that very sentence, and Mr. Mencken's Mr. Nathan said it would never do in the world. Seems quaint, does it not, in these post-"Hatrack" days?

"Hatrack" was the one effort of *The American Mercury* to live up to the reputation which its editor had managed to acquire during his earlier campaigns of moral sniping. Apart from this, our green-dressed messenger of the gods has devoted itself to the accumulation and dissemination of facts and general information with such a serious purpose that one sometimes wonders if the guardian angel of selectivity will arrive in time. Even "Americana" threatens to sink beneath the weight of responsibility and German thoroughness. But "Hatrack" was a shot to the mark.

It was, too, a much more honest and commendable piece of work than were the lubrications of the old *Smart Set* authors. For one thing, its aim was social and political rather than literary, and Editor Mencken's "Prejudices" in these directions are much more enlightened and genuine than his "Prefaces" for books and predilections for music and pictures. What ails the sage of Baltimore is a burning passion for personal liberty. This enables him to discover every new genius who nails the skull and crossbones to the mast. But it makes him uncritical of æsthetic values. Not every buccaneer is seven feet tall. A novel is not necessarily great merely because it enrages the Society for the Suppression of Vice.

Only when he turns to politics, pure and simple, does Mr. Mencken's excessive partiality for the under-dog finally leave him. For music, art, and literature he has only a taste, not too well informed. He has told us that every summer he leafs over the old philosophers, refreshing his memory from a hammock; but he never seems really to have rolled up his sleeves and wrestled with them for their inner meaning. As a matter of fact, he is not much interested in inner meanings, and in the mazes of the abstract he is lost. No, Mencken's genius is that of a statesman, of a sociologist.

In this field he is not so easily to be fooled. "I have known all of the principal gladiators of the [socialist] movement in my time, at least in America," he says.[1] "I have yet to meet one who was not as gullible as a Mississippi darkey, nay, even as a Mississippi white man." Exactly. And Mr. Mencken is not. He sees that "what they [the fathers] dreamed of and fought for was a civilization based upon a body of simple, equitable and reasonable laws—a code designed to break the chains of lingering mediævalism, and set the individual free."[2] And it is that dream—of a balanced government, leaning neither too much to the right nor to the left—which he wants to see come true. I can imagine no better ideal for an American public man.

But of course there is even here that Mencken "prejudice," that shadow of carelessly acquired data, which seems to dim the Mencken spotlight no matter where it is thrown. Rather more individual freedom existed beneath the chains of mediævalism than our sweeping stylist imagines. And if it was not always perfect in practice, that was because the *moyen âge,* like any other age, was sometimes false to itself. But the theory was there in all its pristine splendour, the doctrine of the responsibility and independence of the human soul. Should such mediævalism as we still have cease to linger among us, then would the citizen finally succumb to the State, and have no rights whatever which the *Polizei* were bound to respect. Mencken, though German, has simply picked up the word "mediæval" as it is used in New England and has found its way into Maryland.

He sees readily enough that temporal government must compromise between conflicting interests, that it cannot

[1] "Prejudices," sixth series, p. 98.
[2] *Ibid.,* p. 76.

always wait for the consent of the governed—not when these show a disposition to tread unnecessarily upon their neighbours' toes. He understands, too, that it is folly to sacrifice the citizen to the glory of an abstraction, as if the State were a creature for whose benefit we creatures of flesh and blood were bound to exist. In fact, he knows very well that whenever the demand for such Moloch-worship goes up, some compact little minority is seeking its own meddlesome ends camouflaged as the greatest good of the greatest number, that we have to deal with a band whose opinion is, "The State, that's us!"

But when confronted with the ancient doctrine of absolutism in spiritual truth, he jumps to the conclusion that the theory implies that some men not only have that truth but understand it in all its human applications and must claim the right to impose it upon everybody by force of arms. Men often did make that mistake, even in the Middle Ages—and the Reformation was their just reward. But those qualified to speak never had it in theory, and it was much less evident in practice than Luther-tinted historians would have us believe. The mediæval peasant was allowed to do as he pleased to an extent which would make the modern Rotarian dizzy. I doubt if we still have legs stout enough to stand up beneath such a weight of personal responsibility.

Mencken is really a Superpuritan rather than an Impuritan. That is, instead of carrying Puritan faults to excess and so arriving at licence through the bursting of strait-lacing, in the way which is now so common, he seeks a golden and older mean—to be himself mediæval, in short, without knowing it. He has listened agape to too many Puritan old wives' tales to be able to give his tendencies the right name. Nevertheless he would like to undo some of the harm which a too hasty evacuation of Rome brought upon us, would be very pleased indeed to find at least some substitutes for various useful things which we inadvertently left behind us in our flight. He struggles valiantly to educate the "moron"; to teach him some history, even if it be only his own; to get him to recognize some authority, if it be only the new authority of science not too narrowly understood. Mencken simply cannot live without common sense. Even his pro-sex campaign, undertaken in the days when that dog had a bad name, stopped short of trying to make a god out of glands.

So let us pass over his little follies—not to mention a few big ones—and be thankful for his virtues, especially as every year the follies wither more and more and the virtues wax stronger and more discerning. But why should *I* attempt this panegyric? *The Commonweal,* an avowedly religious periodical, has in its issue for February 15, 1928, an article by its editor, Michael Williams, entitled "A Prayer for a Man Writing a Book." Mencken—he had actually asked for prayers through the *Mercury's* columns—is the man. And Williams prays as follows:

"We Catholics, my dear Mencken, more than a little agree with you, and some of us think you are doing a very useful work for the Church in certain points. And all of us who read you with any judgment and discrimination admire in you a devotion to many very noble things: freedom, truth, honesty, honour, courage, faith and beauty."

Thus ends the man who once tried to pass himself off as having hoofs and horns. The leading American pirate, scourge of wowsers, finds himself hailed as the scourge of God by the leading American layman of the Church of Rome. This is perhaps the saddest thing that ever happened.

CHAPTER X

THE CULT OF THE GOAT

I. JOYCE

"THE tendency to reason things out is but one impulse among many in the human being," says John Storck, in his recently published "Man and Civilization," "and its rôle in determining the contours of our lives both is and should be a relatively minor one."

If by this he means that the cultivation of the mind is a small matter in comparison with the development of character, a truer thing was never said. But it is doubtful if he means this at all. His words more probably express that mood of the moment which sets aside the tendency to reason things out in favour of the tendency to reason things half out or not at all, so that there may result not an increase of sympathy and self-control, but a letting loose of those passions which we commonly regard as animal, though they are much less evident in animals than in undisciplined human beings.

I am speaking, of course, of a mood which is primarily literary, and confined to a certain school of literature at that. By no means all of the public suffers from its infection. We still have our Knut Hamsuns and our Willa Sibert Cathers, and, thank Heaven, they are widely read. Probably, too, in that doubt of reality characteristic of our Weiningers and exemplified in the empty chasm which hides even beneath the concrete art of Proust, we have reached the turning-point in our philosophy, having marked a depth beneath which it is impossible to go.

Strict mechanists, such as Loeb and Watson,[1] tried to build us a rocky bottom, but this has dissolved in the crucibles of the new physics.[2] There are no longer any scientific objections even to Faith. Physics, of course, cannot furnish a foundation for Faith. In itself, physics cannot find a foundation even for itself. Nothing on earth has ever been able to find a foundation in itself for itself. Sociology tries to rest upon biology, biology upon physics and chemistry. So must the natural sciences rest upon the supernatural sciences—which means that the sought-for support from below suddenly turns out to be something to depend on from above. And now, if we can but overcome our recent habit of not reasoning things out, can begin to realize once more that the soul has wings instead of feet, we may be able to escape from the absurd predicament in which half-logic has landed us.

Meanwhile there are those who, instead of making the rôle of reason a minor one, make it relatively nil. These do not attempt to answer the arguments of the all-doubting epistemologists; they simply are not interested in them. What difference, they say, does it make how we know, how we feel? We do feel and know, don't we? At least we feel. Let doddering grandpa sit by the fire, if he will, and puzzle his brains about his brains. He is occupied with the only part of himself which still functions. The rising generation is conscious of arms and legs—legs more especially. So the animalist takes refuge in his body. He is no real animal. That is a level to which we cannot

[1] *Vide* "The Misbehaviorists," chap. ii.
[2] *Ibid.*, chap. v.

JAMES JOYCE
Rotten eggs by fancy laid

innocently return. Decidedly he is a creature who has seen better days. His is the "Portrait of the Artist as a Young Man"; at his worst his name is Stephen Dedalus; his most eminent painter is James Joyce, an Irishman.

"O, come, all you Roman Catholics that never went to mass." [3] For here again we have a Protestant revolt fresh from the arms of the Church, exhausted by no wanderings among the doctrines of Luther.

No doubt these writers, as they shy away from all restraint, have been more influenced (in a contrary sense) by historical Puritanism than they would like to admit. But they have certainly escaped any such degree of intellectualization as artistic young men born of Scotch Presbyterian parents, for example, were forced to absorb even while being suckled by their mothers. These newcomers are more like sudden orphans brought up on nursing-bottles, or on the teats of some she-wolf astray in the forest.

They had, even they must confess, mothers of their own. They are unable to start new-born from the primal ooze. The past continues to trouble them accordingly. They are only reactionists, after all, whose mother let them fall, and out of this situation they manage to get what one may call a considerable kick. How tame it would be to preach nakedness to a world which had never worn clothes! Can you imagine an unbaptized penguin, bird so dear to Anatole France, being much bucked up by a sense of sin?

But these are fowl of a less purely avian description, and that a sense of sin does have a bucking-up effect as

[3] "A Portrait of the Artist as a Young Man," by James Joyce; first published, 1916; revised edition, 1924; Jonathan Cape, Ltd., Bedford Sq., London; p. 39.

to certain faculties is shown by Joyce himself. His "Chamber Music," his "Dubliners," his "Exiles" merely displayed a talent for writing. Only as he became more outrageous, as in the "Portrait," did he give much promise of setting his adopted Thames on fire; and only when, in "Ulysses," he finally threw all decency to the winds, did the water passing under London Bridge (to say nothing of those reaching to Brooklyn) begin actually to blaze with the heat of his inspiration.

It is, for one thing, easier to write pornography than to write "Idylls of the King," even mediocre ones; easier to produce a sensation in the reader's mind when the limit is off than when conventions hold the pen in check. Who can peruse without mental disturbance of some sort these passages which set out in black and white what used to be indicated only by a blank space feebly dotted with asterisks? Such passages have the thrill of novelty—in print, that is, though most of us males were made familiar with their phraseology through early examination of the walls of the old primary-school latrine. True, the novelty soon wears off, but meanwhile the author is stimulated by a sense of his own audacity.

Joyce never did much conscious thinking, even of an evil sort, and so has escaped the blackest curse of all. He merely lets himself sink. At one time he was even interested in affairs, giving almost as much attention to the politics of Dublin as does Mencken to the election doings in the corn, hog, and Bible belts. "Didn't the bishops of Ireland," he enquires,[4] "betray us in the time of the Union, when Bishop Lanigan presented an address of loyalty to the Marquis of Cornwallis? Didn't the bishops and priests sell the aspirations of their country in

[4] *Ibid.*, p. 43.

1829 in return for the Catholic emancipation?" As was to be expected, his was an anticlerical politics. Yet it showed him still concerned with the past rather than with the present or future.

But he tries to bring Dedalus up to date. Here is a hero who is a literary man, as so many novelists' heroes are. But he is that curious thing, a "poet" drawn by what psychologists call an extrovert—that is, by a man whose inner life is meagre, who must feed continually upon outer and material things. He is dizzy with animal passion. Indeed, this vertigo, since it manifests itself in a nature much more simple and thoughtless than Proust, outswings anything to be found in the entire *Recherche*. It takes us reeling through filth with a giddy ecstasy impossible to any fall less abrupt than from unsophisticated Faith to a cesspool.

So Dedalus wanders "up and down the dark slimy streets peering into the gloom of lanes and doorways, listening eagerly for any sound." He moans to himself "like some baffled prowling beast." He stretches out his arms to the street, hoping to "hold fast the frail swooning form that eluded him." The cry that he has been strangling in his throat issues finally from his lips, breaking from him "like a wail of despair from a hell of sufferers," and dies "in a wail of furious entreaty, a cry for iniquitous abandonment, a cry which was but the echo of an obscene scrawl which he had read on the oozing wall of a urinal." [5] Precisely. Nor are these scrawls left to the reader's imagination. Scorning quotation marks, Joyce yet quotes.

He tells how some of the boys were once caught "smuggling"—which is not the word he has in mind, but as daring a one as he is yet ready to venture—in a place that

[5] *Ibid.*, p. 113.

"was all thick slabs of slate," where "water trickled all day out of tiny pinholes and there was a queer smell of stale water." And behind the door there was "a drawing in red pencil." [6] Upon the wall of another closet "there was written in backhand in beautiful writing" a thrilling commentary upon ancient history, as follows: "Julius Cæsar wrote The Calico Belly."

Stirred by things like these, Dedalus wants "to sin with another of his kind, to force another being to sin with him and to exult with her in sin." One night "a young woman dressed in a long pink gown" lays her hand on his arm, detaining him in his walk. She "gazed into his face," and says, "Good night, Willie, dear." His cup of bliss runs over. He tries to "bid his tongue speak that he might seem at ease, watching her. He closed his eyes . . . conscious of nothing in the world but the dark pressure of her softly parting lips. . . . Darker than the swoon of sin, softer than sound or odour." [7]

There are those who credit Joyce with a fine, ironic intent, who imagine him gazing down from some serene Olympus, or at least as thinking all the while puckishly to himself: "Lord! What fools these mortals be!" But to me it seems that the dyer's hand has succumbed to its job, that he becomes his own bad boy staggering beneath the blows of an unholy, ill-taught adolescence. The inspiration of privies and brothels was too overwhelming to be controlled, and so it poured forth in an unparalleled sentimentality which moves one both to gag and to laugh.

Yet Stephen is squeamish, too. Not any and every stink pleases him. True, when once he tried to perform a self-imposed penance, he could find no odour "against which

[6] *Ibid.*, pp. 47–48.
[7] *Ibid.*, pp. 113–115.

his sense of smell revolted" save "a certain stale fishy stink like that of long-standing urine," which was a very remarkable circumstance in view of the aphrodisiac effect already attributed to this very perfume. But consistency is far from Joyce's aim. Stephen no more hangs together than do the fæces of a sheep.

Visiting Queen's College with his father (who was once a medical student there), he sees the word "fœtus" cut in the dark-stained wood of a desk, and "the sudden legend startled his blood," so that he feels himself "shrink" from the company of men capable of having carved such a horror in their youth. Also we are bidden to note that while cows out to grass in the clean fields are well enough, in winter "the first sight of the filthy cowyard at Stradbrook with its foul green puddles and clots of liquid dung and streaming bran troughs" had always "sickened Stephen's heart."

Nevertheless, at the porch of the morgue "he breathed slowly the rank heavy air." On another occasion, " 'That is horse-piss and rotten straw,' he thought. 'It is a good odour to breathe. It will calm my heart.' "[8] Evidently a delicately poised young man, for when he is compelled to watch "three glasses being raised from the counter" of a pub, "as his father and his two cronies drank [beer] to the memory of their past," he is aware that "an abyss of fortune or of temperament sundered him from them." True enough, it did, for "no life or youth stirred in him as it stirred in them. He had known neither the pleasure of companionship with others nor the vigour of rude male health nor filial piety. Nothing stirred within his soul but a cold and cruel and loveless lust."[9] Joyce pauses

[8] *Ibid.,* p. 98.
[9] *Ibid.,* p. 108.

occasionally thus to point a moral—a moral usually without point, since it seldom points to anything better than the evil it points at.

And he pretends that the Jesuits were very anxious that a young man like his hero should join their order *ad majorem Dei gloriam!* Here the anticlerical *motif* sounds forth its antiphonal to the piping of a Pan not yet forest-clean from the degenerate civilization he has passed through on his way to the woods. But Stephen says nay to holy orders. He is, it seems, a poet and no monk. This, in fact, is the portrait of a poet. Not that he writes poetry. He is a poet pure and simple—we have his creator's word for it. So, though the opportunity of learning just "what was the sin of Simon Magus, and what the sin against the Holy Ghost for which there is no forgiveness," and the lure of various "obscure things, hidden from others" but likely to be "murmured into his ears in the confessional under the shame of a darkened chapel," [10] does tempt him for a moment, he elects to deprive the Society of Jesus of his adherence and to matriculate at the University of Dublin. He wishes to be "a priest of the eternal imagination, transmuting the daily bread of experience into the radiant body of everliving life," [11] which means, of course, the ever-living life of unwritten verses.

It is to be noted that, while Dedalus fails to become a consecrated follower of Saint Ignatius Loyola, he is offered as the typical product of a Jesuit school.

That the Jesuits can boast of at least their full share of pioneers and martyrs is a matter of history. That their ascetic remedy for the lusts of the flesh is always success-

[10] *Ibid.* p. 181.
[11] *Ibid.* p. 152.

ful is more than anyone may justly claim. The fact is, the ascetic serum not infrequently fails to "take," by whomsoever administered; and that there has been in the past a too indiscriminate prescription of overdoses of such prophylactic seems fairly obvious. Joyce here for once rises to the heights of irony, and turns against his hero. Disliking the Jesuits has been a favourite world-pastime for a great many years. Did not the Vatican itself once put a temporary extinguisher upon the Order? So why not sling Dedalus at them, as so much mud at a shining mark? He does not seem to me, however, sufficiently characteristic even of Jesuit failures to be likely to stick. Nor do I believe that Joyce really does not love his poet. Unless he loved him, could he have ended by dubbing him Ulysses?

2. A RIOT IN THE CHAPEL

I am unable to understand why the indulgence in typographical eccentricities should be taken as a mark of ultra-modernity. It was all very well in 1895, when Stephen Crane came out with "The Black Riders," printed without the benefit of punctuation marks or of any letters not capitals—all very well to say, as some then did, that the author was mad. But to-day, when Joyce rings what variations still are possible upon the old theme, sometimes Using his capitals Amiss, sometimes not at all, here sp acing in une xpected places, there runningeverythingtogether, the practice seems laboured and imitative.

It has, nevertheless, its uses. Words collected from *ben retiros* and *chalets de nécessité* are seen as in a glass and but darkly if there be confusion in the font, a riot in the chapel, and the printer's devil act as proofreader.

People with normal sensibilities, likely to be in good standing with the police, find the trouble of decipherment not worth their while. Others are therefore more apt to be left alone to enrich their knowledge of vernacular Anglo-Saxon.

For that is chiefly what this pother amounts to. The Anglo-Saxons, you may remember, were conquered once upon a time (to be frank, in the year 1066) by a certain William of Normandy, who turned his generals into nobles and froze the natives out of society by depriving them of all that was stealable in the way of earthly goods. Naturally the "vulgar" tongue became very unfashionable, especially that part of it which referred to those bodily functions of which humanity in general is least inclined to boast. Even nobles have bladders and intestines, without a doubt, but they seldom speak of theirs in the language of churls. The citizenry at large quickly follows suit. A portion of the vocabulary becomes taboo.

It acquires thus a certain immorality and grows poisonous with evil intent—like the earth beneath a drain which spreads pestilence if turned up to the sun. But sunlight soon undoes the harm, leaving this earth as sweet as any earth. So do vocabularies cease to be vulgar in any bad sense once they have had a thorough airing. Infection is to be feared only during the transition stage. Therefore the Joyce vocabulary tends every day to become more and more innocuous. It is rotten with a disease which cures itself, and the ultimate result is likely to be an increased strength and purity in our mother tongue and a healthy habit of calling a spade a spade. All that we will then need to remember is that a conversation exclusively about spades is hardly likely to be edify-

if aided now and then by a little tabloid of cascara sagrada.

Stephen is of finer stuff. He is even reputed to have killed his mother by refusing to kneel down by her when she was *in extremis*. But rent must be paid, though by free men in a towerhold, and Stephen for his share dabbles in journalism, acts as teacher to a class of boys, runs errands for the headmaster. For super-measure, he spouts literary criticism gratis, while realizing thoroughly the degradation of having occasionally to work. Haines, who is one of the towerholders, thinks that Stephen is not a gentleman—sufficient *raison d'être* for Haines, in my opinion. He also raves at night about a black panther, and so introduces the detective-story *motif*. This book is prodigal of *motifs*.

The bullockbefriender watches an old milk-woman "pour into the measure and thence into the jug rich white milk, not hers. Old shrunken paps." (Page 14.) The quotation is avowedly from the befriender's stream of consciousness, but usually the reader is left to guess what stream he is in, and with merely a sporting chance of guessing right.

Stephen goes out to give the day's lessons. He talks with his employer, Mr. Deasy. The boys, playing football before his eyes, enrich the stream: "Jousts. Time shocked rebounds, shocked by shock. Jousts, slush and uproar of battles, the frozen deathspew of the slain, a shout of spear spikes baited with men's bloodied guts." (Page 32.) At such times Stephen is almost a poet after all—of the Gertrude Stein sort. But nothing happens. "Naked eve, boms of sin. Where is poor dear Arius to try conclusions? Warring his life long on the contransmagnificandjewbangtantiality. Illstarred heresiarch. In a Greek water-closet he breathed his last: euthanasia." (Page 36.) No Stein would have written this. Nothing happens. "Ineluctable modality of the visible. . . . Seaspawn and seawrack, the nearing tide, that rusty foot. Snotgreen, bluesilver, rust." (Page 37.) Nothing continues to happen. (End of chapter one.)

The Bloom stream gives us "Sodom, Gomorra, Edom, a dead country, dead as an old woman's." (Page 59.) It seems that his wife, Molly, is deceiving him, for she hides a letter. And the scientific spirit has led him into an intrigue with a shadowy woman who wants to know what brand of cologne is affected by Mrs. Bloom. But he must to the funeral of one Paddy Digham.

This leads his thought-stream to concern itself with rats drinking beer, getting drunk, and puking in the vats, and of how corpses taste to the worms in the cemetery. He sees a dog return to its vomit. He thinks of a man lunching off the scruff of his own head, "cheapest lunch in Dublin."

And so "they drove on past Brian Boroimhe's house. Near it now.—I wonder how is our friend Fogarty getting on, Mr Power said.—Better ask Tom Kerna, Mr Dedalus [Stephen's father] said.—How is that? Martin Cunningham said. Left him weeping I suppose.—Though lost to sight, Mr Dedalus said, to memory dear. The carriage steered left for Finglad road"—and I have attempted to steer my way through this copy without materially improving the typography. The funeral continues to the end of page 111, when variety is introduced by means of heading every paragraph with a caption as little relevant as possible. Also the scene is in a newspaper office, and realism demands that the page shall have a journalistic look, as for instance:

ORTHOGRAPHICAL

Want to be sure of his spelling. Proof fever. Martin Cunningham forgot to give us his spellingbee conundrum this morning. It is amusing to view the unpar one ar alleled embarra two ars is it? double ess ment of a harassed pedlar while gauging au the symmetry of a peeled pear under a cemetery wall. Silly, isn't it? Cemetery put in of course on account of the symmetry.

And so fou no no u forth and so one o forth. Bloom exit. Enter Stephen, who listens while J. J. O. Molloy tells of someone mentioning "the Moses of Michelangelo in the Vatican." There is talk of Blavatsky, and the letterpress is made chromatic by the introduction of semiobsolete English nouns relating to the excretory functions.

Bloom again. "A warm human plumpness settled down on his brain. . . . Perfume of embraces all him assailed. With hungered flesh obscurely, he mutely craved to adore." (Page 160.) He has found a restaurant against whose scenes not even the scientific appetite can contend.

Stephen. He seems to have some theory of Shakespeare. He has to have. The idea that he is a genius must be brought to the fore. Haines well says, "Shakespeare is the happy hunting ground of all minds that have lost their balance," but Buck Mulligan appears to think that when Haines "missed Dedalus on Hamlet" he suffered an irreparable loss. Buck explains Stephen by again blaming the Jesuits. "They drove his wits astray by visions of hell." (Page 239.) We are given to understand that Ann Hathaway was false, that she wooed Will against his Will. Further variety is introduced in the form of a bit of plainsong in the old notation, apropos of nothing. *"Nous ferons de petites cochonneries. Minette? Tu veux?"* (Page 193.)

Introduction of Œdipus *motif*. "A father and son," says Stephen, "are sundered by a bodily shame so steadfast that the criminal annals of the world, stained with all other incests and bestialities, hardly record its breach. Sons with mothers, sires with daughters, lesbic sisters, loves that dare not speak their name, nephews with grandmothers, jailbirds with keyholes, queens with prize bulls. The son unborn mars beauty; born, he brings pain, divides affection, increases care. He is a male: his growth is his father's decline, his youth his father's envy, his friend his father's enemy. . . . In rue Monsieur-le-Prince I thought it. . . . What links them in nature? An instant of blind rut." (Page 199.)

An attendant from the doorway announces that Father Dineen waits without. "Swiftly rectly creaking rectly rectly," Dedalus "was rectly gone." (Page 102.)

Bloom's stream. "Melting breast ointments. Armpits' oniony sweat. Fishgluey slime. Feel! Press! Crushed. Sulphur dung of lions." (Page 227.)

Eloquence *motif*. "Stephen Dedalus watched through the webbed window and the showtrays. Dust darkened the toiling fingers with the vulture nails. Dust slept on . . . bronze and silver, lozenges of cinnabar, on rubies, leperous and winedark stones. Born all in the dark wormy earth, cold specks of fire, evil lights shining in the darkness. Where fallen archangels flung the stars off their brows." (Pages 231 and 232.)

"What is this? Eighth and ninth book of Moses"—in a bookshop down Bedford Row where Stephen has gone, swinging his "ashplant."

"Secret of all secrets. Seal of King David." The wizard *motif,* that hint of the existence of a secret learning, so dear to the unschooled. Simon Magus. Paracelsus. Hocuspocus. Ghost stories in the bright day.

"Bronze by gold hears the hoofirons, steelyringing
Imperthnthn thnthnthn.
Chips, picking chips off rocky thumbnails, chips.
Horrid! And gold flushed more.
A husky fifenote blew.
Blew. Blue bloom is on the
Gold pinnacled hair.
A jumping rose on satiny breasts of satin, roses of Castile.
Trilling, trilling: Idolores.
Peep? Who's in the . . . peepofgold?
Tink cried to bronze in pity.
And a call, pure, long and throbbing. Longindying call.
Decoy. Soft word. But look! The bright stars fade. O rose! Notes
Chirruping answer. Castile. The morn is breaking.
Jingle jingle jaunting jingling.
Coin rang. Clock clacked.
Avowal. Sonnez. I could. Rebound of garter. Not leave thee. Smack.
La cloche! Thigh smack. Avowal. Warm. Sweetheart, goodbye!"

Thus do words pass through the mind linked by superficial association, especially if one be well drunken or mildly insane, drifting like leaves in the wake of some emotion. We glimpse the intelligence of an oyster. But much of the mystery is obtained by printing this prematurely on page 244. The incident which awakened it is not recorded till page 247, when "Miss Kennedy sauntered sadly from bright light, twining a loose hair behind an ear. Sauntering sadly, gold no more, she twisted twined a hair. Sadly she twined in sauntering gold hair behind a curving ear."

More mystery by transposing—now not pages but passages. "Miss gaze of Kennedy, heard not seen, read on. Lenehan round the sandwichbell wound his round body round." (Page 251.) "Miss gaze of Kennedy," for "The gaze of Miss Kennedy." This ought to make a new game. Considering the fate of mah jong, the crossword, and askmeanother, it is not probable that pencil bridge will last for ever.

Variety by old and unrepeatable gags. And then Dedalus senior comes into the bar and sings: "When first I saw that form endearing." Tears. "Through the hush of air a voice sang to them, low, not rain, not leaves in murmur, like no voice of strings of reeds . . . touching their still ears with words. . . . Good to hear; sorrow from them each seemed to from both depart when first they heard." The author tries to appear nonchalant by pieing a few sentences, but we have him now. Sophistication? Merely dung-dust upon an "Abie's Irish Rose." For the veritable "History of the Water Closet" we shall have to go to Cabaniss after all; for horror, to Mirbeau.

What, then, was the object in writing this "Ulysses"?

To demonstrate (*a*) the gullibility of the public, (*b*) the purchasing power of money derived of the fool from whom it so soon parted, (*c*) the limits to which it is possible to go.

Were there any other elements save these of gratification involved?

Yes and no. Ungratifying as to the higher faculties, of necessity as to the lower put in control.

As for instance?

The necessity of a beastly instinct to grow at the expense of its betters, the love of money versus the love of a good name, the instinct to soil clean paper, the rage of the self-condemned against innocence.

Could anybody have done this?

No.

Why not?

Because few have the gall. Also (*a*) a bad painter may make a bad picture, while (*b*) a non-painter would produce no picture at all, and (*c*) only a good painter can produce the worst; moreover, (*d*) this is at least not the ordinary hypocrisy of pretending to have the thoughts and motives we wish we had, but the real inside of a certain skull.

What was the object apart from objects already stated?

To create an opportunity for the writing down of blasphemies, obscenities, immoralities, and more especially the Four Forbidden Words, while preserving face.

How was this saving of face accomplished?

By a smoke-screen.

In what way may a smoke-screen save the face?

By (*a*) obscuring or hiding it, by (*b*) giving it a halo of apparent significance which attracts attention from the features.

Of what is this screen composed?

Of words written out of their common order; of words deprived of their usual companion words explaining the connexion of one with another; of words derived from dictionaries and no longer in common use; of words from foreign languages, notably the French, Italian, and

Latin; of words in dialect argot patois; of words misspelled and botched; of words at times multiplied beyond all reason or belief.

In what manner does this differ from hoax or spoof?

In no manner whatever.

Why, then, is not such mystification denounced?

Because of the fear of mankind to be caught not understanding that which it does not understand, making the individual eternally prone to pretend to find a meaning in that which is meaningless, or importance in that which is unimportant.

Do not, then, exceptional people term Joyce a genius?

Assuredly.

Why?

For (*a*) the reason just indicated, for (*b*) the reason that he is one, for (*c*) the reason that to have read a forbidden book gives the same satisfaction as comes from purchasing an illegal drink, since neither is vended except to those personally known and trusted of the bootlegger, and (*d*) for the reason that not to speak highly of the same is to belittle the privilege thus obtained.

Aside from this, what inducement is offered the reader for incurring such labour?

He is rewarded by the assurance there is no high nor low, and therefore no necessity for attempting to ascend.

And in what consists the joy contained in the receiving of this reward?

The joy of envy, hatred, malice, and all uncharitableness.

Is all this a quotation from the work in question?

No, but it might have been.

Why, then, was it undertaken?

For the sake (*a*) of showing that it is not so difficult, and for the sake of (*b*) of variety.

On page 408 of the Shakespeare Edition, 8th printing —not to be confused with the 2,000 numbered copies of the second printing, of which 500 (see advertisement) were burned by the New York Post Office authorities, egged on by the press-agent or moved by the unprompted instinct of publicity, nor with the 500 numbered copies of the third printing, of which 499 (*vide ibid.*) were seized by officials of the Custom House—Joyce himself, for the sake of more variety still, drops into the dramatic form.

This play within a play lets fall every so often a foul word or two, like droppings in a *vespasiano,* and might most properly be performed in the lazaretto of the violent ward in an asylum for the criminal insane. It introduces not only Stephen and Bloom, but the Scap (unfortunately a small part), Sweney, the Loiterers, the Shebeenkeeper, the Wreaths, a Voice from the Gallery. J. J. O. Molloy, Longhand and Shorthand, the Sluts, the Ragamuffins, the Bawd, the Nameless One, the Jurors, the Quoits (bed-weights), Paddy Digham (deceased), the Bells, Zoe, the Torchbearers, a Millionheiress, a Noblewoman, a Feminist, a Blacksmith, the Peers, Tom Kernan, Pisser Burke, Nosy Flynn, the Mob, the Veiled Sibyl, Alexander J. Dowie, Brother Buzz, a Papal Nuncio, a Dead Hand, the Irish Evicted Tenants, Mesias, the Male Brutes, the End of the World, Elijah, the Gramaphone, the Three Whores, the Beatitudes, the Gasjet, Philip Sober, Philip Drunk, the Cardinal, the Doorhandle, the Fan, the Hoof, the Sins of the Past, the Circumcised, the Nymph, the Echo, the Nannygoat, Shakespeare, the Green Lodges, the Pianola, the Hue and Cry, the Croppy Boy, the Demon Barber, Biddy the Clap, Edward the Seventh, Adonai, old Gummy Granny, the Horse, and many, many others altogether too numerous to mention. It is a feast of words introduced in list-form just for the pleasure which reading gives. Bloom takes Stephen home. Bloom goes to bed. The narrative is resumed.

Follow take-offs: on the Scholastic philosophers; on *Le morte Arthure;* on "Pilgrim's Progress"; on such other masterpieces as happen to intrude memories into the author's stream of consciousness. Then the inevitable result of introducing the Unabridged into Grammar School:

"Universally that person's acumen is esteemed very little perceptive concerning whatsoever matters are being held as most profitable by with sapience endowed to be studied who is ignorant of that which the most in doctrine erudite and certainly by reason of that in them high mind's ornament deserving of veneration constantly maintained when by general consent they affirm that other circumstances being equal by no exterior splendour is the prosperity of a nation more efficaciously asserted than by the measure of how far forward may have progressed the tribute of its solicitude for that proliferent continuance which the evils of the original if it be absent when fortunately present constitutes the certain sign of omnipollent nature's incorrupted benefaction." (Page 367.) He has little wisdom who does not know that the amount of solicitude felt for fecundity is the measure of the strength of a nation. There is no denying it. Which leads us to—

"The National Maternity Hospital, 29, 30 and 31 Holles street, of which . . . Dr A Horne (lic in Midw., F.K.Q.C.P.I.) is the able and popular master." *Dénoue-*

ment. Haines, with certain other gentlemen—of whom "Stephen he was the most drunken"—are here assembled, not in search of professional service, but in the kitchen, there to make merrie with the mead. Meet also Mr. Sometimes Godly, Mr. Ape Swilltale, Mr. Bird-in-the-hand, and Carnal Concupiscence. In the room above lieth Mistress Purefoy, "whose time hieth fast." The author indulges in "words so embiyyrtrf sd yo svvudr in yhrit dprskrt sn unhrslyhinrdd, a flair, for the cruder things of life." (Page 401.) Haines admits that in the first chapter he screamed at the phantom panther because he is the murderer of Samuel Childs. And so, the plot disposed of, we come finally to Mrs. Bloom's stream of consciousness without punctuation.

She is at home in bed by her sleeping husband's side, chewing the cud of old lusts and loves, ruminating more especially upon the well-remembered day of Bloom's proposal at Howth, "and the Spanish girls laughing in their shawls and their tall combs and the auctions in the morning the Greeks and the jews and the Arabs and the devil knows who else from all the ends of Europe and Duke street and the fowl market all clucking outside Larby Sharons and the poor donkeys slipping half asleep and the vague fellows in the cloaks asleep in the shade on the steps and the big wheels of the carts of the bulls and the old castle thousands of years old yes and those handsome Moors all in white and turbans like kings asking you to sit down in their little bit of a shop and Ronda with the old windows of the posadas glancing eyes a lattice hid for her to kiss the iron and the wineshops half open at night and the castanets and the night we missed the boat at Algeciras the watchman going about serene with his lamp and O that awful deepdown torrent O and the sea crimson sometimes like fire and the glorious sunsets and the figtrees in the Alameda gardens yes and all the queer little streets and pink and blue and yellow houses and the rosegardens and the jessamine and geraniums and cactuses and Gibraltar as a girl where I was a Flower of the mountain yes when I put the rose in my hair like the Andalusian girls used or shall I wear a red yes and how he kissed me under the Moorish wall and I thought well as well him as another and then I asked him with my eyes to ask again yes and then he asked me would I yes to say yes my mountain flower and first I put my arms around him yes and drew him down to me so he could feel my breasts all perfume yes and his heart was going like mad and yes I said yes I will Yes."

Curtain.

I have omitted yes Mrs. Bloom's thoughts about garters, drawers, commodes, menstruation, her own intestines O and the pudendum yes in general. There emerges a human being with whom life has dealt harshly, a woman whom Bloom has wronged. She wins our instant sympathy. And in this wild rush of words we get at last that Homeric swiftness with which we habitually talk to ourselves. But Joyce has clotted his text as a sewer is clotted, not inadvertently, but with painstaking intent, and altogether to forgive him is impossible.

3. D. H. LAWRENCE

Some years ago, after long and complacent abuse of his power over the "lesser breeds without the law," the "white man's burden" began to press uncomfortably upon the white man's conscience. It soon became evident that if this inner voice of protest were to be silenced, either

~ D. H. Lawrence ~
Te Demon laudamus

the burden would have to be carried back to the black man's granary or else some compensation offered of a more intangible kind. Admiration, for instance. What could be cheaper than that, or more acceptable to right-minded dependents? A thing, too, which it was as blessed to give as to receive. It excused the shirking of any part of the burden which might prove irksome and define itself as duty, and at the same time permitted the white to ease himself of not a few burdens of his own. He had but to choose his objects of admiration carefully, darken his face—or at least his habits—and wallow in comfort.

Of course the idea that the masses of mankind, whatever their breed or colour, were stretched at ease in some primitive slime, was a convenient fiction, like that of the savage as a primitive mammal, living without law or religion in sylvan, yet muddy freedom. The bed, however, promised to be comfortable for the discouraged Aryan. If neither Negroes, Indians, nor the proletariat in general were already enjoying it, no matter. There must, it was argued, be such a bed somewhere, and on it we were eager to stretch our civilization-tortured limbs. Whereupon Youth, discovering that here was not only a bed but a marriage-bed, and one with whose rites no tiresome clergymen need venture to interfere, took up the refrain: "*Te Demon Laudamus.*" Devil-worship had been rediscovered under the name of Something New.

Why new? Because it was so old. Our Impuritans knew that it was old. They even fancied that it lay at the very roots of things. But they were confident that the respectable middle classes had never heard of it, or at least had never permitted themselves to learn how comfortable it was.

D. H. Lawrence, the Englishman, did not reach the

ooze at once, nor without effort. No longer ago than "Sons and Lovers," first published in 1913, we find him merely sickening with its malaria, not yet acclimated, and as ill at ease as a pair of satin slippers in the Everglades. Far from yielding whole-heartedly to the demands of the gonadal apparatus, he shrank like any other sick author from even its healthy manifestations. Men are brutes—healthy men, that is. Their insistence upon marital rights—always a thorn in the flesh of the invalid male's side—is an outrage which Lawrence felt certain their wives must resent. He therefore took up his cudgel on the wives' behalf.

Before Gertrude Coppard's marriage to Walter Morel, "the dusky, golden softness of this man's sensuous flame of life that flowed off his flesh like the flame from a candle, not baffled and gripped into incandescence by thought and spirit as her life was, seemed to her something wonderful, beyond her." [1] Morel was "well set-up, erect, and very smart . . . soft, non-intellectual, warm," cutting a dash at a Christmas party, dancing well, and swept off his feet by "that thing of mystery and fascination, a lady." Right and natural, so far. But, though one would never think it from this description, Morel is a common miner, and after the marriage the lady discovers that he drinks beer.

What Lawrence means is that the marriage is consummated, and he cannot repress a shudder—which he duly attributes to the lady-bride. Here she was with a husband, and suddenly she realizes that her own father was just like that. She can remember very well how she used to hate him for his "overbearing manner towards her gentle, humorous, kindly-souled mother." So she turns

[1] "Sons and Lovers," p. 10.

for consolation to her sons, one after another as they arrive and grow up—William, who dies just in time to prevent his committing matrimony himself; Paul, the hero of the book; and a third son, who enlists in the army.

Wyndham Lewis thinks that we have here an "incest motive." I think not. Sons are better than husbands because their love is Platonic, sexual only in a non-sexual sense. I should call it the philandering motive, with frankly physical Sex cast in the rôle of villain. What we see is Luther's concupiscence, as an evil *per se,* once more performing its antics upon the stage.

There are times when Lawrence probably considers himself a satirist, and certainly the plea will be entered in his behalf, as it is in behalf of all other sentimentalists of his sort. Indeed, it would seem most reasonable to suppose that he is slyly making fun of his Gertrudes, so ladylike in their own estimations, so afflicted with fathers and husbands of the male gender. But the theory lacks support. The "overbearing manner" of these monsters resides too exclusively in the author's *obiter dicta,* too little in evidence which he is able to produce. One is driven to conclude that the facts of normal life were too much for Lawrence at this stage to stomach. Eliminate the author from "the bottoms" where the Morels live, and everybody would be able to worry quite comfortably and cosily along.

He fairly revels, however, in making people peevish and dissatisfied with life. The air is shot with nervousness, which, while striving to appear like outraged virginity, has the gait and manner of sex-starvation coupled with malnutrition of a swollen sense of self-importance. Of course there are just such folk living in just such bottoms, but they are exceptional, pathological, antitypical. They get into this kind of literature merely because the world is a looking-glass, and many a writer who believes himself to be holding a mirror up to nature is in fact regarding his own grimaces.

Paul falls in love with Miriam, a girl to whom his mother objects because said girl wants something more than his body and therefore threatens to poach upon the mother's sentimental preserves. Then he falls in love with Clara, a married woman, to whom less objection is found for the reason that only the body is here involved. Mother cannot be made jealous by the thought of losing that which she neither possesses nor desires.

As to Morel, the only humanly human being beneath the roof, the other inmates unite in treating him as a leper. The children leave the room when he enters. The family life is sordid, for no apparent reason except the necessity of blaming pa for something. There is great harping upon the lack of money, yet there is always plenty when it is required.

When the mother dies, the model Paul, who has deserted both his mistresses, finds himself alone, a derelict who just manages to resist the temptation to commit suicide. He is of the "artist type," like Stephen Dedalus—an artist who, horrible to relate, has been compelled to assist in the manufacture of artificial limbs for the sake of keeping soul and body together. We are given to understand that somehow he begins life all over again, but whether as an artist or manufacturer we are not informed.

To begin life over again, without any of those aspirations and limitations which civilization has imposed—that is the remedy, though we are asked to swallow it only later, in the pages of "Mornings in Mexico." This means that Lawrence, finding himself sickly civilized, has decided—not to cure his civilization but to abandon it. He is a perfect example of the discouraged Aryan who, beginning to doubt his right to go on living as he is, solves his dilemma by a plunge instead of a climb. It is the remedy of moral suicide, the eternal temptation of those who have lost all power of enjoying real life through dint of trying to feed upon an idealism which denies the facts of life. They seek surcease in a world of carnal dreams. As there is to be no strain upon the physique whatever, let the dream be wild and its action fierce. The loudest shouts will be heard as whispers in a medium as thin as this.

So the shouting begins—from over the border. "The commonest entertainment among the Indians," we learn from "Mornings in Mexico," chapter on Indians and Entertainment, "is singing round the drum, at evening." These, then, are mornings when the sun is about to set rather than to rise, though it looks like an innocent way of passing the time. But "it is almost impossible for the White people to approach the Indian without either sentimentality or dislike," and "the common healthy vulgar White usually feels a certain native dislike of these drumming aboriginals," while "the highbrow invariably lapses into sentimentalism like the smell of bad eggs."

If one is high-browed, one becomes sentimental, like a bad egg. If one is low-browed, one dislikes the performance. Why? I should say it was probably because the performance was bad, listened to with realistic ears. But it becomes romantic, that is, strange and charming, if there is a brow to add excellences which are not actually there. Good for the brow. And yet it is a romance of the rotten-egg variety. The brow is not so good after all—though I take it the author means, not that it is a rotten egg, but that it has a taste for things of that description, an acquired taste of a worse than natural sort, for rotten eggs by fancy laid, diluted with unreality to that merely high flavour necessary to please a jaded palate and a coated tongue. From highbrows of this kidney, good Lord deliver us. All hail the common healthy vulgar White. But where does Lawrence stand? Nowhere in particular. It is a land of warm, copper-coloured fogs. We take at random from that grab-bag into which has been dumped whatever of the wreck of old systems still retains an agreeable emotional association. Sight no longer bothers, nor do contradictions fret. This is the pursuit of happiness, understand—but be careful of understanding too much. Understanding mars the enjoyment of no end of untoward things.

The white fishermen of the Outer Hebrides "approach the Indian way" of drumming, and manage thus to suggest the habitat of "beasts that . . . stare through . . . vivid mindless eyes. . . . But even this is pictorial, conceptual far beyond the Indian point. The Hebridean still sees himself human, and outside the great naturalistic influences." He therefore merely approaches the Indian, who "sings without words or vision," but does not by any means manage to equal him. No. The Indian drummer, with "face uplifted and sightless eyes half closed and visionless mouth open and speechless," has a consciousness in the abdomen. No cerebellum may hope to catch him, and the cerebrum is entirely out of the running. So Lawrence arrives at his conclusion that "the Indian way of consciousness is different from and fatal to our way of consciousness." The White, however degraded, retains some measure of the power of thinking and seeing, nor ever learns to do his observing exclusively with a visionless open mouth.

Lawrence obviously regrets these white limitations—that is the remarkable fact—more remarkable even than the slander of our southern neighbours which he manages to derive from nothing more awful and mysterious than a few brunets pounding pigskin—or maybe snakeskin—around a campfire in the evening.

His excuse is that he doesn't consider it slander. He considers it a compliment. This highbrow romances by trying to idealize the Indian downwards instead of upwards, but first he has reversed his scale of values. For if once we arrive at the conclusion that there is no high nor low, that what passes through the duodenum is as fit for sentiment as what passes through the mind of a Homer or a Dante, it is inevitable that we go further and assert that the lower is the higher, the gut more noble than the brain. Nature abhors equality, and man destroys one hierarchy only to worship another.

Indians that I have met are not quite so intestinal as those with whom Mr. Lawrence seems to be acquainted. Real Indians, as a matter of fact, no more think with their guts than we do. But what if they did? Then certainly their way of consciousness would be fatal to ours. And what ought we to do about it? See to it that the non-human, without words or vision, lays no strangling hold upon the creature who sees and speaks? No, says Mr. Lawrence in effect, white meat should give way to dark. "The mind is . . . merely . . . a servant. . . . The mind bows down before the creative mystery."

Here is what one might call a "beautiful" confusion of thought. Certainly the mind is an instrument. Certainly it should bow down before the creative mystery. But the creative mystery has somehow fallen to the foot of the class, the dunce instructs the teacher. By sinking below

higher faculties will thus cause exultation in the lower. Yes, Satanism pure and simple, though ritualized with great gusto and art.

4. LAUGHTER AND SHERWOOD ANDERSON

Sherwood Anderson (it was Mr. Mencken who nicknamed him Sherwood Lawrence) transposes to America the Englishman's doubt of his right to live. In his hands the bright squawks of the parrots become the dark laughter of the house servants; and the laughed-at, like the squawked-at, acknowledge the corn, accept the criticism, apologise, and promise to do worse in the future.

But—again paralleling Lawrence—Mr. Anderson had to grope awhile before discovering that the Indian drum, or, say, the banjo, was the solution of all life's puzzles. "Dark Laughter" was preceded by "Windy McPherson's Son" (1916) and by "Tar," two interesting sets of variations upon "Sons and Lovers" (1913). Sherwood Anderson is no plagiarist; he is an example of bilocation, as William McFee is Conrad reincarnate, and Thomas Beer an avatar of Stephen Crane. What makes the case especially intriguing is the fact that the apparently derivative talent is the elder. Mr. Anderson was born in 1876, Mr. Lawrence not until 1885. But then Haydn preceded Beethoven.

Windy McPherson, however, is a rather better effort than Walter Morel, and, like Morel, he is the only character one could call a man and a brother on a stage crowded with splenetic phantoms. He is "war-touched," a veteran of the struggle between the North and the South, who cannot forget that he once "commanded a company through a battle fought in ditches." Anderson thinks that

Lawrence obviously regrets these white limitations—that is the remarkable fact—more remarkable even than the slander of our southern neighbours which he manages to derive from nothing more awful and mysterious than a few brunets pounding pigskin—or maybe snakeskin—around a campfire in the evening.

His excuse is that he doesn't consider it slander. He considers it a compliment. This highbrow romances by trying to idealize the Indian downwards instead of upwards, but first he has reversed his scale of values. For if once we arrive at the conclusion that there is no high nor low, that what passes through the duodenum is as fit for sentiment as what passes through the mind of a Homer or a Dante, it is inevitable that we go further and assert that the lower is the higher, the gut more noble than the brain. Nature abhors equality, and man destroys one hierarchy only to worship another.

Indians that I have met are not quite so intestinal as those with whom Mr. Lawrence seems to be acquainted. Real Indians, as a matter of fact, no more think with their guts than we do. But what if they did? Then certainly their way of consciousness would be fatal to ours. And what ought we to do about it? See to it that the non-human, without words or vision, lays no strangling hold upon the creature who sees and speaks? No, says Mr. Lawrence in effect, white meat should give way to dark. "The mind is . . . merely . . . a servant. . . . The mind bows down before the creative mystery."

Here is what one might call a "beautiful" confusion of thought. Certainly the mind is an instrument. Certainly it should bow down before the creative mystery. But the creative mystery has somehow fallen to the foot of the class, the dunce instructs the teacher. By sinking below

higher faculties will thus cause exultation in the lower. Yes, Satanism pure and simple, though ritualized with great gusto and art.

4. LAUGHTER AND SHERWOOD ANDERSON

Sherwood Anderson (it was Mr. Mencken who nicknamed him Sherwood Lawrence) transposes to America the Englishman's doubt of his right to live. In his hands the bright squawks of the parrots become the dark laughter of the house servants; and the laughed-at, like the squawked-at, acknowledge the corn, accept the criticism, apologise, and promise to do worse in the future.

But—again paralleling Lawrence—Mr. Anderson had to grope awhile before discovering that the Indian drum, or, say, the banjo, was the solution of all life's puzzles. "Dark Laughter" was preceded by "Windy McPherson's Son" (1916) and by "Tar," two interesting sets of variations upon "Sons and Lovers" (1913). Sherwood Anderson is no plagiarist; he is an example of bilocation, as William McFee is Conrad reincarnate, and Thomas Beer an avatar of Stephen Crane. What makes the case especially intriguing is the fact that the apparently derivative talent is the elder. Mr. Anderson was born in 1876, Mr. Lawrence not until 1885. But then Haydn preceded Beethoven.

Windy McPherson, however, is a rather better effort than Walter Morel, and, like Morel, he is the only character one could call a man and a brother on a stage crowded with splenetic phantoms. He is "war-touched," a veteran of the struggle between the North and the South, who cannot forget that he once "commanded a company through a battle fought in ditches." Anderson thinks that

Lawrence obviously regrets these white limitations—that is the remarkable fact—more remarkable even than the slander of our southern neighbours which he manages to derive from nothing more awful and mysterious than a few brunets pounding pigskin—or maybe snakeskin—around a campfire in the evening.

His excuse is that he doesn't consider it slander. He considers it a compliment. This highbrow romances by trying to idealize the Indian downwards instead of upwards, but first he has reversed his scale of values. For if once we arrive at the conclusion that there is no high nor low, that what passes through the duodenum is as fit for sentiment as what passes through the mind of a Homer or a Dante, it is inevitable that we go further and assert that the lower is the higher, the gut more noble than the brain. Nature abhors equality, and man destroys one hierarchy only to worship another.

Indians that I have met are not quite so intestinal as those with whom Mr. Lawrence seems to be acquainted. Real Indians, as a matter of fact, no more think with their guts than we do. But what if they did? Then certainly their way of consciousness would be fatal to ours. And what ought we to do about it? See to it that the non-human, without words or vision, lays no strangling hold upon the creature who sees and speaks? No, says Mr. Lawrence in effect, white meat should give way to dark. "The mind is . . . merely . . . a servant. . . . The mind bows down before the creative mystery."

Here is what one might call a "beautiful" confusion of thought. Certainly the mind is an instrument. Certainly it should bow down before the creative mystery. But the creative mystery has somehow fallen to the foot of the class, the dunce instructs the teacher. By sinking below

the fishermen of the Outer Hebrides, who still see themselves as human and therefore outside the great naturalistic influences (that is, see themselves created by a superior), and then by sinking further, at first to the level of the Indian drum, and then further still, beneath even the songs-without-words-or-vision of the Mex, we shall find out God. The primal forces, it seems, spring from the ground. The hole throws out the dirt and creates the cellar; the cellar creates the foundations; the foundation creates the masons; the woodwork creates the carpenters and the architect. And so we get a house—which is described as worse than the hole.

Mr. Lawrence puts this theory of evolution into poetic form by imagining a lot of bursting suns, each producing its peculiar "consciousness." There was at one time My Lord the Parrot, "shrieking about at midday, almost able to talk"—on the point, you might say, of renouncing his birthright of visionless open beak. "Then someone mysteriously touched the button, and the sun went bang, with smithereens of birds bursting in all directions." The bird was saved from talking in the nick of time, though at considerable expense, like a gentleman who clings to his traditions in spite of revolution, taking the consequences but hoping that his children may live to see a brighter era. There were left, in fact, "a few parrots' eggs and peacocks' eggs and eggs of flamingos snuggling in some safe nook, to hatch on the next Day, when the animals arose."

Among these animals is to be noted Corasmin, a "little, fat, curly white dog." The parrots, their noses broken, take to the trees and answer his yap-yapping with screeches. "The third Sun burst in water," and "out of the floods rose our own Sun, and little naked man."

Corasmin—a smithereen himself now, and woefully lacking in parrot-pride—consents to follow at man's heels. The parrots say to themselves, in parrot talk, I suppose, since these were no shamefully educated birds: "Hello! . . . Must be a new sort of boss."

This is an intriguing drama, emergent evolution set to the music of a cosmos groaning in parturition. But Lawrence does not accept the theory that, for one species to develop into another, something better had to be added from the general store of things. He admits the general store, but he turns the whole scheme upside down. These additions are subtractions. The parrot was unrighteously dispossessed. The dog was superior to the man who forced him to heel. The black men and the red men—black men and red men, be it understood, of the mouth-gaping, eye-closing, blind, and speechless literary sort—were better than the whites who eventually got the upper hand. Not the lowbrow but the browless comes nearest to the naturalistic influences which brought all this bursting of suns about.

Now why such humility on the part of the Nordic? Evidently for the sake of escaping from that bad conscience aforesaid. If he can only make himself believe that his higher aspirations are artificialities leading him away from the eternal dayspring from beneath, why, then he will be able to indulge himself. He will arrive at an animal sort of innocence. But he can't quite make the down grade. A ghost of bad conscience remains.

Very well. Even this can be utilized, once it becomes sufficiently shadowy. We hardly want actually to beat the Indian drum. It would be too much like work. But we can hearken to it in our musings. The shivering of our

higher faculties will thus cause exultation in the lower. Yes, Satanism pure and simple, though ritualized with great gusto and art.

4. LAUGHTER AND SHERWOOD ANDERSON

Sherwood Anderson (it was Mr. Mencken who nicknamed him Sherwood Lawrence) transposes to America the Englishman's doubt of his right to live. In his hands the bright squawks of the parrots become the dark laughter of the house servants; and the laughed-at, like the squawked-at, acknowledge the corn, accept the criticism, apologise, and promise to do worse in the future.

But—again paralleling Lawrence—Mr. Anderson had to grope awhile before discovering that the Indian drum, or, say, the banjo, was the solution of all life's puzzles. "Dark Laughter" was preceded by "Windy McPherson's Son" (1916) and by "Tar," two interesting sets of variations upon "Sons and Lovers" (1913). Sherwood Anderson is no plagiarist; he is an example of bilocation, as William McFee is Conrad reincarnate, and Thomas Beer an avatar of Stephen Crane. What makes the case especially intriguing is the fact that the apparently derivative talent is the elder. Mr. Anderson was born in 1876, Mr. Lawrence not until 1885. But then Haydn preceded Beethoven.

Windy McPherson, however, is a rather better effort than Walter Morel, and, like Morel, he is the only character one could call a man and a brother on a stage crowded with splenetic phantoms. He is "war-touched," a veteran of the struggle between the North and the South, who cannot forget that he once "commanded a company through a battle fought in ditches." Anderson thinks that

when some true historian finally "comes to write of our Civil War," he will "make much of our Windy McPhersons . . . will see something big and pathetic in their hungry search for auditors and their endless talk." He certainly will if he understands his business. But Sam, Windy's son, evidently lacked this historic sense, for "the realization of the fact that his father was a confirmed liar and braggart . . . for years cast a shadow over his days."

Windy does stretch it a bit. He is given to grand gestures, a mute, inglorious Homer. And upon a certain Fourth of July he writes his epic in brass. For he has subscribed so extravagantly to the celebration fund that he is permitted to mount upon a white horse, ride through the village streets, and blow the reveillé at dawn. Even Sam is moved to the extent of buying the old man a bugle.

The dawn arrives. "Windy, sitting very straight in the saddle and looking wonderfully striking in the new blue uniform and the broad-brimmed hat, had the air of a conqueror come to receive the homage of the town"—the "little corn-shipping town of Caxton." In Main Street, "the people were packed on the sidewalk. Heads appeared at the windows. . . . Slowly and with stately stride the horse walked . . . between the rows of silent waiting people. In front of the town hall the tall military figure, rising in the saddle, took one haughty look at the multitude, and then, putting the bugle to his lips—blew." [1]

There was once another hero who "set the slughorn to his lips, and blew: 'Childe Harold to the Dark Tower Came.'" But Windy cannot play a note. "It is doubtful if he had ever had a bugle to his lips until that moment. But he was filled with wonder and astonishment that the

[1] "Windy McPherson's Son," p. 31.

reveillé did not roll forth. He had heard the thing a thousand times and had it clearly in his mind; with all his heart he wanted it to roll forth, and could picture the street ringing with it and the applause of the people; the thing, he felt, was in him, and it was only a fatal blunder in nature that it did not come out at the flaring end of the bugle."

But it doesn't. Instead, a great shout of laughter rolls down the street—not dark laughter as yet—and Sam sneaks home, shamed, determined that nobody shall ever laugh thus at him. One cannot help sympathizing with all concerned. Surely, it is of such scenes as this that great novels are made.

But Anderson cannot permit himself to remain healthy and agreeable. He wants to be important. So he takes us to Windy's home. No laughter of any sort there, nor humour, nor courage, only dull distaste of life. That fatal blunder of nature, endowing Windy with imagination but no technic, makes it necessary for the wife to take in washing. All the children look down upon their father as a moral outcast—even Kate, who manages to get her a husband and a baby, all within the space of thirty days. What shall Sam do? For he, too, is of the artist type—as, indeed, we all are, with our eternal desire to express ourselves, to make people applaud and hold their laughter, at least until we have passed out of earshot. But Life decides that Sam shall peddle papers and become a captain of industry.

Whereupon John Telfer, aged 45, an ex-student of Latin-Quarter Paris, who now lives upon his milliner-wife, is stricken to the soul. He calls Sam "a little mole that works underground intent upon worms," and reminds him that "an artist is one who hungers and thirsts

~ SHERWOOD ANDERSON ~
Civilization is the butt of the joke

after perfection." Telfer has hungered and thirsted thus all his life, without, however, making any effort to appease either thirst or hunger of this particular sort. What Sam needs, he says, is to hear an older man "talk about love."

Sam does hear an older man talk about love, Telfer, to wit. But he complicates matters by reading the Bible betweenwhiles. "Left to himself," he "might have sensed its meaning." But there is a thin-lipped minister at the brick church, and there are shouting, pleading, evangelists hard by, who insist that the Bible means that souls should be saved. So Sam's native ability as theologian is lost to the world. He drops the Bible without ever discovering what it does mean (nor does Anderson tell us what he would have found had he found what is really there), and begins to look shyly "at the ankles of women crossing the street." This, of course, was some time ago. He also looks shyly "into dictionaries for words that appealed to the animal lust in his queerly perverted mind." To which the author adds: "Yet Sam McPherson was no evil-minded boy." Why, then, speak of his mind as "perverted"?

It is now that Mike McCarthy has a fight with the husband of one of twelve women who he claims have listened to him when he, like Telfer, was moved to speak of love. In jail for assault and battery, he evangelistically shouts his gospel through the bars:

"I have had a philosophy of life, O Father! I have seen men and women here living year after year without children. I have seen them hoarding pennies and denying Thee new life on which to work Thy will. To these women I have gone secretly talking of carnal love. . . . Are vou there, O dwellers in the cesspool of respectability? I have been with your wives. Eleven Caxton wives without babies have I been with, and it has been fruitless." Fruitless. Alas, poor Yorick! "The twelfth woman I have just left, leaving her man in the road a bleeding sacrifice to Thee. I shall call out the names of the [other] eleven." [2]

He does. And Telfer takes pains that Sam shall hear, because "the truth won't hurt" him, and "this McCarthy has a brain. Although he is half insane now, he is trying to work something out." But he doesn't work it out. Telfer doesn't work it out. Mr. Anderson doesn't work it out. And certainly I can't work it out. Sam apparently can and does, for no sooner had he listened to McCarthy's message than immediately he "felt that he had been shriven. His mind, his heart, even his tired body seemed strangely cleansed. . . . Where the church had failed, the bold sensualist had succeeded." The boy retires to his room, and prays: "O Father, make me stick to the thought that the right living of this, my life, is my duty to You."

It may be admitted that Mike has voiced some part of a truth which the thin-lipped minister and the shouting, pleading evangelists had missed. I hold no brief for thin-lipped ministers nor for shouters. In this world of ours the flesh undoubtedly has its place. But what of "right living" as exemplified by the shouting, would-be impregnator? Mr. Anderson is fairly bristling with moral indignation about something. It seems to be birth-control. A surprising position for a modern novelist. His remedy is more surprising still—a sterile lover!

Sam goes upon the indicated way as far as to exchange kisses with a girl, but Telfer warns him against women, "whose purposes are not man's purposes." Is it

[2] *Ibid.*, p. 52.

people whose lives remain blank and empty even when the care of babies is added to their dish-washing, their scrubbing-boards, and their yokels? But the worst does not befall until our shadowy despair-makers try their own hands at dreams of reform. It is then that these idle females "are to be seen drunk with emotion amid the lurid horrors of a French Revolution, or immersed in the secret whispering, creeping terror of a religious persecution. At their best they are mothers of half mankind."

Let us take them, then, at their best, giving as wide a berth as possible to the mothers of French Revolutions and the secret terrors of religious wars.

"Wealth coming to them, they throw themselves into garish display of it, and flash upon the sight of Newport or Palm Beach." Who? The mothers of the best half of mankind? Seemingly so. "In their native lair, in the close little houses [we here turn, evidently, to the mothers of the worse half], they sleep in the bed of the man who has put clothes upon their backs and food into their mouths." 'Tis true, 'tis pity, and pity 'tis 'tis true. They ought to sleep in other beds—say, those of the husband at large, the man who has not been snatched from society. "They do not love, they sell, instead, their bodies in the market-place and cry out that man shall witness their virtue because they have had the joy of finding one buyer instead of the many of the red sisterhood." I see. It is only the red sisterhood who love. Beware of the woman who sells you her body by becoming the mother of your children.

"A fierce animalism in them makes them cling to the babe at their breast, and in the days of its softness and loveliness they close their eyes and try to catch again an old fleeing dream of their girlhood, a something vague, shadowy, no longer a part of them, brought with the babe out of the infinite." I see again. It is a fierce animalism that makes them cling to their babes and try to catch at the dreams of girlhood. But—

"Having passed beyond the land of dreams, they dwell in the land of emotions and weep over the bodies of unknown dead or sit under the eloquence of evangelists. . . . Along streets they go, lifting heavy eyes to peer into the lives of others and to get a morsel to roll upon their heavy tongues." Anything "touching the lives of such as walk in the clean air, dream dreams and have the audacity to be beautiful beyond the beauty of animal youth, maddens them, and they cry out, running from kitchen door to kitchen door and tearing at the prize like a starved beast who has found a carcass."

What, really, is our author driving at? These women, deprived of the vague dreams of their girlhood, are fierce animals when they try to find these dreams fulfilled in their children. When beyond dreams, they seek emotions by going to funerals and listening to sermons. Who, then, are they who walk in the clean air and have the audacity to be beautiful in that unyouthful way which alone seems capable of awakening envy?

"Let but earnest women found a movement and crowd it forward to the day when it smacks of success and they [the domestic French Revolutionists] fall upon it with a cry, having hysteria rather than reason as their guiding impulse."

The beautiful ones, then, must be the Leaders of Movements, but not of revolutions—movements, say, for stopping the snatching of men from society. They know the smacks of success. But the ugly snatchers "for the most part . . . live and die unseen, unknown, eating off rank food, sleeping overmuch"—notwithstanding yokels,

~ CARL VAN VECHTEN ~
Conducts the slumming-party

dishes, dirty clothes, children, the fomenting of religious persecutions, the hearing of sermons, and the funerals which they have to attend. "In them is all of femininity—and none of it." They may be seen "sitting through summer afternoons rocking in chairs [is this, now, at Newport or at Palm Beach?] and looking at people passing in the street. In the end they die full of faith, hoping for a life to come."

No more need be said. No wonder Mr. Anderson thought that any and all objections might logically be made to them. They hope for a life to come!

Sam escapes the female determination to be by-man-fed-and-clothed by going to Chicago, becoming one of the big men in the Rainey Arms Company, and marrying Sue Rainey, Colonel Rainey's daughter, who has money in her own right. He also escapes from a love-affair with a girl who tells him that "books are *not* full of pretence and lies." Lucky Sam.

Yet even Sue has a purpose of her own. "Her idea was one of service to mankind through children. . . . She had thought it all out and had tried to plan for herself a life . . . and wanted a husband in accord with her ideas."

"Can you," she asks on page 186, "accept my beliefs and live for that I want to live? . . . I can find a man," she goes on, "whom I can control. . . . My money gives me that power. But I want him to be a real man, a man of ability, a man who does things for himself, one fitted by his life and his achievements to be the father of children who do things." This idea of a real man of ability, who does things for himself and can be bought with money and controlled, even to the accepting of beliefs which are somebody else's, "seemed wonderfully

simple and beautiful to Sam." To me it seems somewhat complicated. Anyway, they decide to give Sue's wealth and Sam's ability to the children who are to come, though it means, she warns him, "giving up [his] dreams of power." That is, to have children who do things, the father must cease to do things.

"You will have to make a mother of me and keep making a mother of me," the bride-elect continues. "You will have to be a new kind of father with something maternal in you." Nursemaid as well as paterfamilias. "You will have to live wholly for me because I am to be their mother. . . . And then when they come you will have to give all these things to them day after day in a thousand little ways." It begins to look almost as if Sam were to be snatched from society after all.

But motherhood is no longer the dreadful thing it was in those small, unaired houses. Sam is no yokel, to kiss anybody in a darkened room, well ventilated or not. No. "Sam took her [Sue] in his arms, and for the first time in his memory the hot tears stood in his eyes."[3] "Sex," he tells himself, "is a solution, not a menace—it is wonderful." I presume he means that sex-indulgence is a solution. The passion itself has been thought by some to offer rather a problem.

Be that as it may, the marriage takes place, and during the honeymoon the happy pair sleep in the open, thus avoiding the risk of becoming the despair of reformers. But not a single little stranger consents to arrive. In vain is the stork-call sounded from the muezzin tower. Evidently here was a case where the unborn saw their parents first.

Sue takes refuge in civic betterment. "We must make ourselves units," she says, "in the great modern move-

[3] *Ibid.*, p. 189.

ment for uplift." But Sam rebels and leaves Sue to her own devices. He even goes to work, and becomes the head of a gang of unscrupulous men engaged in big business of the predatory sort. Then he turns unbeloved vagabond and wanders forth incog, searching, we are told, for truth and for God. He finds neither, though he explores the possibilities of a great many things, including manual labour and whisky. What he does find is the deserted wife of a plumber. She has three children for sale, Joe, Tom, and Mary. Sam buys them, goes back to his wife, and lives happily ever after. It has taken him four years to think of adopting a family.

A novelist may well depict imbeciles, but he should be chary, I think, of letting their imbecility refract the angle of narration. If ever there were an occasion for dark laughter, it is Sam. A little of it might have made "Windy McPherson's Son" a great book. But, as has already been suggested, it was Haydn who came before Beethoven—in this case a not very authentic Beethoven, and a Haydn dipped in "Tar."

"The mother pig," Tar noted, "had stiff white hairs growing on her nose, and her eyes were heavy with weariness. Often Tar's mother looked like that. . . . And then the new Moorehead baby was born. . . . His mother groaned softly. She stirred in her bed. What was going on? Tar knew because he had seen the pigs born in the field, knew because what was happening in the Moorehead house was always happening in some house. . . . It happened to neighbour women and to horses, to dogs, to cows." Hiding his face in the pillow on his own bed, Tar tries not to believe. "Birth," he told himself, "was a thing belonging to the world of pigs, to cows and horses, and to other women," not to his mother. "What

was happening in the next room was not happening to her. . . . He did not want his mother to have another baby."

The theme now is "the secret inner life of pigs . . . revealed to . . . children," and the result of such a method of education does not appear to have been a happy one. Has Mr. Anderson abandoned his brief in the cause of fecundity? More likely his conscious object is to show the evils of Tar's bringing up, though I have no idea in what he believes the root of the evil to consist. Just such little human pigs as Tar are unquestionably to be found, not always on the farm, either. But once again the inherent nastiness of the page seems to come more from the author than the character. It rather looks as if Tar were being used to enable the adult reader to revel in dark fancies all his own, that the spectacle of a sow giving birth to a litter has been wrested from nature and handed over to depravity.

In the telling of a tale, we are warned in the Foreword of this very book, truth is apt to be "utterly lost" in the writer's fancy. Fiction, Mr. Anderson declares, "is in a strict sense nothing but lying." Maybe so. But certainly the great masterpieces of the art are not thus composed. When the real giants of the pen begin to "lie," it is like the sun piercing a cloud, light shining where before was darkness. As matters stand, Mr. Anderson has merely succeeded in moving the sty into the house and spattering repulsive mud into the face of human motherhood.

Whereupon he proceeds to do a similar service for womanhood in general. He discovers the body of an old crone naked in the snow, and presents it to Tar's view (i.e., to ours) after it has been worried by dogs. "Neither of them [Tar nor his brother] had ever before seen a

woman's body." The men turn the body over, and then "Tar had seen everything." What is the object of all this horror? Why not let us look at pigs and cadavers through the eyes of physicians, coroners, or farmers? Because then such scenes would seem natural and tolerable, or no more than lamentable. Bringing in a child increases the sense of outrage, and the sense of outrage is what we are catering to.

After this, "Dark Laughter" seems like a return to health, albeit of the new pagan sort. Gone are the terrors of childbirth, the theatrically transposed fecundity of pigs, the rapacity of female home-makers. We are nearer to the red sisterhood with all its freedom and stainlessness.

There is a husband, "Fred", in this case, to take the responsibility of breadwinning from the shoulders of the leading characters. Fred's wife employs a gardener, a former newspaper-man of Chicago. The garden, however, is in the too, too sunny South. Fred is away. Comes love. The Negro servants see it coming. And then "a high-pitched Negro laugh rang through the house. . . . The air on the hill-top was filled with laughter—dark laughter." Oh, Lord!

"Oh, Lord! Oh, Lord! Oh, Lord!" one of the servants cries to another—a comment difficult to improve upon. "The older Negro woman tried to quiet the younger, blacker woman, but she kept laughing the high shrill laughter of the Negress. 'I knowed it, I knowed it, all the time I knowed it,' she cried, and the high shrill laughter ran through the garden and into the room where Fred sat upright and rigid in bed."

"Why couldn't Fred laugh?" enquires the author. "He kept trying, but failed." I suggest that it was because he knowed it too. He was insufficiently philosophical to hear

in this merriment the welcome extended to a new-comer by the "great naturalistic influences." He merely felt that he had lost face below stairs.

Fred's wife could not laugh, either. "About the Negro women it did not matter," she thought. "They would think as their natures led them to think, feel as their natures led them to feel." Still, it was unpleasant to realize that even servants could have natures so low as to be unable to appreciate the poetry of that act of high adultery. I fear these Negroes were not as free from prejudice and conventionality, in their ideals at least, as were the parrots and Mexican drummers of Mr. Lawrence.

Yet Mr. Anderson seems to hear in all this laughter the glad, triumphant shout of an all-conquering Pan. Let the Negroes laugh for whatever why they may, Anderson will laugh with the Forest. Civilization is the butt of the joke. This is the whole point of the story. Something seems to be wrong with our civilization, in fact. But has our author exactly put his hand upon the canker?

5. THE MCKAY AND VAN VECHTEN BLUES

I wonder if we are really in danger of becoming a race of quitters—if our habit of scrapping old machinery and skyscrapers, and building new rather than bother with tinkering and repairs, is to be applied to institutions. Didn't we even begin by applying it to an institution? Yet we don't scrap old knowledge—of machinery. We merely replace and improve. Perhaps that would be a good way to treat civilization.

There is something appealing in that poem of Tennyson's—

"We did so laugh and cry with you,
I've half a mind to die with you,
Old Year, if you must die."

But there is nothing poetic in desertion, in giving up the ship the moment she springs a leak. True first principles are things not to be abandoned—never, under any circumstances, for from them we spring. What has to be annulled eventually is not the original marriage but some later divorce. Does not Michelet warn us that all things must from time to time return to their origins or die? So it might be well to go on trying to behave like human beings, for a little longer anyway—even to go back and try again.

Messrs. Joyce, Lawrence, and Anderson think, on the contrary, that we ought to secede. In a rough sea, with scurvy on board, they would neither return to port for fresh supplies nor stop to patch a broken shaft, but would jump overboard and hurry to the bottom. The latter two even suggest that the dark-complexioned races have already done so—or rather have never subscribed wholeheartedly to the fashion of not crawling on the bottom, on all fours. But if we really could get beneath these richly pigmented skins, what should we find? Any such sympathy with "nature" as this?

In America, the Negro has always been our great tragedy, but such a gay, humorous tragedian, up to now, whose laughter was simply laughter, aimed chiefly at Old Man Trouble. The slave with his banjo, singing beneath the gum-trees down in Dixie, wrestler with the angel of the Lord on the camp-meeting ground, hoping for dem golden slippers and dem golden stairs—if his consciousness differed from ours, it was only in being so carelessly brave. He had a better excuse than even the savage's for embracing animalism as a creed, but he chose instead to embrace the creed taught in the little A. M. E. Zion and A. M. E. Bethel chapels.

Just as literary material, he promised the American author a unique mine. And when he turned author himself, and began not only to compose spirituals and blues, but novels and plays, it looked as if, give him a little time, and the world would know a poet "such as it had in the ages glad, long ago." His was to be the romance of Africa espoused to our own South, the savage's sense of the nearness of the spiritual world purified by all that trial, discipline, and ultimate success could give of knowledge as to what God may humanly be conceived to be. And many coloured workers in the arts and in literature are doing their best to realize this dream, though their opportunity is too recently come and their educational advantages are still too slight for any measure of the race's ultimate capacity as yet to be taken.

But along with this we have recently been brought face to face with a new development—the black man, not oppressed, not cringing beneath the white man's vices, but corrupted by them. The result is an almost total loss of identity. Claude McKay, coloured, writes, in "Home to Harlem," just about as well and just about in the manner of Carl Van Vechten, white, in "Nigger Heaven." Their material is the same, and though the characters of both have dark, or at least high yaller, skins, they differ only superficially from the dregs of any great city, and might as well be cuticled in red, pink, or green.

On Pacific Street, San Francisco, there used to be, and probably still is, a Negro dance hall called the So-Different Café. The name was deceptive. It was not so different from any other slum-hole. A bitch parlour is tediously the same, whether it be in Harlem, lower Manhattan, London, Paris, Berlin, Rome, Athens, Pekin, or Timbuctoo. There is no possible variety in degradation, as Dante knew when he shaped Inferno like a cone, its circles winding smaller and smaller as they approached the depth. The wide glamour of the hells of Saignon, Benares, or Stamboul is seen only by those to whom they are happily unfamiliar, or who know of nothing better.

So human sluts and bullies are of importance to art only because they are human beings, with an inner sanctuary, eternally aloof and inviolable. Packed into a mass, they are nothing. It seems like a paradox, the way we understand each other, are valuable to each other only as we draw apart in an individual aloofness. And yet it is a truth—one with which modern philosophers seem unable to grapple. They want egoism, yet refuse to seek it in the one place it may be had—in selfless superiority. The fact is, we are all more or less strangled with Brahminism, and bad Brahminism at that, which teaches that approach to God is an approach to annihilation.

And yet we know that evolution always progresses in the direction of increased differentiation; that wireless telegraphy is best carried on between well-organized stations, not between machines reduced to one general and indistinguishable wreckage. When it is said that he who loseth his life shall find it, it sounds like an idle play upon words. But nature plays, by no means idly, upon the same words. We are confronted by the fact. By losing our limitations we acquire others, more definite and far-spreading. An insect is more finely articulated than its grub. Progress is always towards the clear, the conscious, the intelligent, the more highly and perfectly organized, with ever widening communications. Thus we reach that resilient flexibility so characteristic of strength, of sensibility and life, so opposed to the brittle rigidity or flabby inertia of death. But when we try to think of losing our limitations altogether, we become like hurriedly overblown bladders, and burst.

Thus even other people's virtues may puff us up if we only pretend to have them. Thus it happened to the frog, who wanted to be an ox rather than a good frog. Swelling is not always growth. If these virtues of other people really become ours, they become engagingly different, original, and our own.

Now the Negro should remain engagingly different. Those who look forward to an earthly paradise composed of standardized citizens all of a shade, mingled in an undifferentiated hodge-podge, have neither science nor history on their side. They can never have looked closely even at two peas. Could McKay have been really at home in the Harlem he depicted, he might have made himself the nigger-hell articulate, and have written, if not a great novel, at least a valuable human document. After all, it makes little difference where you start. He could have shown us that in the case of black trash as well as white trash, there is, in spite of the temptation to let go and disintegrate, the determination not to become lost in the shuffle, the aspiration to remain clean-cut, individual, unmixed with things in general—or, as we say, pure, in the only true moral sense of the word. And he could have shown that wherever this aspiration is on the wane, all hope, even the reason for being, is passing into eclipse. It is the tragedy of despair, the moral of the awful warning.

But no more than Carl Van Vechten, or the author of "Dark Laughter," does he seek to do anything of the kind. Like them, he merely conducts a slumming party for the entertainment of buckra jig-chasers anxious for an excuse to be base. His talent, which is beyond question, might have reflected great credit upon his race. At times it does, in its crude, singing way, just as Howard W. Odum's "twelve-string Laura in the Rough" occasionally strikes up a tune worthy of his cry, "There's a Rainbow round My Shoulder." We could not have expected to keep for ever the romantic Negro of our own imaginations, the Jasbo Brown of DuBose Heyward.

"Yer got to know
I ain't de kine fer stayin';
Always I is movin',
Always playin'.
For Gawd's lonely chillun
What got er song,
Life is jes' hello
An' so long!"

Like Cooper's Indians, he was bound to disturb the picture by stepping out of it, by saying something for himself. Why couldn't McKay have said a little more for himself? Instead, I find him borrowing the bardacious ofay idea of a peculiarly real reality existing in nothingness, coupled with that other undigested notion so eminently ours that there is a truer than true truth in tumescence, and solid solidity only in that no-ness of the not which is by abdominal thinkers said to be the fecund parent of thingless things.

A coloured person—and by implication an uneducated person of any tint—has, according to McKay, "simple, raw emotions, and real. They may frighten and repel refined souls, because they are too intensely real, just as the simple savage stands dismayed before nice emotions that he instantly perceives are false."[1] Simple, raw emotions, and real, which may repel refined souls, are all right enough —in their place. But why suggest that they are any realer than the nice emotions which the dismayed savage instantly perceives to be false? What does McKay know about savages? Though born in Jamaica, he is an American college man and lives in Europe. And why must a nice, refined emotion necessarily be false? Does he mean that we are false to ourselves when we have such emotions, that they are condemned by our intelligence? Or does he mean that they are false in the sense that we only pretend to have them? But this is like the charge which the musically illiterate sometimes bring against classical compositions—that nobody really likes them. But even Beethoven has now become so popular, at least when spiced with a few extra syncopations, that this is no longer said even in Harlem. No, it is love, not music, which McKay has in mind; it is love which he assumes must be raw if it can really be felt.

Were this philosophy distilled from his own experience, it would be worth notice—as an indication of his rank in the scale of being. But he bootlegs it from the stills of alien degenerates.

He calls his hero, Jake, "a black Pan out of the woods." Pan! And Jake "took what he wanted of whatever he fancied, and kept going"—from woman to woman. So Ray, the sub-hero and somewhat civilized, envied him his "reality."

Nevertheless, "life burned in Ray perhaps more intensely than in Jake." Ray "drank in more of life than he could distil into active animal living." One is glad to

[1] "Home to Harlem," p. 338.

hear it. "No nigger strut for me," he would mutter, "when the feeling for Agatha [a decent domestic woman] worked like a fever in his flesh. He saw destiny working in her large, dream-sad eyes, filling them with the passive softness of resignation to life and seeking to encompass and yoke him down just as one of the thousand niggers of Harlem. And he hated Agatha and, for escape, wrapped himself darkly in self-love." [2]

It is not so well with Ray, then, after all. His belief in Jake's "reality" betrays him—betrays the author too. Here is a sophisticate in the bad sense, another Windy McPherson's son, another Sherwood Anderson railing against roof-loving women who want to snatch him from society. Thousand-lot niggers in Harlem have no characters because they stoop to supporting wives and pickaninnies. Not even a fever working in the flesh is "real" when it threatens to lead to responsibilities. What is real? Why, "dark self-love," the "I" reduced to the vanishing point, ego-worship, zero-worship.

So McKay tries, and almost succeeds, in making his talent a white talent—white as leprosy is white. It would be absurd to single him out for especial blame. He reflects a part of his literary material, even if more often than not the worst part—"pink-chasers" who try to "pass." It is not kopasetee. But it is inevitable that prominence, or even any sign of promise, should expose the coloured artist to-day to an excess of blond influence, and natural, I suppose, that the worse should prove more infectious than the better. Perhaps McKay will yet learn to shame the devil and exploit the true McKay vein. Let us hope so.

[2] *Ibid.*, chap. xviii.

Meanwhile there is, it seems to me, something peculiarly sad and out of character in an unspiritual Negro, one whose only religious knowledge is evidently a knowledge of cant, and whose very blues are jazz.

CHAPTER XI

DIVINAMORE

WE have followed now the modern idea of love, from the infusoria to the mammal and to man. It is a false idea, written backwards. Seldom has it risen even to the genuinely human plane, to what we mean by love in ordinary speech. For it all is based upon the hypothesis that sex created not only itself but the celestial empire, instead of being merely one of the rungs upon a very tall ladder, taller than all of us, and quite as firmly fixed at the top as at the bottom. We even seem to have lost the ability to distinguish one end from the other.

The ladder is still there, however; and, after all, this blinding smoke proceeds from the smouldering of a very few dead leaves. The masses of mankind will always have a collective wisdom, to which they return after each passing winter. They must. Because of Divinamore.

"There is another *amorino,* who is sometimes mistaken for that One: but in reality he is a dæmon and he is called Desire. In appearance they are the same; in action they are the same. But in effect they are not the same. . . . It is a matter of heart.

"One or the other comes into your heart; and there he makes his home. It depends on your own will, whether you admit him, or no. If you keep him out, your heart withers away. . . . If you admit Desire, you regret afterward. If you admit Divinamore you do the best action of your life, and you are never sorry any more.

"Yet it is a difficult task to tell the one from the other. . . . For, at first, they come to you in the form of a little child, sweet, innocent, asking for a home. You take in this little child, and show him kindness. . . . In your heart, he grows to boyhood; and, on the sly, when you are not looking, he makes weapons, arrows, and bow, like an archer, and wings bloom upon his arms, so that he may fly away and leave you when the moment comes. . . . And, then, at last, he gains his full strength; and he is vigorous, and terrible: and he arises in his majesty; and, with his arrow, he wounds your heart, and strikes you down. . . . When he has flown away, your heart burns, and craves a medicine to heal its wound.

"And only now can you be certain of the god whose wound you bear. The wound itself is the desire for happiness. And, if the god who gave it was Desire, then you will strive and struggle for the happiness of yourself, and of yourself alone. But if Divinamore has wounded you, then there must be another beside yourself; and for that other you will gladly strive, gladly suffer, gladly die, or very gladly live, which is the hardest thing of all."

So wrote Frederick William Rolfe, Baron Corvo.[1] I do not know to what extent he understood his own words.

[1] *Vide* "In His Own Image," chap. xii.

APPENDIX A

THE ORIGIN OF DOMINANCE

The process may be roughly pictured thus: Let us suppose a chromomere loaded with a unit trait, which may be called *a*. This divides into two chromomeres, *a* and *a*. The chromosome which contains them divides, one *a* going into one half and the other *a* into the other. The cell divides, and each of its halves contains an *a*. Thus far it is plain sailing. But suppose that the original chromomere was itself the product of a union, of a contention between this *a* and another unit trait, or factor, relating to precisely the same feature but having something slightly different to say about it, though the difference might amount to no more than comparative weakness on the one hand and strength on the other. The chromomere will then be loaded with *a*1 and *a*2, 1 standing for dominance and 2 for recessiveness.

Suppose further that reduction-division, the prelude to a new possibility of sexual union, is now in progress, instead of simple division. The chromomere containing *a*1 will go into one chromosome (nobody knows exactly how), and that containing *a*2 will go into another, and one of these chromosomes will go into one gamete of the dividing cell, and the other into the other, so that both gametes will have a unit character with something to say about the feature *a*—since otherwise this feature would be entirely lacking, and if it also happened to be lacking in the gamete with which union was subsequently made, the feature would be lacking in the offspring.

Accident may possibly sometimes bring this to pass, with consequent monstrosity, but it is enough here to concern ourselves with the normal. The point is that reduction-division followed by union increased the likelihood of difference between *a*1 and *a*2. In pure-bred creatures it remains very slight, so that it is impossible to tell whether a given trait was inherited from one parent or the other. In crosses the difference is often enormous. In neither case is it likely that the same trait was derived from both parents. There seems to be no blending of hereditary units.

Another interesting fact is that the word pure-bred is a relative term. There is almost always a little difference between *a*1 and *a*2, though in certain creatures, like the cockroach, for instance, the difference has become so slight that, judging from fossil remains, there has been no appreciable change in bodily form for millions of years. Most creatures, however, vary slightly from generation to generation. The streams of heredity from the two parents are slightly different, and have not quite settled down to uniformity. Quite possibly variation is a phenomenon of this narrow sort of hybridization.

APPENDIX B

SEX AND HORMONES

Weininger notes ("Sex and Character," p. 20) that "we cannot deny altogether the occurrence of a certain degree of effeminacy when the crucial operation of extirpation of the human testes has been performed. . . . So also in the opposite case, it cannot be wholly denied that ovariotomy is followed by the appearance of masculine characters."

Nobody, except perhaps the Weiningerites, wishes to deny it. Here is nature's closest approach to arrhenoplasm and thelyplasm, and the action of these secretions, showing what power the essential sex-characters have over the general growth of the body, completely upsets the notion that each body-cell has its own specific load of a particular plasm. Thus it happens, whatever Weininger may have said to the contrary, that we are not confronted with the social problem of the hereditarily male uterus and female phallus.

But he is puzzled (*Ibid.*, p. 18) because "the most recent experiments of Sellheim and Foges have shown that the type of a gelded male is distinct from the female type, that gelding does not induce the female character." Further confusion arises in his mind "as to those cases of *eviratio* and *effeminatio* which the sexual pathology of the old age of men has brought to light."

But all these cases are negative cases. The gelding thickens, coarsens, develops in a non-sexual way, indicating a surplus of energy now that one particular drain upon energy has been stopped. When the opposite sex-characters seem to be produced either by age or by surgical intervention, it is usually because the receding tide of sex in the primary features tends to make already existing secondary features perhaps not quite in harmony with the whole more conspicuous than formerly—as the falling tide of the sea brings hidden islands to the surface. But there is no release of suppressed traits except in so far as an inhibitor has been removed, and no new trait except with the introduction of foreign organs.

H. L. Mencken

Super-Puritan

Lend him your prayers